# Ancient Mysteries and Modern Revelations

BY

## W. J. COLVILLE

# DEDICATION TO HALLEY'S COMET.

Bright harbinger of glorious light,
Illumining both morn and night,
Fair messenger thro' vibrant space.
Running thy rapid wondrous race,
Untiring as the ages roll,
Suggesting our undying soul.
Witness to Heaven's all-constant law,
From thee we inspiration draw.
Welcome, thrice welcome, in our sky,
Pointing to days of freedom nigh,
As on thy radiant form I look,
To thee I dedicate this book.

May 18, 1910.                    W. J. COLVILLE.

# CONTENTS.

# CONTENTS.

# AUTHOR'S FOREWORD.

In presenting the following pages to the world I desire to offer a few explanatory words concerning the form in which this book appears.

During my 6 months' residence in the city of Washington, U. S. A., which comprised the winter of 1909-10, I was earnestly entreated by many friends to compile a volume which should embody the gist of a very large number of lectures delivered during that period, especially those which dealt particularly with the Sacred Books of the world.

Owing to the very large amount of space required for even the barest outline of treatment of the Scriptures venerated by Jews and Christians alone, to say nothing of the Sacred Books of other faiths, I have attempted to present in this volume only discourses on those themes which have been specially brought to my attention by friends and students in many different places which I have visited and where my earlier books have widely circulated. To take up this entire subject at any length, or even to treat any portion of it with anything like fullness, would necessitate the publication of quite a long series of volumes, to which the present fragmentary work may possibly consitute an introduction. This particular book aims only

at presenting, in meagre outline, a view of revelation and inspiration which renders it easily possible
for us to admire and venerate the Bibles of all
peoples, without in any sense making a claim for
their infallibility or finality.    One of the chief
objects of all these discourses or essays is to increase interest in universal aspects of religion and
philosophy, and wherever possible to throw some
light on doctrines which are still occasioning much
perplexity in many quarters.   So much general interest is now evinced regarding all that pertains to
the psychic side of every subject, and so many
curious and conflicting views are still expressed
concerning matters designated "occult" and "psychical," that it seems a highly important duty to do all
we can to clear up mysteries and present our ripest
and most helpful thought to the enquiring multitude, whatever may be our special viewpoint.   One
cannot keep in any degree abreast with current
literature without encountering the most extraordinary ideas concerning the unseen universe, the
mysteries of which the modern world is making
desperate endeavors to unravel.   It is all in vain, in
these days, for religious teachers to tell the masses
that "secret things belong to God" and we have,
therefore, no right to enquire into them, for were
such a text to be pushed to its logical extremity,
in the hands of many theologians it would mean
putting an end to all investigation and blindly
accepting the dictum of some pretentious hierarchy.
It was this very attitude insisted upon by Dr. Pusey,
but repudiated by Dean Stanley, which drove Mrs.
Annie Besant to Atheism, from which Theosophy

eventually rescued her. If we cannot believe in the reality of a Spiritual Universe and at the same time use our reason, then thinkers must of necessity take refuge in some form of Agnosticism which can never satisfy the affection and never permanently content the intellect. If Bibles will not bear examination then the sooner they are consigned to the limbo of desuetude the better,—but if, as is maintained in the following pages, we can find much that is excellent in all of them, but the whole of truth in none, we do well to broaden our human sympathy by comparing Book with Book and System with System, to the end that we may at length discover a common religious and philosophical denominator. Magic as well as Mystery is dealt with in these lectures, chiefly on account of the great interest now prevalent in mysterious phenomena and the very misleading views in circulation concerning a topic which always lends itself readily to the exploitation of doctrines calculated to terrify the timid and support theories of the Universe utterly incompatible with any sane and wholesome views of life here and hereafter  Ancient and modern authors have been freely drawn upon to illustrate the many subjects briefly treated, and many valuable works are named, with the hope that those who read this treatise will derive benefit from studying the various questions herein outlined at much greater detail if time and opportunity permit and interest incite.

In my judgment, the chief benefit to be derived from travel (and I have traveled considerably) is the evidence it furnishes of the oneness of our

humanity; and if literal material travels contribute
to that important end, much more do mental excursions into many fields of diverse schools of Thought
bring us mentally and sympathetically closer together; and it is this intimate sense of togetherness
which must ultimately banish warfare and bring to
pass the fulfilment of the glorious prophecies
common to all illumined prophets, that a day will
dawn when all humanity will be so united that tho'
nations may remain as distinct communities, they
will be in spirit completely unified.  It is impossible
to predicate any ultimate unification of humanity
on any less exalted basis than that of the essential
goodness of human nature.  Nothing keeps us apart
so completely as false theology, on the one side, and
gross materialism on the other.  Could we once for
all realize our common humanity vitally, as an indisputable spiritual reality, we could not continue to
indulge either race or class hatred.  Race and class
consciousness there may be, within reasonable
limits, but race and class antagonisms are inconceivable if we realize our oneness.  Speculative theology
and philosophy which results in no widening realization of human unity, may be a scholastic exercise
agreeable to certain active intellects, but it may well
be dismissed as a superfluity by practical philanthropists who aim directly at benefiting human
beings here and now.  One by one the strongholds
of partialism and exclusivism are being broken down
and human unity is standing radiantly disclosed.
All the pitiable makeshifts of partialist theology are
losing their hold on the thinking, loving, masses
who are becoming more and more imbued with the

beauty and dignity of Abraham Lincoln's majestic saying, "All or None." This was that noble emancipator's answer to the question put to him by narrow-minded theologues concerning his views of human ultimate salvation. The stupid arrogance which imagines that some human beings will be finally blotted out, while others will enjoy everlasting conscious blessedness is intolerable in the light of all our deepest insight into the unity of our humanity. "Pilgrims of various probations," as Eliza Pitzinger calls us in her magnificent poem, "The Song of the Soul Victorious," we may be, and as such it is the privilege of the maturer to guide the less mature, and in the words of Lucy Larcom in her exquisite song, "Hand in Hand with Angels," we can well go thro' life "clinging to the strong ones; drawing up the slow." Nothing could be more ridiculous than to claim that we know all about the processes whereby the ultimate glorification of the entire human family will be accomplished, but, to quote once more from Eliza Pitzinger, "Side by side we are marching onward, and in time we will all agree." In dealing with ancient Oriental Scriptures, or even with the most recent works couched in Oriental phraseology, we find an abundant use of metaphor; it seems therefore incredible that any even slightly educated person to-day can experience any very great difficulty in translating the imagery with which all Bibles abound. "Fire" is no more to be taken literally when referred to as a means for purifying souls, than "sheep," "goats," "pieces of money," and a multitude of other symbolical expressions are to be taken literally; but they convey definite ideas allegorically, and are quite readily understood by all who have even a very small accquaintance with the significance of similitudes. There is much obscurity in much that is put forward as modern revelation, a fact which by no means proves that there is no truth in it, tho' it cannot fairly be foisted upon us as absolutely and irrevocably the final word on the subject of which it treats. Deeply grateful as we ought to be for every gleam of light that shines upon our mental and moral pathway, we miss the purpose of our educational experience directly we cease to investigate claims for ourselves and blindly endorse the dictum of another. My own researches in the Psychical field, which have been continuous from my childhood, have convinced me that however useful external phenomena may be in some cases, the only satisfactory assurance of immortality which can come to an individual—I mean an assurance that nothing can possibly overturn—must come thro' a development of one's inherent ability to discern spiritual relatities spiritually. The scientific world owes it to itself and to the larger unscientific world outside to fearlessly investigate all varieties of phenomena, and we have good reason to predict that present investigations will soon have led to radical changes in the popular belief concerning the constitution of our universe. Life continuous beyond physical dissolution is being proved on every side despite the incredulity of some investigators and the trickery of many mountebanks. Clairvoyance cannot be ruled out of court because tricks are played by greatly overlauded "mediums," nor can any mental phenomenon be affected should it be proved that alleged physical phenomena are often spurious. We need not be dismayed at anything external if our inner faculties are well developed, and one of the most hopeful signs of the times is that more and more attention is being given to cultivating faculties within us which we have allowed to lie fallow, but which are now asserting themselves with rapidly increasing vigor and distinctness. Our horizon is not properly limited by the outermost physical senses which are all that many people imagine they possess; there are interior faculties bursting thro' and when these shall have made themselves more generally known and honored we shall have entered upon an age of spiritual unfoldment to which the period of doubt and conflict now passing has surely led the way. With boundless confidence in the Power that makes for righteousness, and without a doubt as to the finally blessed outcome of all life's manifold and strange experiences, I throw this book upon the world trusting it will help in some slight measure to increase confidence in the "Divinity that shapes our ends, rough hew them as we may."

W. J. COLVILLE.

May, 1910.

# ANCIENT MYSTERIES AND MODERN REVELATIONS.

## CHAPTER I.

### BIBLES UNDER MODERN SEARCHLIGHT.

Nothing can be more evident than that two diametrically opposite mental tendencies are now figuring prominently on the intellectual horizon. We note everywhere an intense and sometimes even fanatic interest displayed in everything marvelous or mystical and at the same time we cannot but be impressed with the distinctly rationalistic, often amounting to an evidently agnostic, trend of thought in many influential directions. Modern Mysticism presents many curious aspects, for it is undoubtedly a strange compound of a very ancient love of the marvelous, for its own sake, with the truly modern scientific spirit which is satisfied with nothing less than a critical and impartial investigation of whatever claims to carry with it divine, or indeed any superordinary, authority. Between Mysticism and Occultism the famous Dr. Rudolf Steiner of Germany, declares there is this essential difference. The Mystic is one who realizes truth

in some interior intuitive manner, while the Occultist takes delight in observing and producing extraordinary phenomena, by means of which he hopes
to gain some added insight into the laws and
principles of the universe.

The sacred literature of all ages and of all peoples
abounds with striking illustrations that both Mysticism and Occultism were widely known and highly
prized from the earliest periods, concerning which
history informs us.  The mystic element in all Bibles
may be called truly religious in the deepest and most
spiritual meaning of the term; while all records of
miracles may be classed as spectacular occurrences,
calculated to impress the minds of many whose
interior life may have been largely undeveloped,
while their tendency to analyze external manifestations of any unusual sort may have been quite as
keen as we find it in the case of our most distinguished modern scientists.  We need always to
remember when handling the complex problems of
biblical criticism and psychical research (the two are
far more closely allied than many scholars seem to
imagine) that there are now among us just those
very same distinctive types of human nature which
co-existed in ages long gone by; therefore, while it
is quite permissable to discriminate between higher
and lower states of mind, as well as between differing degrees of spirilual and moral enlightenment,
we need to be extremely cautious lest we appear to
condemn a certain mental attitude which is positively inevitable in the case of many of our honorable
neighbors, even though we ourselves may have no
active sympathy with it  We hear a great deal in

these days of Liberalism and of Modernism, but as a rule those terms are very loosely employed; the former being used quite blindly and indiscriminately to cover every conceivable phase of thought which people choose to call "unorthodox or unconventional," while the latter is applied in particular to certain theological opinions which have recently met with papal condemnation.

We need as far as possible, within the limited scope of our literary endeavors, to define these terms a little more precisely so as to give them a much clearer and more readily intelligible standing in our popular vocabulary. By Liberalism is properly meant not a destructive or simply lax philosophy, but a system of thought which is sufficiently elastic to stretch without breaking, and also good-natured and broad-minded enough to see good in many systems of thought and practice, not merely in those to which we ourselves are from some cause or other especially attached. By Modernism we ought to mean simply the opposite of Ancientism, a word not yet often met with, but one that is capable of rendering much valuable service in any debate where it is found necessary to define clearly the modernist position. While it would sound churlish to call all our intellectual opponents illiberal and ourselves liberal, no offense need be taken if we divide for convenience sake, into Ancientists and Modernists while discussing the most vital points at issue between debaters who need never be belligerents. Those who take the ancient position may well be called faithful sticklers for certain views which have been handed down to them through many gener-

ations of venerated ancestors, and who are so conservative by intellectual bent and sympathy that it
is highly distressing to them to even contemplate
a change from the positions which these venerated
ancestors have, in their opinion, sanctified.   Modernists, on the other hand, have no such blind reverence for antiquity, not because of any lack of
affection and respect for their progenitors, but because of their intense conviction that days of old
were no holier than to-day and ancient countries no
more sacred than the lands we now inhabit.   Very
few indeed among us probably go the full length
in either direction, for we almost invariably find
ourselves at one time led by sentiment to revere,
perhaps unduly, some romantic work of old, while
at another time we are led by intellect to turn our
backs upon the positions of our forefathers and
boastfully declare that the achievements of the
present day are far greater than those of any period
in the past.   Let us now endeavor to analyze quite
fairly the claims of antiquity and the claims of
modernity to our sympathy and love.   Our affection
for the antique is almost always based upon some
endearing associations with the past that no amount
of didactic reasoning ever suffices entirely to dispel.
We cannot rationally analyze it any more than we
can give a satisfactory analytical account of any
other deeply rooted sentiment.   Probably the best
account of the great affection felt by so very many
people for the Bible is contained in the beautiful
song, "The Old Armchair."   "A Mother sat there
and that's why I love it, that old armchair."   The
singer goes on to tell us that that beloved mother

"turned from her bible to bless her child." This is quite sufficient to explain the deep fundamental hold which the ancient Bible continues to exert over the hearts and minds of quite a multitude of distinctly liberal thinkers who positively repudiate all attachment to traditional authority. For this reason the subject of biblical criticism is one which is necessarily attended by many sentimental difficulties which do not surround the candid investigation of any other literature in English speaking countries; for very few of us have any strongly sympathetic attachment to the Classics or to the Sacred Books of the East which the famous scholar, Max Muller, so finely edited; but were we to find ourselves in some Asiatic country the state of thought would be exactly reversed, for there our Bible could easily be treated quite impartially while certain other Scriptures which are also made up of divers elements Americans are almost entirely ignorant, would be surrounded with the same sort of sentimental halo with which we have encircled the Jewish and Christian documents. Whenever any one of us can effectually dismiss this widely prevailing sentiment and examine the many distinct books which go to make up the compendious literature we have long been accustomed to designate Holy Bible, we find that very much that it contains is no holier, and no less holy, than important portions of many other literatures which are also made up of divers elements brought together no one knows exactly when or how. We need not be either surprised or shocked to find that the same glorious ethical teachings which make many portions of our Bible magnificently superb

are couched in almost identical language with
equally high and noble moral precepts enunciated
elsewhere; nor need we experience the least aston-
ishment when we begin to trace a subtle mystical
element running through all the widely venerated
Scriptures of the world.

Let us now endeavor to place ourselves in the
mental attitude of those who have never seen, until
to-day, the Sacred Writings we are properly called
upon to impartially examine, and let us be perfectly
straightforward in dealing with these ancient records, precisely as we ought to deal with the newest
prose or poetry submitted for our consideration.
Bible worshippers and Bible haters are alike
fanatical, though their fanaticism is diametrically
opposed; for no one can judge any matter impartially if he approaches the study of it with his
mind already made up to either glorify it or condemn it.

Whether the Bible can pass through the scathing
ordeal of modern criticism safely and serenely, may
not yet be fully decided, but it may be safely predicted that the new aspects of criticism which are
rapidly coming to the front will much more nearly
agree with ancient kabbalistical interpretations than
with the now almost antiquated iconoclastic method
which was bound to prevail in the tempestuous days
of the French Revolution, when Voltaire, Thomas
Paine, and many other brilliant intellectualists were
seeking to prove that bibliolatry had long been the
cause of an intellectual servitude which they felt it
to be their special mission to overthrow. "The Age
of Reason" is a purely Deistic treatise which under-

takes to prove that divine revelation never can depend upon either books or priests, for Nature itself is the revelator of God to Man, consequently we of to-day have quite as much opportunity for enjoying a divine revelation as had any ancient prophets who lived under somewhat different conditions from ourselves. The works of Swedenborg, which had been circulated many years before the writings of Paine were issued, were no more in harmony with any blind worship of the letter of the Bible than were the words of Paine, but Swedenborg wrote from an entirely different standpoint, and distinctly claimed to be a specially illuminated man, divinely influenced to restore to the world a knowledge of those interior senses of Sacred Scripture well understood by many peoples several thousand years ago, but at the time of his writings almost entirely unknown to scholarly theologians as well as to the great multitude of the relatively uninstructed.

The modern Theistic position, rendered popular in New England by Theodore Parker in the middle of the nineteenth century, and since then widely accepted in nearly every section of the globe, does not differ radically from either the rationalistic position on the one hand or from the mystical on the other, provided that neither rationalist or mystic endeavors to set up any particular man or woman, or company of men and women, as infallible censors to whose dictation the multitude must bow. Every consistent Theist stoutly maintains that no one has any right to impose his or her opinions upon any other, seeing that no genuine human development is attainable apart from intellectual and moral

freedom; for if we simply bow to the alleged
authority of others, be they either ecclesiastics or
agnostics, we allow ourselves to suffer, to a large
extent at least, the loss of that exercise of individual
conscience and reason without which any real
human development is impossible. It is, of course,
quite true that some people are more highly enlightened than others, and are therefore quite capable
of functioning in the capacity of teachers, but no
arbitrary dictator is really a teacher, because if we
accept the say-so of another without individual
examination of what that other teaches, we positively learn nothing, but place ourselves mentally
and morally in the abject position of human parrots
or phonographs. Now it is often argued that as
there have always been Blessed Masters upon the
earth who have communicated oracular teaching to
their special disciples, we can only obtain knowledge
of important truth regarding spiritual matters
provided we accept the presumably authoritative deliverances of these heaven-inspired oracles, but such
a statement is entirely ridiculous, because if we
blindly accept something as true which we are quite
unable to understand, we accept it only in an illusory
manner, seeing that we do not feel within us any
vital response to the outside appeal; therefore, we
are only echoes and liable at any time to be switched
off our present mental track and diverted into quite
a foreign channel.

Whoever feels any real confidence in the intrinsic
and abiding value of the Bible must be strangely
inconsistent if he is afraid that a perfectly honest
and altogether impartial examination of the sacred

text can ever weaken its hold upon the hearts and minds of fearless truthseekers; but if anyone secretly entertains serious misgivings as to the ability of the Bible to withstand whatever attacks may be made upon it, he surely confesses his own serious doubt as to the real sacredness of the Scripture he ostensibly endeavors to uphold.

The spirit of frank investigation is the only spirit worthy of esteem, and whatever cannot stand the searchlight of such investigation as this spirit necessitates and prompts, must in the nature of things soon come to be regarded as far more of a human fetish than divine revelation.  It is certainly true that a superficial view of any collection of Sacred Writings reveals them as of very unequal value and abounding in traces of the particular errors common to the places and periods when and where they were produced.  It is, however, quite reasonable, when taking into account the circumstances of their production, to explain these seeming discrepancies and traces of unreliability not so much to lack of wisdom or inspiration on the part of the authors as to the actual need for appealing to humanity in a language not far removed from the average comprehension of ordinary men and women, while at the same time conveying an interior meaning to all who can read below the surface by means of the employment of a system of parable or metaphor which is, to this very day, the common practice of all teachers in the East.

We are now confronted with the task of examining the Hebrew and Greek records which constitute our Bible in the light of this twofold method,—the rationalistic and the mystical,—the former having reference to the outward text, the latter to the interior intention of those who employed it for the express purpose of handing down through succeeding ages certain vital truths which do not essentially vary, no matter how widely outward circumstances may change.

Probably no intelligent person to-day believes that any great moral purpose can be served by simply studying ancient history and committing to memory the names of certain patriarchs whose general character was certainly not outwardly in all cases of the highest stamp. Then again we have no definite assurance that any event occurred exactly as it is described in the external narrative. But when we come to regard these personages and incidents as far more than simply historical, we find them all capable of conveying important lessons to us to-day. The geographical and chronological elements in the Bible may well be regarded as extremely doubtful, but only in the sense that we need not look for local and historical exactitude in a great novel, a mighty poem or an elevating play, into which the names of certain persons and places have been freely introduced, but chiefly with dramatic motive—i. c., for the sake of making the teaching conveyed stand out boldly before the eye of the reader or the ear of the listener as it could not stand were it not for this vivid external drapery. When we read Shakespeare we need not care whether Hamlet, Prince of Denmark, or Timon of Athens were or were not actual historical persons. Somebody lived in Denmark and somebody lived in Greece during those periods to which the plays incidentally refer, but the object of these great dramas is certainly widely different from that of a school history, the avowed object of which is simply to acquaint the students with what actually occurred in certain countries at certain times.

All history is valuable provided we learn the lesson that it is capable of conveying to us; but the distinctive value of a work of art, written with the sole intention of embodying important moral teaching in attractive outward form, is far higher than that of any work which is undertaken from the standpoint of the historian simply.

We are all familiar to-day with the extreme doubt which is often expressed in learned circles concerning the authorship of every great literary classic. The plays of Shakespeare have been attributed to Bacon, while the Iliad and Odyssey of Homer have often been tentatively referred to unknown authorship, but no caviling as to authorship can ever detract one iota from the intrinsic merit of the suublime poetry thus skeptically dealt with, for it does not make any real difference to us to know or not to know who wrote a certain book or when or where it was written, seeing that the only great value of any literary production, which aims at elevating the moral tone of humanity, consists in the appeal it makes to our inherent moral instincts, which can usually be reached by fear if we are in an undeveloped and almost savage mental condition, but only by veneration and love if we are more highly evolved intellectually.

It is now not uncommon to find gifted teachers of

mental science and moral philosophy entirely ignoring the simply historical elements in ancient
Scriptures during the course of Bible lessons, which
they deliver with the one intention of aiding their
students to overcome diverse limitations and prove
themselves superior to the weaknesses and temptations which surround us in the modern world. We
need not wonder that this method of teaching is
sometimes looked upon by rationalists as unwarranted and by extreme conservatives as heretical,
but a little sober thinking will soon convince us that
we have all a perfect right to make the most practical use we possibly can of the world's most widely
circulating religious literature. Nothing can be
further from the truth than to declare that the
Bible in these days is not read as much as formerly,
though it is certainly the case that it is not read so
exclusively, and it is being read far more critically.
This change of attitude toward the venerable book
is quite inevitable when we take into account the
enormous literary output of the present day and the
resolute determination on the part of modern
scholars to ventilate as widely as possible the results
of recent criticism. We can quite sympathize with
all persons who object to the Bible being read in
public schools as a book entirely different from all
other books, alleged to contain a divine revelation
which no other literature can hold, for such a claim
for a particular volume is clearly an attempt on the
part of Bible worshipers to compel many of their
fellow-citizens who do not share their views to
submit the whole of the rising generation to a kind
of course in dogmatic theology, which while it may

meet with the complete approval of some parents and guardians, is thoroughly distasteful to others Were the Bible placed on a level with other avowedly Sacred Books and treated with honest impartiality, there could be no objection to selecting from it for school reading many noble passages, but the volume as a whole is far too obscure in many places, and it also deals with too many subjects unfit to be discussed by children of school age, to be placed in their hands either as a complete divine revelation or as a standard text book of faith and morals which they are expected to peruse from Genesis to Revelation. We know well enough that there are very many beautiful stories in the Bible which are well adapted to childish comprehension, and which by their dramatic intensity make a strong and altogether salutary appeal to juvenile imagination. Such tales could profitably be included in a judiciously compiled selection from many venerable writings where they would stand side by side with similar stories taken from other Scriptures: But admirable though such a selection from the various Sacred Books of the world might be, such a volume could never receive the sanction of those exclusivists who have set their faces determinedly against the study of comparative religion, unless it be so conducted as to put their own system in the most favorable light possible, while all other systems must be relegated to the shades of at least semi-darkness.

When it was seriously proposed to Mrs. Annie Besant that she should compile such a book as we are now advocating, she very frankly informed her friends that she could compile it without much difficulty, but she saw little chance of its being accepted after she had written it, in those particular places into which her friends were most desirous of introducing it.   Any gifted man or woman who has traveled widely and studied deeply might gather together, without any onerous labor, a large amount of valuable matter from the immense bulk of the world's sacred literature, and a very great good service could be rendered thereby to the cause of mutual understanding between the representatives of different religious systems, but though such a result after its accomplishment could only be beneficial in the long run, it could not be brought about at present on any extended scale without arousing ferocious controversy, by reason of the enthusiastic self-conceit which we find manifested by professedly orthodox advocates of every religious system beneath the sun.   Nothing seems more difficult than for those who profess to admire and fully accept the most exquisite portions of their own beloved Bible to act as though its finest inculcations were really true, for if they would but admit what their greatest prophets and apostles have clearly stated, they would immediately consent to trace divine revelation impartially through the myriad channels along which it has been flowing without cessation through all the ages.   Could we all agree to dispense entirely with both jealousy and prejudice it would not be long before we could all unite to form a worldwide Study Class, in which all venerated Scriptures could be employed and quoted side by side in such a manner as to greatly and quickly help forward that mighty spiritual movement looking toward the establishment and maintenance of universal Peace which we are assured by all true Theosophists, and all other workers for the unification of humanity, is the one movement beyond all others most calculated to enable all of us to practically realize the divine origin and constitution of our common humanity.

Nothing can surely be more detrimental to the interests of universal peace than an arrogant belief that some one nation has been appointed sole custodian of celestial verities, for such a claim made by any body of people inevitably inclines them to an overweening sense of their own importance coupled with a more or less contemptuous attitude toward all the rest of humanity. "Poor benighted heathen," is a phrase we often hear at missionary meetings, not simply applied to certain benighted elements in any given population, but indiscriminately used to designate all non-christian peoples regardless of their intelligence or moral excellence. The only reason given for speaking of them thus is because they have never seen our Bible, or accepted' our particular views of religion, though in many cases they have actually embraced the identical teachings which we frequently declare are the crowning glory of our vastly superior civilization. Were we to really understand the Scriptures of those so-called "heathen" nations, we should find in them very much to admire, though also much to criticize, but were they fairly examined we should soon discover that their worst passages are no worse than the worst in our own Bible, and even those are not bad at all if we regard them as containing some interior meaning which lies far below the surface of their letter.   No intelligent person can possibly believe that any true God ever told people through any instrumentality whatever to slaughter hosts of innocent women and children; therefore, whenever we read that such commands were given from God, we may be quite sure either that the record is false or that it is conveyed in mystical language.   We can accept which alternative we please, provided we adopt the same method of interpretation when dealing with various records; but in no case can we have the right to assume that what is right when contained in one Bible is wrong when found in another. Bibles in all cases possess some amazing element of vitality which has enabled them so far to withstand all the censure which has been brought against them that they go on living despite all efforts made to crush them.   This may be due to the simple fact that they contain so much truth, intermingled with a large amount of error, that that truth keeps them alive while the error has a tendency to work their destruction, or we may go so far as to believe that in all cases they are portions of some great universal literature which owes its value, as well as its enduring character, to the spiritual element which is its permanent soul, and which enjoys immortal life though outward bodies may be far from capable of enduring everlastingly.

Whichever view we take we must be extremely careful not to indulge in any special pleading for our own Bible, while holding up to scorn or ridicule the equally venerated Scriptures of hundreds of millions of our fellow beings; and when we come to deal with the subject of idolatry we must again be equally careful to avoid the very common error of declaring that our own images represent certain spiritual truths, and are only regarded by those who honor them as emblems or symbols, while we most unjustly infer that other images in other parts of the world are actually "false gods" of wood and stone which the "wretched heathen" worship because they are destitute of all genuine spiritual illumination. It is quite pardonable that Europeans and Americans should, for the most part, be largely ignorant of Oriental faith and worship, but if that be so, surely some becoming modesty should be exercised and we should refrain from passing judgment where our knowledge is so extremely small. We need not claim to endorse or advocate doctrines and practices with which we are unfamiliar, but we may well be reticent concerning them, and were a wise reticence generalyy observed, we should enjoy the advantage of a total absence of all ill-feeling toward our Asiatic neighbors and we should also be quite open to learn from them as they may also be open to learn from us concerning spiritual realities.

# CHAPTER II.

A very remarkable Chart, intended to describe the progress of religious ideas and varying forms of worship among all nations, was long ago issued by Major General Forlong, by means of which he traced out with considerable clearness what he believed to be the stream of human religious progress from as far back as 10,000 B. C. The earliest forms of worship included the Tree and the Serpent as objects of world-wide veneration, and with these emblems were associated all the symbols connected with Phallic worship. It is quite easy to trace in these primitive and wide-spread emblems the natural tendency of humanity to deify all those agencies through which the stream of life is constantly flowing from some mysterious unseen fountain-head into manifold manifest exterior expressions. According to Forlong's calculations the worship of Fire somewhat preceded the adoration of the sun, and these two forms of closely related worship he traces back to about 6,000 B. C. Regarding the chart carefully we soon become familiar with many interblending lines showing how Sun worship, Tree worship and Serpent worship were so interblended as to have been well-nigh, if not entirely, inseparable. Ancestor worship, according to this reckoning, dates back only to about 3,500 B. C, and seems to have immediately followed the more ancient Egyptian Sacred Ritual which paid special homage to all phases of creative fertility. Mountain worship is still more recent and is said to have prevailed everywhere at the time assigned by Jewish tradition to the giving of the Law from Sinai, and immediately after that period Animal worship became everywhere prevalent. This seems to be in strict accord with the narrative in Exodus which informs us that the people worshiped the golden calf after the Law had been revealed to them from the mountain top, and we may also well believe that the sacredness of mountains appealed especially to men of prophetic type, while animal worship was the common practice of the unenlightened. We can never entirely get away from these forms of worship which grow up instinctively and are therefore no more artificial products than are any other spontaneous natural productions. We have all some instinct of veneration within us which in its earlier and less refined condition is sure to lead us to pay extravagant homage to those external objects which most naturally and powerfully seize hold upon our imagination and cause us, by their unique impressiveness, to regard them as divine agents in more than ordinary degree.

This consideration alone may lead us far on the highly desirable road of kindly consideration for the many aspects of faith and forms of worship which have survived unto this day, and which seemingly satisfy, in some considerable measure, the religious aspirations of multitudes of our contemporaries. Though the very highest idea of Deity which the human mind seems capable of entertaining is well expressed in the majestic words "God is Spirit and they who worship Him must worship Him in spirit and in truth," what constitutes spirit, and how spiritual worship may be offered, is not usually very clear to the average intellect, hence men have always devised some concrete figures which they have placed before them, not intending thereby to represent Deity in fullness, but only to assist them in concentrating their attention upon some venerated object which to their minds clothes or embodies at least some special divine attribute which they most admire and which they most desire to share. Modern scholarship universally inclines to an acceptance of the thoroughly reasonable proposition that beyond all localized and limited divinities the great nations of antiquity acknowledged and venerated one Supreme Being whose attributes were variously embodied in multitudes of subordinate divinities, and though it is the proud boast of the most advanced nations in the modern world that they acknowledge only one God as the proper object of human worship, we can hardly fail to recognize a very definite continuation of ancient Paganism in modern Christianity. By this declaration we are not intending to infer anything disrespectful to the Christian system, though we cannot admit that in its present form it is other than hybrid. Primitive Christianity may have originated with some definite determination on the part of a few intensely zealous men and women to carry into effect the exact teachings of a great Master whom they desired implicitly to follow, but no student of Christian history can fail to note that very soon indeed the early Church began to associate itself with the civil power of the Roman Empire, and from the moment it did so it must have ceased to preserve, even in semblance, its primitive simplicity.    All the great religions of the world appear to have originated with some great inspiration received through some illustrious Founder, whose followers very soon began to drift away from the primal purity of the system established by the Founder, and in so doing they invariably committed themselves to an endorsement of prevailing ideas and customs, which had already taken so firm a hold upon the minds of the great bulk of the populace where the new religion was introduced, that a formulated system soon grew up and flourished which was a compromise between the new revelation and the older hierarchy.    We can readily see traces of this blending of new and old in every Bible we may be called upon to study, and the fact of its universality should dispose us to take a kindly as well as a rational view alike of its origin and purpose.    Though worship of external objects, no matter how majestic and sublime, must be ultimately superseded by a purely spiritual form of adoration, we can clearly see that in the course of human conscious evolution lower concepts of Deity must of necessity precede higher ones, and for this reason we should be ever ready to put the most favorable construction possible upon ancient and modern religious beliefs and usages alike.    It is a great, though a very common, error to suppose that so eminently rational and charitable a view means indifference to all essentials of faith or doctrine, for such is surely not the case. The most thoroughly sympathetic view of all religious systems is the one always taken by the most thoroughly devout and conscientious upholders of those essential and fundamental verities, which an impartial investigation of Comparative Religion can only serve to endear more and more to the hearts and minds of all who are liberal and intelligent enough to appreciate, in some vital manner, the splendid words attributed to the Apostle Paul, "GOD has never left Himself without witness." As we trace the widely spreading boughs of Forlong's imaginary tree, and seek to appreciate the manifest significance of its widely ramifying branches, we cannot fail to note how many strange beliefs and practices are often marvellously interlinked. Human progress in civilization seems always to have proceeded along a circuitous path; never does it seem to have gone straight forward. This fact must be well digested before we can possibly estimate truly the career of religious ideas and ceremonies through centuries and milleniums. It has long been a gross mistake, and a fatal error, to suppose that one religious system has necessarily borrowed from another because we can trace extremely close resemblances in many instances between one system and another. This close relationship both in doctrine and ceremonial by no means necessarily proves anything more or other than that different peoples in different countries may have simulanteously reached an almost identical altitude of mental, moral, and spirit-

ual attainment.  It is clearly evident that between
five and six centuries prior to the commencement of
the Christian Dispensation a mighty spiritual, intellectual and moral wave of inspiration and illumination was sweeping voluminously over the Earth, lav-
ing Europe, Asia, and the Northern Coast of Africa
with its effulgence.  Then were the days of the
latest of the Buddhas in India, of Confucius, the
eminent moral philosopher, and of Laotze, the profound Mystic, in China ; also of the greatest of the
Philosophers in Greece.  How came it about, we
may well enquire, that so many illustrious lights
were shining contemporaneously in different sections of the world?  Surely there are mental,
moral, and spiritual tides in the history of Humanity which have their periodic ebb and flow as surely
as have the tides of oceans, which most of us have
learned to trace.  To ascertain the cause and
periodicity of these mysterious Psychic Tidal
Waves may yet be well within our average power,
but up to the present the ability to do this has been
claimed as an exclusive possession of certain highly
trained or well developed Adepts or Initiates, who
can peer within the veil of mystery which has for
ages shrouded the inner sanctuaries from the gaze
of all the uninitiated.  A mighty question is now
agitating the minds of rapidly increasing multitudes,
viz., Has the time now come for the great unveiling
long predicted, and eagerly anticipated by enquiring
throngs to-day?  The signs are manifold, and
they are rapidly accumulating, that we are on the
immediate verge of a new Cycle in human history.
    To quote the language of Forlong, "There may be

observed from the synchronizing of the history of
faiths a remarkable tidal wave of intensity which
seems to acutely affect the race physically and mentally and with remarkable regularity every six hundred to six hundred and fifty years, reminding us of
the Sothic and other cycles, but especially of the
mystical phœnix or Solar eras of Egypt and the
East.   The ebb and flow of this tide is shown on the
chart by light broad bands embracing a width of one
hundred years."

With the beginning of the Christian era we notice
a determined effort to unify, as far as possible,
every system older than Christianity.   This tendency is so familiar to all students of the Fathers
of the early Church, that it seems almost incredible
that any graduate from a well equipped divinity
college can be ignorant of the fact that what he has
been taught to call Christianity is both a compound
and a continuation of many ancient faiths and ceremonies; but though this is unmistakably the case
we   are   not   thereby   justified   in   characterizing
Christianity or the New Testament as in any sense
fraudulent, though that serious charge is often
brought by vigorous iconoclasts, who can readily
trace existing parallels but seem unable to interpret
their real significance.   The publishers of Forlong's
chart were very careful to publish in connection
with it the thoroughly truthful statement that it is
neither orthodox or heterodox but simply chronological, therefore suitable for general use in all
schools where classics are taught; but though it is
simply historical in its manifest design, no one who
peruses it thoughtfully can fail to trace its distinctly

universal implications. Its chief object is professedly to exhibit a gradual evolution of ideas from
rude material and elemental symbolism to abstract
spiritual conceptions. Several colors are employed,
each one denoting some great leading idea which,
though long continuing, tends to diverge and at
length become lost in some wider common stream.
The streams are called merely "Lines of Thought,"
neither national nor ethnographical in their arrangement, for certain streams of tendency are steadfast
while all religious systems are progressive, in consequence of the fact that human nature progresses
and one generation of men and women will inevitably put some new construction upon doctrines and
ceremonies alike, by no means in strict accordance
with the views taken by their predecessors in the
same communion.

We are altogether too much inclined to speak of
people as Jews, Christians, or Mohammedans, as
though such broad designations completely describe
as well as effectively label them; but such a mistaken
inference can never hold sway over the minds of
soberly thoughtful people, seeing that nothing can
be more self evident than that there are as many
varieties of Judaism, Christianity, and Mohammed-
ism, for example, as there are distinctive types of
people professing each of these varied systems of
religious thought and practice.

We are often apt to think that should we travel
in Eastern Asia and mingle freely with Brahmins,
Buddhists and Parsees, we should find certain rigid
kinds of people professing certain definite doctrines
and observing certain ancient and unvarying cere-

monies with scarcely anything to distinguish one
individual from another among professors of a
certain creed.  This might prove true, to some extent at least, were we to associate exclusively with
the uneducated and largely unthinking rank and file
of some specific population, but should we enlarge
the scope of our acquaintance, till it included the
best educated and most highly representative members of any Oriental community, we should soon discover quite as wide a dissimilarity of thought and
practice as we are ever likely to encounter in the
West.   That fertile author, James Freeman Clarke,
whose splendid text book, "Ten Great Religions," is
a most valuable mine of rich historical information,
often took occasion to remind his hearers, in the
course of his always instructive sermons, that we
greatly need to remember that though institutions
seemingly remain permanent, with their confessions
of faith unchanged and their ceremony unaltered,
yet because the living members of those institutions
are not the men and women of past centuries, we
have no right or reason to expect that the personal
conduct of any body of people to-day will necessarily be identical with the behavior of the men and
women who bore the same distinctive titles in the
past.   This is, of course, self-evidently true, but as
every organization extant to-day contains many
widely diversified elements, so was it in even the
distant past; consequently the more thoroughly we
study history the more clearly convinced do we
become that there never was a time when all the
professors of a distinctive creed came up to a uniform standard of either intellectuality or morality.

Quite recently the beatification of Jeanne D'Arc, the Maid of Orleans, by the Church of Rome has called much attention to two distinctly separate aspects of the attitude of that Church to the heroic girl who was indeed a deliverer of France, and then a Martyr through the perfidy of the very King and his attendants who owed their exaltation and their safety to the brave inspired damsel without whose valiant leadership the French Army of that period could never have been victorious.

We often hear it said that the Church burnt this maiden as a witch a few hundred years ago and now enthrones her statue above its altars as an object of veneration for the faithful, while priests call upon their people to invoke the intercession of the very girl who was so bitterly denounced and cruelly masacred in a by-gone century. This statement is by no means altogether true, for while it may be a historic fact that those particular persons who put the maiden to death professed the Roman Catholic faith, we cannot learn from any reliable historian that the high dignitaries of the Church as a whole were in any way concerned with her unjust martyrdom. Personal jealousy and other equally base motives animating the corrupt minds of certain men in authority at the time of her condemnation, were the direct external causes of the unjust sentence passed upon her; it is not therefore true to relate that a great Church as a whole condemned the Maid of Orleans in one century and canonized her in another, but it is a fact that the general temper of these times is less barbaric than that of four or five hundred years ago. Yet even now it does not seem impossible that harsh injustice might be meted out to some modern deliverer of France, or any other land, were corrupt men to be in power and in a position to cast a deciding vote as to the fate of a new emancipator.

We can all understand what Felix Adler, President of the New York Society for Ethical Culture, meant when he gave a book the title of "Deed vs. Creed," though that saying cannot always be endorsed at its full face value. What Dr. Adler clearly intended to convey was that good deeds can be performed regardless of creed, and any sort of creed can be intellectually maintained regardless of the behavior of its advocates. We sometimes hear it said that it is of no consequence what we believe provided we live good lives; this is a very shrewd saying requiring very close examination, by reason of the fact that it seems to contain a sort of catch which, however, we soon discover when we penetrate below the surface of its obvious letter. Much good was undoubtedly done some years ago through the columns of the London Daily Telegraph by the publication day after day, for several months, of numerous letters from all conceivable varieties of scribes in answer to the query, Do we Believe? "Of course we all believe something," is the only possible general answer which can be given to this question, but two other inquiries directly follow it, What do we Believe? and, Why do we Believe what we Believe? to which a third may be added, What Influence does our Belief exert over our Conduct? To answer these four queries, not merely to discuss the first in the series, must be the work of the

philosophic student, and it will surely not take us
very long to make the uncomplimentary discovery
that our average beliefs are largely due to nothing
else than blind unreasoning compliance with accepted notions entertained by a large majority of
persons among whom we have been brought up.
Such beliefs cannot well be vital; they are usually
little if any better than intellectual lumber, a kind
of mental furniture which we take for granted
because we have been accustomed to seeing it in our
surroundings from our early childhood.   Once we
begin to think seriously upon the nature and import
of belief, we find that our beliefs, if they are in any
sense living, cannot be entirely unimportant, because they always do exercise a considerable amount
of influence upon our actual life.   We cannot really
believe in an angry God or in useless and endless
misery without being to some extent demoralized
thereby; such beliefs, therefore, are decidedly
dangerous in their inevitable tendency, because if
they are seriously entertained, or even passively
accepted, their necessary tendency is to brutalize
instead of humanize those who hold them.   When,
on the other hand, we really believe in a God of
love and wisdom, who is in essence entirely beneficent, also in the remedial nature of all chastise-
ment involving suffering both here and hereafter, such a conception must have a tendency to
ennoble and purify our own attitude toward our
fellow beings.   In all our arguments in favor of
simple Theism as immeasurably superior to every
narrower and cruder faith, we base our claim for
its reasonableness and goodness, not upon any meta-

physical subtlety, but upon the appeal it makes to all the sweetest and noblest sentiments in our common human nature. People must be dense indeed if they cannot see that a higher idea of divine government, extending throughout the universe, must exert a better influence upon humanity at large than can any lower concept.

Tracing, as far as we are able, the career of the God idea in history, we do not find so much of widely separated streams of thought as we trace a blended current, due to the fact that the greatest teachers of humanity have appeared and worked among all conditions of human development.

To go no further back than the period referred to in the Christian Gospels we are told that a great spiritual luminary blazes forth in the Roman Empire, of which Judea is then a province. This spiritual light shines freely for all and is poetically designated "the Sun of Righteousness arisen with healing in its wings," a prophetic metaphor which clearly gives evidence that the disciples of a great Master believed his mission to be entirely universal in its intent. So it consistently follows that evangelists record that this great teacher commissions his emissaries to go forth as ambassadors into all nations proclaiming good news, or joyful tidings, to every creature. But how do the same evangelists tell us that this Master and his teachings were received? Multitudes at times flocked to his standard and crowds of common people heard him gladly, but there were also many who regarded him as a sorcerer, or as an imposter, and stirred up a conspiracy against him, even as certain vicious elements in

Greek society at an earlier day had branded Socrates a foe to religion and virtue and an enemy of the State worthy only of banishment or death.  We may well believe that some people both in Greece and in Palestine were actually sincere in their benighed protests against the life and teachings of the great teachers whom they hounded out of physical existence, but in all probability the great majority of those who joined in the clamor for the removal of those who were continually doing good were actuated by far from honorable motives, foremost among which was the constant fear that their own temporal power, which they knew they held unjustly, would soon be wrested from their grasp did they allow a high moral philosophy to win increasing triumphs in lands which they desired unrighteously to govern.  But be this as it may, it is not possible that a low type of intellect can ever grasp a very high idea of either divine or human government; thus it often happens that quite sincere, but undeveloped, natures believe that harsh coercive measures are essential to the welfare of the Family and of the State, therefore, from their standpoint, those who teach the Law of Love and adopt a higher policy than that of warfare are looked upon as dangerous fanatics who, if their influence should greatly spread, would quickly undermine and overthrow the safeguards of society.  Those who entertain such views, and we have some such human fossils in our midst to-day, cannot see anything but a dangerous menace to morality in the breaking up of the old traditions to which they slavishly adhere, fearing that if these be even weakened a deluge of

vice and anarchy will speedily overwhelm the earth.
Many preachers who represent the extreme of sur-
viving religious orthodoxy express not the slightest
hesitancy in declaring that apart from some element
of dogmatic theological teaching interfused, all
advance in secular education must eventually result
in weakening instead of strengthening the ramparts
of morality.

This contention, though ultimately unsound, com-
mends itself with easy readiness to the minds of
timid and highly emotional people who have never
sought to soberly sift the groundworks of morality.
Dogmatic theology has long been so closely associated with moral training in the minds of large rural
populations in many countries that it must be difficult for many parents, who belong to an old regime,
to understand the attitude of the Ethical Culturists
of the present day, and some show of reasonableness attaches to their fears because of the fact that
during a transition period like the present, when an
impulsive rising generation breaks away from time-
honored moorings it is very likely to plunge un-
thinkingly into an abyss of folly from which it
can only be recovered through the agency of a
wiser mode of treatment than is yet widely comprehended by the masses.   It is, however, only fair
to state that the present generation is guilty of no
crimes or follies which were not often perpetrated
in the so-called "good old days" when the parson
was supreme in the village, the Bible regularly read,
and family prayer punctually offered.   There are
evidently two causes for modern religious and social
unrest; one is unmistakably due to the spirit of the

age, which no attempt to quench can prove successful; the other proceeds from a certain careless
impetuosity, begotten of that very restraint which
so many short-sighted persons believe to be the only
safeguard of youth and upholder of morality. Take
us as a whole we are undoubtedly deeper and more
serious thinkers than were our forefathers, though
we may not have among us any very large number
of particularly eminent men and women; but this
seeming absence of distinguished geniuses may be
fairly attributed to the causes which Bulwer Lytton
in his famous novel, "The Coming Race," says the
Vril-Ya gave for the absence of distinguished genius
in that mysterious subterranean world into
which that highly romantic author has introduced
his often awestruck readers. Where the general
average of intelligence is high we cannot reasonably
expect that lofty mental attainments will stand out
so conspicuously as where it is comparatively low;
likewise where the general moral attitude is fairly
lofty we seldom pause to contemplate with great
esteem some distinguished moral hero; and again
we must not lose sight of the fact that true and
lasting morality can never be secured where individuality is suppressed and the people cowed into
submission by threats of terrific punishment if they
dare to disobey the mandates of their commanding
officers. We are certainly nearer to the long predicted Golden Age than we have ever been before.

But what is really meant by this romantic figure
of speech? we may well enquire. An age in which
literal gold is worshiped, as though it were veritable
Deity, must ever be an age of dire calamity, and

such it has ever proved whenever and wherever
this popular idol has been enthroned for adoration.
Gold in the Alchemical sense means something far
different indeed from any precious material metal,
though it can scarcely be seriously disputed among
students of Alchemistic Philosophy that all its chief
exponents have admitted the possibility of the
literal transmutation of baser into superior metals,
and all eventually into gold.  The symbolic mention
of gold, however, directs our thoughts far away
from all external treasures and centers them upon a
celestial inheritance, in comparison with which all
worldly possessions must sink into utter insignificance; therefore we are perpetually assured by
Mystics of every rank and name, that the true
object of Alchemical research is the regeneration
of individual human beings immediately, and ultimately of the entire Human Race.  "I believe in
the resurrection of the Body and in the Life Everlasting," originally meant far more than it means
to the average Creed-reciter of to-day, who is
usually one who scarcely seeks to find any interior
meaning in the mighty mystic words which rise
so glibly to the lips of all who have simply learned
to utter published phrases.  In like manner Baptis-
mal Regeneration is taken only as to its most
external garb, when in reality it has true reference
to that marvel of interior transformation which it
has always been the object of the Mysteries to
progressively unveil.  The first body to be considered when we are dealing with Mystic Initiation
is, of course, the inner body of the Neophyte or
Candidate, one who is sometimes termed a Cate-

chumen; but as no selfish desire for exclusive individual salvation or enlightenment can ever be approved spiritually, it has always been the *open* as well as the *private* teaching of real Initiates that Social Regeneration is the great intent of all true Mystic Schools.

Turning again to Forlong's Chart for illustrative examples, we find the colors employed are Red, Blue, Green, Pink, Brown, Violet and Yellow. Worship of Fetiches is marked at the very beginning of the record and takes historic rank with Charms and Amulets, which were venerated everywhere in the remotest ages of which we possess any definite or authentic record.   Three quite distinct, but for long contemporary, objects of worldwide veneration were the Tree, pictured appropriately in green; the Lingam and Yoni, sacred to Phallic Faiths, portrayed in yellow; and the Serpent, portrayed in brown, doubtless to suggest the earth on which the serpent moves.   These three especially ancient Emblems all interblend and at length become merged, or at least united, in the Sacred Ritual of ancient Egypt, accounts of which are now quite easily procurable.   About 3000 B. C., according to Forlong's reckoning, there were great wars between Jovites and Titanites and between Solar and Lunar worshipers.   At this distance of time it is not necessary to attempt to enter elaborately into the causes and nature of these conflicts, but it does certainly appear that the position of the opposite sexes, as objects of veneration, was often a burning point of controversy in olden times.

With recent dissertations concerning Atlantis the

antiquity of ancient Faiths seems much greater than before that once mighty submerged Island-continent became a subject of popular research. as it had not become when Forlong's Chart was originally issued, but though LePlongeon and other indefatigable students of antiquity quite clearly trace all Oriental and Occidental beliefs and practices to their common home in Atlantis, it is highly probable that the dispersion of religious systems rapidly spread at the time of the breaking up of that mysterious land. the last remnants of which are said to have finally collapsed very nearly 10,000 years before the commencement of the Christian Era.

This great event may well account for the existence of a specific traceable chronology carrying us back to 10.000 B. C., but no further.

Definite and simple Theism, within the present historic period (traced in vivid red on Forlong's Chart) is not made to appear earlier than 2,400 B. C. Intensely interesting, and instructive also, though these graphically formulated statements prove there must always be some doubt as to precise historic accuracy, though none whatever as to the real prevalence of different Religious Systems and very little as to the effect which each is logically calculated to exert upon its faithful devotees.

This point conceded, we must be prepared to go a definite step further, and consider that all Systems have their letter and their spirit, and while the letter is always crude, and sometimes even barbaric, the spirit is pure and gentle, reminding us of nuts, which have hard indigestible exterior shells while they are inwardly delicious and nutritious.

"The letter killeth, but the spirit giveth life," is not a text that can apply alone to the Mosaic Law, or to any other portions of the Bible of the Jew and of the Christian; it is applicable to every record accounted sacred by any section of mankind.   Is there then no place remaining in these modern days for missionary enterprise?   There is a vast new field opening for missionary endeavor, but the coming missionary must be a man or woman widely awake to the actual needs of our present humanity, which greatly needs convincing of the unity of all religious systems at their core.   The letter of all systems is in process of sure disintegration and in this dissolving process many observers think they see the growing disappearance of religion itself from earth In this surmise they must soon find themselves mistaken, for actual discovery of the roots of all religious trees is leading multitudes to accept, not Atheism but Theosophy.   Annie Besant is not the only brilliant worker in the ranks of Atheistic propaganda who has discovered its pitiful unsatisfactoriness, though she has proved an exceptionally prominent and influential example in this connection.   Prof. Charles Eliot, President Emeritus of Harvard University, has undoubtedly, to some extent, correctly outlined the religion of the future, but that religion may have many other excellent aspects besides those which this kindly veteran educator has vigorously emphasized.   The religion of the future is certainly in the making, and though it can be neither wished nor expected that it will be an entirely new production, it is not unduly optimistic or presumptuous to predict that it will contain all

that is worth preserving in the heritages we have
gathered from the past, but as new times require
new applications of eternal verities, we must not
imagine that anything worth preserving is being
swept away because old truth is being freshly gar-
mented and the present generation is voicing the
Wisdom of the Ages in a language of its own.

# CHAPTER III.

Though the true meaning of a revelation is simply a disclosure this obviously simple word has long been one to conjure with, and it is still to-day a veritable storm-center wherever theological matters are discussed.

Scientifically, however, the word presents no difficulties, for in scientific circles it is always used as the synoynm of discovery. We may truly say that we receive a revelation of the heavens when we gaze through telescopes into the midnight skies and trace the process of the constellations, but no one imagines for an instant that the stars are deliberately showing themselves to astronomers and hiding their faces from all other persons. But it remains a fact that certain astronomers actually see far more of the heavenly bodies than is beheld by the general bulk of any population.

Let us apply this simple illustration to those great seers or prophets, who may well be termed the spiritual star-gazers of our race. Such men and women are figuratively represented as climbing to the tops of mountains, and delving into caves of the earth and clefts of rocks, just as astronomers and geologists literally ascend mountain eminences, and dive into the depths of the crust of the planet, that they may in the one case have a wider view of the sky and in the other a bettre opportunity to examine the layers or strata of the globe.   We know quite well that certain places are particularly favorable for astronomical observations; among these deep wells have always occupied a foremost place, for we can see the stars at midday if we descend into a well and at night-time we can only have a wide sweep of the heavens if we plant our observatories on lofty heights.   Natural similitudes have always been employed by bards or psalmists to describe their realization of the nearness of the spiritual universe, which does indeed interpenetrate as well as encircle all material orbs.   The nineteenth psalm, and some majestic portions of the Book of Job, won the admiration of Thomas Paine, who quotes some splendid passages in his "Age of Reason," in which much controverted volume he levels biting sarcasm at many other portions of the Bible, which he deems entirely inconsistent with the glorious conception of the Supreme Being set forth in the quotations he admires.   "The heavens declare the glory of God and the firmament showeth his handiwork," is a superb tribute to its author's sublime idea of Nature, and yet more does it testify to his realization of human ability to scan the heavens and read, in their outspread beauties, the caligraphy of the Almighty.   The cattle in the fields are just as near the sky as the shepherd who is tending his flocks on the same pasture ground, but we have no reason to suppose that sheep or oxen contemplate the heavens as did the shepherd king of ancient Israel, and we have no ground for surmising that even the average human traveler who ascends to the summit of some lofty peak has anything like the same idea of the starlit skies as those Magi or Wise Men of ancient Persia or Chaldea, who are said to have discovered the Star of Bethlehem at the time of the birth of Jesus. Every age has had, and the present undoubtedly has, its particularly earnest and qualified inspectors of the widely open book of natural revelation, which is never for an instant closed except in the face of ignorance and indifference. Were we all equally open-eyed and open-minded we should all receive an equal revelation, for Nature holds no secrets shut away from some, which are purposely revealed to others. Who, let us ask, were those prophets of old, who saw and heard so much more of the ways of Deity than did the hosts of their contemporaries, to whom they always appear as almost unfathomable enigmas, strange beings like "super-men," to be either blindly venerated or ruthlessly persecuted, according to the temper of those among whom they mingled. These mystic visionaries, and stalwart champions of right-eousness, have ever been the glory of the lands on which they have set foot, and their record is handed down through successive centuries and milleniums as bearing special witness to divine interposition in the ordinary affairs of men. But science, perhaps, will not allow us to use that word interposition, see-ing that it gives color to a belief very much at vari-ance with general scientific reasoning; let us then in-terpret the history of those romantic dwellers on the

borders of the unseen universe in reasonable terms,
easily understood by all who are diligently seeking
to show that unity exists between the physical and
superphysical at all times.   We may well afford to
discard the adjective "supernatural," unless we give
it a significance quite at variance with much that
passes for theology.   There are higher and lower
planes of nature; thus it is not incorrect to call some
*super* and others *sub,* when we are comparing them
with a genreal average level of human intellectual
attainment, which claims to have a certain amount
of acquaintance with a very limited portion of
Nature, but freely speculates regarding other
realms, which are beyond the scrutiny of ordinary
observations.   There is nothing unscientific, and
certainly nothing irrational, in lending a willing ear
to the testimony of the ages on behalf of spiritual
revelation, provided we always admit that what was
possible in the past is equally possible to-day, and
that however strange to us certain phenomena may
seem, we have no ground for supposing that because
they are (to us) mysterious, they are not as much
in harmony with the operation of undeviating law
as the erratic movements of a celestial visitor like
Halley's Comet, which comes to visit our skies
only about once in every seventy-five years, instead of appearing regularly in the heavens like
those familiar planets Jupiter, Venus, Mercury,
Mars and Saturn, who are old friends to every one
of us.   Whatever we are accustomed to regularly
behold we are quite certain to call natural, but anything unusual or previously unknown to us we are
apt to dub supernatural, thereby exposing a strange,

but familiar, combination of ignorance and self-conceit. What right have we to claim to so far know the limits of the natural as either to deny the possibility of some curious phenomenon or else rashly attribute it to some miraculous intervention of divine providence, as though God changed or suspended universal order every time we encounter something we are not wise enough to explain? The growing thought of to-day in cultured circles is drifting ever further and further away from atheism, and from supernaturalism also, and is coming to a reasonable conclusion that the unseen universe has never been entirely invisible to the whole of humanity, though very few apparently have anywhere at any time penetrated to any large extent into its mysterious depths. The honored names of Sir William Crookes, Sir Oliver Lodge, and many other distinguished modern scientists immediately summon forth the idea of fearless and industrious seekers after truth coupling psychical research with general mundane occupations. These good and great men, and many others associated with them, have during many years of indefatigable investigation accumulated an enormus quantity of facts which have already gone immensely far to dispel the clouds of superstition and negation which still, to some extent, obscure the public intellect, even in Great Britain and America where intellectual progress has supposedly reached a very noble pitch. Soon after the breaking forth of the movement known as Modern Spiritualism in America, in 1848, a large number of highly distinguished men of light and leading in various communities under-

took a searching investigation of the claims of the
new cult, which from its inception has always embodied within itself the most curiously heterogeneous elements.   Among distinguished authors on
both sides the Atlantic a foremost place is deservedly given to William Howitt, whose compendious
work, "The History of The Supernatural in all
Ages and Nations, and in all Churches, Christian
and Pagan, demonstrating a universal faith" may
well be styled a monumental tribute to ripe painstaking scholarship.   In this great work, issued in
two large volumes both in England and America,
we have an account of spiritual manifestations of
the most widely diversified character, ranging from
the truly angelic to the distinctively diabolical, and
as the author was one of the best known scholars of
his day, and a man who wrote much of the best
standard educational literature published in Great
Britain during the middle of the Nineteenth Century, his testimony cannot be lightly brushed aside;
nor can we justifiably ignore the works of those
famous Americans, Mapes and Hare, or the writings of Judge Edmonds and many other equally
well known and highly reliable members of the
learned professions, all of whom from a worldly
standpoint risked much, but could gain nothing, by
giving their endorsement to the genuineness of
marvels which were rudely scouted, not only by
the ordinary people but by the great majority of
college professors and graduates who would not
condescend to seriously investigate them.   No one
doubts that a vast amount of fraud has been introduced in the name of Spiritualism, and we cannot

close our eyes to the fact that many honest people
are sometimes subject to hallucinations, but there
is unmistakably a large residiuum of fact which conclusively proves the existence of a spiritual life in
humanity which far transcends all materialistic
theories of human origin and destiny.   Prof. Alfred
Russel Wallace,—himself an earnest Spiritualist
as well as a world-renowned Naturalist—has sometimes expressed his opinion that our humanity to-
day does not essentially differ from the humanity
expressed on earth during the Stone Age or some
other remote geological period.   If this be a fact,
and we see no reason to dispute it, we can very
readily understand how it has come to pass that we
find ourselves to-day invited to share experiences
common to ancient nations and individuals who
have left behind them extraordinary testimonies to
the commingling, to some extent at least, of dis-
carnate spiritual entities with physically embodied
humanity.   Without presuming to deny the exisit-
ence of multitudinous orders of intelligencies in the
Universe belonging to very different planets and
systems than our own, we have certainly the right,
and it is indeed our imperative scientific duty, to
weigh the alleged evidence brought forward in
fancied support of the oft-repeated allegation that
the Angels of light, and also the Demons of darkness, constantly referred to in our Bible, and in a
multitude of other venerated Scriptures, belong to
other orders in Creation than ourselves.   It seems
almost unaccountable, in the face of the Biblical
record itself, that anyone should ever have imagined
that the authors of the text ever had in mind the

appearance on earth as Angels, of beings of any other Order than ourselves, for the narrators always describe celestial visitors as men, or at any rate as human, for there is no definite allusion to sex in any original. The masculine and plural genders are very much confused in English versions of Hebrew Scriptures, and this is often due to the fact that a great many Hebrew words fail to give any idea that one sex rather than the other is indicated. Nothing but senseless bigotry and old-fogeyism can have led ecclesiastical commissioners to reject statues representing angels, as occurred at one time in New York, because the sculptor had chiseled some of them in male and others in female shape, and for educated Christians to take so ridiculous a stand would be quite incomprehensible were it not for our painful familiarity with the strenuous endeavors of intolerant males in many ages to consign their mothers and sisters to comparative oblivion while they filled all important offices themselves and derived their adequate support very largely indeed from the work and income of the female members of their flocks. A very old and powerful weapon is wrested from the grasp of masculine ecclesiastical monopolists immediately we prove to the world that the very authority on which they have relied to sustain their fictitious claims is actually against them. People have a perfect right to openly dispute the doctrine of Biblical authority, but there can be no fair play if we misrepresent the teachings of any documents and then base our own dogmas on such misrepresentation. The first chapter of Genesis emphatically declares that

original Humanity is equally male and female.
There can be but two intelligible explanations of
this fact, viz., the ancient belief, still entertained
by many Mystics, that human beings were originally
super-sexual, sex differentiation only beginning with
some departure from an original condition, and the
much simpler view, which we can all appreciate
without plunging into any deep waters of Mysticism, that whenever and wherever human life first
made its appearance on this planet males and fe-
males were existent side by side on terms of complete equality.   Who then are the Bible angels who
so frequently appeared to patriarchal families of
old?   Young men, in our English text, they frequently are called, and so perfectly human in all
their attributes did they appear that frequently we
are told the inhabitants of cities in which they
manifested mistook them for ordinary travelers,—
a circumstance which once for all disposes of the
claim that they were something other than human, or
that they appeared in any startling, because unfamiliar, guise   We have no justifiable reason for deciding that all the Biblical Angels were even human
spiritual entities disrobed of flesh; it is quite rational
to maintain that the word "angel" is often used to
designate a messenger from some Spiritual Order,
one who merely held high rank as a teacher or
ambassador and who was entrusted with some particular commission to a special place and people.
There seems good reason for admitting the contention of Edward Irving,—founder of the body
of Christians styling itself Catholic Apostolic
Church,—that the primitive Chrisian Church ac-

knowledged four Orders of Ministers, the highest
of which was termed Angels. This doctrine
proclaimed successfully in the Nineteenth century,
first in Great Britain, and then in several other
lands, by the intrepid Irving and his devoted followers, derived much sanction from the opening
chapters of the Apocalypse, which speaks of the
message of the Spirit being sent to the Angels of
the Seven Churches of Asia, the plain inference
being that the overseers thus designated must have
held a rank similar to that of bishops in many
Christian communities to-day. It seems, however,
certain that though the simplest definition of angel
is, broadly speaking, messenger, ancient Scriptures
give us frequently to understand that beings ordinarily unseen occasionally made their appearance in
materialized form, and when they did so they were
not generally distinguishable from ordinary human
beings. Whenever we are led to suppose that they
were seen by common vision we may rationally suppose that they were actually young Initiates into the
Temple Mysteries of antiquity, commissioned by
the Heads of the Orders to act as ambassadors or
intermediaries. This very simple commentary on
some, otherwise highly mysterious, portions of the
Bible text explains lucidly and simply the oft-repeated title "Angel of the Lord," which occurs with
great frequency, and though it may come as a
decided shock to Bible-worshipers to be offered so
simple a commentary, even the most orthodox of
such,—if in any way connected with one or other
of the sacerdotal Churches,—will soon begin to see
that if such were the case in days of old, this fact

only bears witness to the antiquity and continuity of a priestly system, and priesthoods are, as we all well know, much more ancient than either Christianity or Judaism.  According to the ideas we are now expressing, we must take into exact account the original meaning of terms and titles variously translated GOD; the Lord God; the Lord; and the Angel of the Lord.  These designatory titles are by no means correctly interchangeable, and the fact that they have been so largely regarded as synonymous has led to an immense amount of bewildering and acrimonious controversy.  We can scarcely believe that any man, woman, youth or maiden, possessed of ordinary intelligence and fairly well acquainted with the English language, would ever imagine that these four plainly distinctive titles were used as synonyms originally, any more than one is inclined to believe, when reading general history, that an envoy is the monarch whose commissions he has been appointed to fulfil.  Every student of Kabbalistic literature knows thoroughly well that the oldest Hebrew documents treat largely of various Orders of Intelligences who execute Divine commissions and take actively influential parts in directing the affairs of Earth.  No one can read a modern Jewish Prayer Book, belonging to the orthodox or conservative school, without finding frequent mention of several Celestial Hierarchies, in accordance with very ancient terminology.  For example, we will turn to the standard popular orthodox Jewish Prayer Book in use throughout the British Empire, and to a considerable extent also in the United States.  In the course of the Morning Service for Sabbaths and

Festivals, occur the following majestic words, which are verily a beautiful link between the more prosaic present and the richly-storied and imaginative past: "Be thou blessed, O our Rock, our King and Redeemer, Creator of holy beings. Praised be thy name for ever, O our King; Creator of ministering spirits, all of whom stand in the heights of the universe and proclaim with awe in unison aloud the words of the living God and everlasting King. All of them are beloved, pure and mighty, and all of them in dread and awe do the will of their Master; and all of them open their mouths in holiness and purity, with song and psalm, while they bless and praise, glorify and reverence, sanctify and ascribe sovereignty to the name of the Divine King, the great, mighty and dreaded One, holy is he; and they all take upon themselves the yoke of the kingdom of heaven one from the other, and give sanction to one another to hallow their Creator; in tranquil joy of spirit, with pure speech and holy melody they all respond in unison, and exclaim with awe; Holy, holy, holy is the Lord of hosts; the whole earth is full of his glory; and the Ophanim and the holy Chayoth with a noise of great rushing, upraising themselves towards the Seraphim, thus over against them offer praise and say Blessed be the glory of the Lord from his place."

The above quotation, which would find no exact parallel in any Prayer Book compiled by Rabbis of the Reform school, is an interesting survival, both in sentiment and language, of very ancient Jewish thought, tho' we would presume to suggest that improvements in the English version would in no way obscure the meaning of the Hebrew original, which still remains the unrivaled tongue of orthodox Israelitish worship. · Such a word as "dread" finds a better substitute in "reverence," and it is highly important to keep this thought in mind when we undertake to criticize the Bible texts, from the sublime imagery of which such utterances have been collated. Ezekiel's visions are responsible for such passages as the one just cited, and it is, of course, very largely open to conjecture how far it was formerly believed in Israel that these visions were actually revelations of life in the Spiritual Universe, and how far the language was designedly symbolical. But however much room there may be for controversy in this particular regard, no doubt whatever can exist in the minds of those who have made themselves familiar with the records of antiquity, that the Jews, in common with all other historic peoples, had firm confidence in the real existence of unnumbered legions of spiritual cmopanies, who were often called the Legions of the Skies. It has remained for Le Plongeon, and a few other indefatigable modern investigators in the Western Hemisphere to prove conclusively the enormous antiquity of similar convictions in Western as well as Eastern lands. Though at first sight it may appear to unreflecting minds that there is little else than primitive superstition in these allusions to manifold Orders of spiritual existences, it surely requires but a very little intelligent meditation on the scientifically revealed arrangement of the universe to put to flight so vapid a conclusion. Harmony is everywhere self-evidently dis-

played in the systematic organization of solar
systems which stud the immensities of infinitude,
and in all the myriad systems of worlds discovered
through the piercing eye of the most far-reaching
telescopes, we find no two globes exactly similar tho'
all are constructed of a single primary substance
and all revolve with such perfect regularity that
astronomers know exactly when to expect the re-
appearance of even the remotest star in the gigantic
aggregation of constellations which make up our
universe.   This indisputable natural revelation well
comports with all that we are accustomed to call
Natural Religion, and when it is fairly weighed it
serves to explain, without denying the primal basis
of Revealed Religion, because when both are rightly
understood one dovetails into the other.   Natural
Religionists invariably claim that they derive all
their ideas from a contemplation of natural phenomena without the interposition of any priests or
angels, but they who make this claim to possess
more information than the majority of their fellows
are simply placing themselves in the ranks of what
may well be called a scientific priesthood, and nothing is more self-evident than that avowed Rationalists place extreme reliance upon the authority of
great names and point to scientific discoveries with
immense satisfaction, though they were made by
others than themselves.

There is very little difference at core between this
attitude and that of the most confirmed Theosophists, for the latter only claim that their authorities
are peculiarly endowed individuals whom they term
the Elder Brethren of our race.   Recent Theo-

sophical publications are far less difficult to read and understand than are the older writings of the Alchemistical Philosophers, who had a double object for concealing the inner meaning of their teaching within a cloak of hieroglyphical symbology.  The "jargon of the Mystics," as this allegorical method has been vulgarly termed, was rendered necessary during the Middle Ages in Europe on account of the ignorant fanaticism then and there prevailing, for without the employment of a mystic glyph there would have been no safety for the writers and also no means of communication between fellow students of the Mysteries.  We glibly speak of the great discoveries made by Bruno, Galileo, Herschel, Newton, Kepler, and many other highly endowed men who lived but a few centuries ago, and we praise them none too highly when we pay glowing tributes to their research and industry; but there is no valid reason for continuing to assert that the heliocentric system of astronomy was not known long ages before modern Europe was a home of learning.  We are far too apt to claim some monopoly for discovery or revelation, which always covers a much larger area than can be bounded by any special time or place.  We ought now to be ready to recast our theories concerning the spread of religious ideas and practices, many of which may have sprung up simultaneously in different parts of the world instead of having been borrowed by one nation from another.

Astronomers in their observatories need not make each other's acquaintance, or even know of each other's existence, to make similar observations of celestial phenomena, for it is quite possible that different men in various places at the same time may be turning their eyes to the heavens and watching the same celectial panorama.

The Egyptian and Indo-Germanic theories of the transit of religions and languages have often been pitted against each other as rival candidates for universal acceptance, but as the Atlantian theory is very much older than either, we may find in it a very fair solution of many difficult problems which a less universal theory of origins will fail to supply. The kings and queens of very ancient days may have indeed ruled by that divine right of individual qualification for supremacy without which all nominal rulership is the next thing to a farce. The Gods and Godesses of ancient Greece and Rome are now often looked upon as glorified rulers of Atlantis, whose memory had been handed down with ever increasing glorification, just as we are prone to glorify our national heroes and heroines until from a basis in actual history we construct mental images of almost divine personages whose anniversaries we celebrate as public holidays and whose memories we extol so highly that many of them shortly become saints and even demigods in our esteem. When we read Homer's Iliad and Odyssey we are at once impressed with the very earthly attributes assigned by that great poet to the divinities of the Pantheon. Such beings as are therein described are so entirely human in all their feelings and conduct that we can well belive that their idealized existence in the Empyrean was founded on records of their actual life on earth, a conclusion

easily reached by all who know how firm  a hold
ancestor worship has held and still holds upon the
hearts and minds of multitudes.   There is much
more that is historical, and consequently much less
that is fabulous, in the views of Mythologists than
many of us have been brought up to believe, for we
are now experiencing a reaction in thought from
the extremely materialistic views which for many
centuries held undisputed sway in nearly every
Western seat of learning.   So dense has been the
darkness in which college professors were engulfed
where the Classics were concerned, and so relentless
was the prejudice against Oriental religions, that in
every European university students were taught to
believe that there was no truth whatever in the religious concepts of even the most illustrious Pagans,
apart from some concession being made to the excellence of a portion of their moral philosophy.
Now it is becoming the fashion to treat the pagan
divinities very much as we treat the Christian saints,
who were certainly human beings with an actual
earthly career, though it is very doubtful whether
such narratives as we find in the "Lives of the
Saints" published with ecclesiastical sanction, could
in all cases be verified by historic scrutiny.   Our own
contemporaries may be, some of them at least, quite
as intelligent and also quite as saintly as their
greatly revered progenitors, but as distance always
lends enchantment to a view, we are rarely if ever
anything like so ready to canonize those who are
living among us as those who have long since
departed from this mortal state.   There are, however, four distinct elements in mythology without

due regard to which we are unable to make much progress in Biblical and Occult research. These are, first, Astronomical and Astrological; second, Historical and Biographical; third, Spiritualistic and Idealistic; fourth, Esoteric and Intuitive. We can read any ancient story in the light of this four-fold method of interpretation without doing violence to reason or good judgment, for we must always remember that there were no cheap printing presses in days of old or in Classic lands making it easy for every item of unimportant information to be recorded in a daily paper. Scribes in olden times were exceptionally capable people and the art of writing was looked upon as sacred, therefore, only the very important events in the life of the people would be permanently recorded, and that portion of their literature which would be produced on well-nigh imperishable tablets would be the work of those exceptionally learned ones to whom was entrusted the custody of those affairs which were generally esteemed as of the highest moment. Trivial incidents are often mentioned but not for their own sake, only for the purpose of illustrating important teachings which the wise men gave to their students through the agency of a double cipher, which enabled those who were in the inner ring of the students' conclave to ascertain the teachers' esoteric meaning, while all outside that consecrated circle would only hear of common-place events of no exceptional significance. When this fact is thoroughly digested and we consider the parabolic teaching still universal in the East, our examination of ancient records will become both edifying and fascinating and we shall be able to escape the Scylla of unreasoning scepticism and also the Charybdis of blind unquestioning belief in the Divine authority of all that any record holds.

# CHAPTER IV.

## VARIOUS SPIRITUAL ELEMENTS IN THE BIBLE AND CLASSIC LITERATURE.

In that highly authentic work by William Howitt, "The History of the Supernatural," that learned and painstaking author, whose reverence for the Jewish and Christian Scriptures was extremely great, justifies his employment of that old-fashioned theological term,—now frequently superseded by the far simpler word superphysical, in the following graphic language: "The author of this work intends by the supernatural the operation of those higher and more recondite laws of God with which, being yet but most imperfectly acquainted, we either denominate their effects miraculous, or, shutting our eyes firmly, deny their existence altogether. So far from holding that what are called miracles are interruptions, or violations of the course of nature, he regards them only as the results of spiritual laws, which in their occasional action subdue, suspend, or neutralize the less powerful physical laws, just as a stronger chemical affinity subdues a weaker one, producing new combinations, but combinations strictly in accordance with the collective laws of the universe, whether understood or not understood by us. At a time when so many objections are raised to portions of the Scripture narrative, which unsettle men's minds and haunt them with miserable forebodings, the author has thought it of the highest importance to bring into a comprehensive view the statements of the most eminent historians and philosophers of all ages and nations on the manifestations of those spiritual agencies amongst them, which we, for want of farther knowledge, term supernatural." This extremely fertile author completely fulfilled his promise to his readers to acquaint them with well-nigh universal testimony to the reality of spiritual occurrences which have taken place, sometimes plentifully, and at other times but rarely, in every section of the globe, and though William Howitt may well be ranked among Christian apologists as well as among Bible elucidators, he was an un-compromising, though never a fanatical or un-reasoning, Spiritualist. The American edition of the famous English book to which we are now alluding was published in Philadelphia in 1863, by the celebrated firm of J. B. Lippincott & Co., at a time when the British and American publics were intensely agitated over religious scepticism on the one hand and the stupendous claims of modern Spiritualists on the other. Had it not been for William Howitt's wide and high reputation al-ready achieved in literary circles, it is doubtful whether his explanations of Spiritualism would have excited much attention, but the name and fame of this distinguished author were unquestionably such that whatever he published was always perused thoughtfully by intelligent persons in all stations. The unique value of such a treatise is in the light it throws upon the universality of spiritual unveilings. How the claimant for *exclusive* revelation can derive any satisfaction from so broad a testimony we are at a loss to see, but to the student of Sacred Literature in general, rather than of a single volume, the extent of territory covered in the narrative must prove thoroughly welcome as well as enormously enlightening. Good and evil spirits are acknowledged in all records of spiritual intercommunion during modern as well as ancient days, but by "evil" is never corectly meant "hopelessly depraved," for the unanimous testimony of all truly enlightened teachers in all climes and ages has been in complete condemnation of the hideous doctrine of endless and useless suffering and its boon companion, total depravity. These nightmares of false theology have never received support or sanction at the hands of any illuminated teachers, and it is quite safe to aver that there never was a really enlightened spiritual teacher on earth at any time who endorsed the garbled misinterpretations of Sheol, Gehenna, Tartarus, and other Hebrew and Greek terms for states of post-mortem purification, which are found either in the Bible or in the Classics. But however true the statements may be that "the door of reformation is never closed" and that "the pathway of progress lies eternally unobstructed before every human soul,"—as certain Spiritualist Societies declare that it does,—such an affirmation by no means disposes of the darker aspects of spirit-communion, though it does suggest to us a reasonable attitude to take toward those "dwellers on the threshold" who are frequently mistaken, by credulous persons, for some mighty angelic beings who are supposed to be amazingly advanced along the path of progress. We cannot curtly dismiss the doctrine of "obsession," disagreeable though its contemplation may be, with the mere snap of a contemptuous finger, but if dark as well as bright unseen influences are around us, whether we know that such is the case or whether we are ignorant thereof, we may rest well assured that the incessant operation of the undeviating law of spiritual affinity must ever be the factor which determines the class of influences to which we yield, and this same law must inevitably at all times regulate our closest psychic intimacies. "I will fear no evil," says the composer of the twenty-third psalm, a phrase which would be meaningless did the word "evil" convey no meaning to its employer's mind. Good and evil are to our understanding relative, not absolute terms. Absolutely there can be no evil but relatively all discord or disease is evil, while all harmony or health is good. This concept is so entirely universal that in all lands and through all ages the demonstrated healing of the sick, through some ordinarily uncomprehended agency, has furnished satisfactory proof that the operating intelligence was of beneficient character. Among Jews and Romans alike this test was considered quite conclusive at the beginning of the Christian era, and all through the following centuries, including the present, the same idea has remained so widely prevalent that works of healing are always triumphantly referred to as evidences of the holy source

whence mysterious abilities are derived.   "Can a
devil open the eyes of the blind?" is a question just
as pertinent to-day as when propounded in the time
of Jesus.   Miracles of healing are only performable
by magicians of the "white" variety; those of the
"black" order can produce genuine manifestations
of many dubious kinds; they can startle but they
cannot heal, because healing being a work of harmonizing is not within the range of rites performable by those who live in discord, and as the great
divide between Leucomancy and Necromancy, *i. e.*,
between light-dispensing and death-dealing magic,
is that the former is always operated with benign-
ant and the latter with malign intent, it is not very
difficult to discriminate intelligently between a
righteous Spiritualism and an unrighteous Sorcery.
At this point many would-be Bible interpreters have
appeared almost insanely blind, for even in this day
we often read reports of sermons against Spiritualism displaying such crass ignorance on the part of
the preacher that we know full well that nothing but
blear-eyed prejudice or sheer stupidity could have
allowed such utterances to pass as "gospel preach-
ing" when we all know "gospel" is a synonym for
good news and joyful tidings.   It is indeed an important part of a prophetic ministry to warn the
unwary against dangers which lurk in their path,
often unseen and unsuspected, but there are but
two ways in which such warning can be profitably
given; one being to counsel the highest moral integrity and the other to recommend firm development of individuality, neither of which good purposes can possibly be served by diatribe and the

hopeless confounding of things which radically differ.  It must certainly be frankly admitted that there are many statements in various parts of the Hebrew Scriptures fiercely condemnatory of Babylonian magical arts as they were practiced during the Jewish Captivity, and it was almost immediately after the return of the Jews to Palestine that there arose great prophets in Israel who strongly urged upon the people an immediate recantation of their errors and an instant return to the pure monotheism which was from the very first the pride and glory of Israel.  No doubt there are many passages in various portions of the Bible which can be so construed as to make it appear that every form of divination was condemned by the prophets in the name of God, but if so strained an interpretation be placed on doubtful passages, what can we say concerning Joseph and his divining cup which was found in the sack of his younger brother Benjamin, when this same Joseph was held up for admiration as a true prophet and one through whose gracious influence famine was averted in Egypt and his own brethren, despite their cruelty to him in his youth, most hospitably received and kindly treated in the time of their necessity?  What can we say concerning Samuel who was not only clairaudient in childhood but grew up to be a mighty prophet, one to whom the people resorted, and never in vain, for wise direction in times of difficulty; and what indeed concerning a whole host of prophets who were all diviners in some respects but who righteously adhered to the moral law and only employed divination for honorable and praiseworthy ends.   It surely needs no unusual acumen to discriminate between prophesy and witchcraft, seeing that the original of the word witch means one who exerts unholy spells with malicious purpose, a practice not entirely absent from the ranks of unscrupulous persons in the present day.   No matter whether the spells worked or not, the true prophets of every age and people have entiely condemned every practice actuated by any desire to work injury upon man or beast, and they have also condemned all those highly objectionable methods resorted to in the Babylonian Empire which had for their object entering into communion with unseen beings through the arts of necromancy, which were so entirely different from all respectable Spiritualistic practices that it is manifestly unfair to in any way confound them.   We hear a good deal about "malicious mesmerism," and much else that is uncanny when the inner workings of some modern societies are divulged and one party undertakes to criminate another, and though it is a very open question how far such charges can ever be substantiated, we have a right to set our faces very decidedly against all endeavors to misuse any occult agency with which we may be familiar.   Nothing can well be more weird and despicable than to endeavor to pervert telepathy or mental telegraphy to the base end of harming someone against whom we feel resentment; but on the other hand we can readily see how truly kindhearted may be the action of benevolent and conscientious people who give what they term "absent mental treatments" for the sole purpose of assisting others to gain or to recover health and to

rise superior to all sorts of temptations and difficulties.   The cry of danger is sure to be raised in some
quarters whenever the mysterious is mentioned, and
the faint-hearted are very readily alarmed at any
cry of "wolf," no matter by whom that cry is raised;
but we should like to inquire of those alarmists, who
are always prating of real or imaginary dangers,
whether they know of any domain in the whole wide
field of scientific and mechanical progress in which
there is no danger   Let calamity-howlers and
other scarecrowists be consistent and they must of
necessity warn us against the use of steam, electric-
ity, and every other appliance of civilization, and
they must also veto every advance in the art of
navigation, especially that of the air, because of the
perils actually encountered by sailors and aviators.
We have no right to suppose that we are entirely
immune from danger until we have reached the
height attained only by great adepts in any line of
enterprise, but such elevated conditions have never
been reached by cravens; only the strong and the
brave are fitted to scale the heights on which now
stand the triumphant heroes whose motto is ever-
more Excelsior.

Alluding again to the work of William Howitt
we can easily follow him in his daring assertions
that miracle is "the eternal heritage of the church,"
but let us always remember that the Latin word
*miraculum* only means something wonderful because unexplained, though not inexplicable.   People
marvel greatly whenever they witness anything they
fail to comprehend, but if they use their reason
they do not therefore attribute it either to jugglery

or diablerie.  A great mass of testimony has recently
been collected proving that works of healing similar
to those described of old are now taking place among
us, some of them within the pale of organized
churches, but very many entirely outside of all
recognized organizations.  Christian Scientists and
other would-be monopolists of the healing power
may well point with satisfaction to their own
successes, but they can have no right wahtever to
claim that they alone are gifted with power to heal,
or that similar wonders wrought by people outside
their ranks are due to "malicious magnetism" or
some other scarecrow which they have trumped up
in the interests of their monopoly.  There are very
good people within the ranks of all parties, who
because of their earnestness and faith do truly
accomplish wonders, but no single denomination
or institution whether it be a church or a school,
has a shred of evidence to support its bombastic
claim if ever it attempts to prove that it alone is
a repository of divine grace or healing energy.
The power to heal has ever been regarded as both
a divine gift and a scientific attainment, and far
from these ideas being mutually exclusive they are
in complete accord, the thought of a divine gift
referring properly to our inward containment, and
scientific skill to the results of human industry
making use of the gifts latent within us.  No one
can read that portion of the Book of Exodus which
recounts the tale of Moses and Aaron on one side,
and Pharaoh's magicians on the other, without at
once discerning that the narrator considered it a
self-evident proof that Moses and Aaron were under

the patronage of heaven, while the emissaries of the
King of Egypt received no divine sanction, because
the former could and did heal the sick, while the
latter with their enchantments could only add to the
sufferings of afflicted men and animals.    Whatever
those wonders were which preceded the outgoing of
Israel from Egypt, they were certainly considered
by Josephus and other eminent historians as clench-
ing the matter in favor of the Hebrews, seeing that
they possessed among them prophetic leaders who
could disarm all antagonism and triumph over every
obstacle by supplying those credentials which were
always demanded in ancient times of all who pre-
sumed to speak to the nations as divine ambassadors.    We may well claim that there are phases of
spiritual healing, such as the reformation of
character, much more important from an ethical
standpoint than even the removal of the most
serious bodily distempers; but all the varied works
of healing recorded in ancient and modern scriptures seem manifestly to proceed from a single
central source.    That beautiful modern classic, "Ben
Hur," by Lew Wallace, very clearly portrays the
world-wide and age-long feeling that every divinely
inspired messenger must accomplish some real good
to humanity in more than one direction; and the
higher the station and the greater the power of the
messenger in question, the mightier must be the
miracles accomplished; therefore it is quite harmonious with universal sentiment in this regard to select
a case of two lepers who were healed by a Master
when they placed implicit confidence in him, and
thereby availed themselves of his healing potency.

All mere wonders which simply excite surprise and apparently benefit no one, carry no manifest credentials with them; they may be "wheat" or they may be "tare," and until they have proved themselves by their effects, we have no right to judge them definitely; but whenever actual good is accomplished we are stupid indeed if we do not attribute it to a benevolent origin, and our position is equally absurd if we refuse condemnation to practices of any sort which bring disaster in their train.   We must use our reason concerning miracles just as we use it in the ordinary affairs of life, judging trees by the fruit they bear, and when this test is faithfully and universally applied we shall no longer stumble blindly as of yore over approbations and prohibitions encountered in the Bible or elsewhere.   It would be a very interesting story, though a very long one, to consider the full significance of all the names ascribed to the various characters in the Bible, and in other Sacred Books, with a view to ascertaining as far as possible, the esoteric bearing of these many peculiar titles, at the same time paying particular attention to the purposeful changing of names, either by enlargement of the number of syllables, or by complete alteration.   The modern world is becoming greatly interested in nomenclature, and many are the classes held in London, New York, and other influential cities for the study of name values. What's in a name? is a very serious question in the esteem of many present-day enquirers into esoteric mysteries, and when we take into account the very large amount of interest now taken in astrology among highly intelligent people, we are quite ready to actively revive all that is innocent and useful in the methods of divination practised by the Ancients. In that remarkable treatise "Art Magic" presented to students of Spiritism and Occultism by Emma Hardinge Britten, in 1876, and more recently distributed widely through the enterprise of that singularly comprehensive weekly paper, "The Progressive Thinker," of Chicago, we read of many sorts of divination which the author regards as highly repulsive to refined feelings, though by no means unworthy of attention from the standpoint of research into the possible amount of control which highly trained ascetics may gain over their subjugated material organisms. With such harsh and repulsive methods as those practised by Hindu Fakirs and Mohammedan Dervishes do not care to deal, as their frantic rites are not the ceremonies performed by the refined Esoteric Confraternities, who studiously cultivate a love of the beautiful and the wholesome, and of naught beside. In the ancient temples of Greece and Rome, as well as of Egypt and India, there were many various arts of divination practised, ranging from the sublime to the disgusting, not indeed all at one time in any single class of temples, but at different periods, and to some extent at the same time also, by different bodies of practitioners. Just as there are many highly variant schools of religion and medicine in the leading countries of the world to-day, so was such the case in lands and ages of antiquity, and such it has continued to some extent at all times everywhere. Divination by examination of the entrails of slaughtered animals was very common in the Roman Empire, and though this was not a truly refined, it was not an altogether abominable practise, as animals were killed for food, as they are still, and after the breath has left the body there is no crime in examining the carcass; nevertheless we must always remember that the most lucid seers were vegetarians who would utterly refuse to have any part in the slaying of animals or birds and to whom contact with a corpse would be intolerable. These pure-minded and exceptionally refined Sensitives of old were the seers and seeresses through whose instrumentality oracular teachings were given which won for the Schools of the Prophets, wherever such were established, a reputation for immediate contact with veritable divinities. The atrocious practices of vivisectors and other flagrant violators of natural order may bring about certain psychical results of a highly detrimental character, but never can brutal outrages on man or beast result in any other sort of consequences, in the long run, than the fate which invariably overtakes every "black magician." That exquisite story of Parsifal, known to all music-lovers as the grandest of all modern operas, sets forth, with unmistakable lucidity, the exact distinction between the contradictory varieties of magic symbolically designated "white" and "black." Parsifal becomes a prince among Adepts, worthy to be the Supreme Head of the Knights of the Holy Grail, only after his fierce encounter with Klingsor, which resulted in the complete destruction of a palace of necromancy. Kundry, at one time a servant of the Knights and at another time a slave to Klingsor, previous to her final deliverance by

Parsifal, is a good illustration of an unbalanced sensitive, liable at any time to be swayed by a temporarily predominating influence.   When as a guileless youth Parsifal goes forth with bow and arrow and thoughtlessly slays a sacred swan, he is reprimanded sharply by Gurnemanz, a guardian of a sacred enclosure, and henceforth the lad shoots no more birds.   At that moment when he accepts reproof and resolves to live by a higher rule than the ordinary he has "entered the Path," and is verily on the mystic road to eventual adepthood.   We cannot too forcibly insist that the great difference between the state of the simple Medium and that of the Adept, is that the former is subject to the sway of varying external influences, while the latter has learned the art of psychic navigation and can therefore determine what influences shall or shall not sway him.   Amfortas, a weak (and therefore incompetent) Leader of the Knights, must resign his office to a stronger and worthier successor.   When Parsifal ascends the throne he instantly heals the wound of his afflicted predecessor by touching it with the Sacred Spear, which Amfortas had lost during an unsuccessful struggle with Klingsor, and which Parsifal had recovered at the end of an equally sharp encounter with the necromancer, a battle which ended in the complete destruction of a dangerous institution of iniquity.   No story illustrates more fully than Parsifal the magical antipodes, for on the one side we find the spirit losing to the flesh and on the other the spirit triumphing over it; and again, on the one hand a vacillating woman subjugated to the ends of evil, and on the

other hand that same woman rescued and strength-
ened and adapted henceforward to gladly serve, in
perfect freedom, the cause of righteousness.

The curious story of the Witch of Endor is one
of those Bible narratives which have given rise to
endless controversy by reason of the highly involved nature of the narrative itself, for it is by no
means clear that that extraordinary woman was an
untruthful or disagreeable personage, though King
Saul, by no means a model monarch, had put all
women of her class under the ban of his displeasure.
There is no moral lesson taught by endorsing the
popular clerical view that Saul committed a great
sin by consulting this woman, rather is the moral of
the story to be found in the statement that neither
she, nor the spirit of Samuel whom Saul invoked,
could save him from the consequences of his own
long-continued disobedience to divine direction.
Samuel had long and often remonstrated with Saul
and urged him to turn from iniquity to righteousness, but the obstinate king persistently and steadily
refused to heed the prophet's admonitions, and to
such a pass had he brought his own condition by
long-continued obduracy that at length it became too
late for him to retrieve his fallen fortunes; thus it
was all in vain that he strove to gain an interview
with the departed Samuel who, great prophet though
he was, had no power to save the transgressor from
from the accumulated consequences of his now ripe
trangressions.  There are crises in all histories,, both
personal and national, and when a harvest is ready
for the sickle it is then too late to endeavor to avert
the result of what has culminated in a conspicuous

output. We must take the consequences, painful and bitter though they may be, just as on the other hand, when we have acted wisely and righteously, we cannot escape the blissful effects of our long-continuing harmonious activity. Up to a certain point we are all free to change our course of action, but when certain seeds have already matured and trees are already in fruit, though we may resolve that our next harvest shall be a very different one, we cannot avert the immediate doom which now confronts us. The oracles and sybils connected with all ancient temples were accustomed to warn their clients of impending catastrophes, and, if we may place any reliance on history, their warnings were often useful in helping those who consulted them to avoid continuance in a path of danger; but sometimes the consultor of the oracle arrived too late to take advantage of that benevolent seership, which when resorted to in season saved many from falling over psychic precipices. The woman at Endor (who is not a witch in the original but only a clairvoyant) told Samuel that she saw with him in spirit a form which he recognized as Samuel, but she had no power to induce this spirit to answer to her demands. That very fine drama, "The Shepherd King," in which the highly gifted actor, Wright Lorimer, has starred so successfully, gives a version of this Biblical incident wonderfully convincing and strikingly in accordance with the purest esoteric teaching. In that superb play, the woman in her cave declares she has no power to summon Samuel, but he appears to Saul entirely of his own volition, a perfectly reasonable conclusion if we take into

account the obvious fact that the prophet would be
in a spiritual condition far superior to that of any
possible familiar spirit who might be at the beck and
call of any ancient seeress or modern medium.
Moses Hull, a prominent American Spiritualist,
pointed out very clearly in many of his lectures and
writings that the word "witch" was only among
those headings of the chapters in the King James
Version of the Bible which were manufactured
about 1611, nowhere in the text itself even in that
particular version.   Nothing can be more ridiculous
than to declare that because there were laws against
witchcraft three hundred years ago in England that
therefore every woman accused of witcheries, regardless of place or conditions, was other than
respectable.   Samuel Putnam wrote a fine history
of witchcraft in New England in which he proved
conclusively to all fair-minded readers that at
Salem, Massachusetts, and in several other places
in America fanatical Puritans condemned to death,
after having committed to torture, many innocent
victims of their insane intolerance not many centuries ago.   The original object of legislation
against witchcraft may have been entirely praiseworthy, as it was evidently intended to effectually
discountenance all unholy practices having for their
object human injury, but we all know how very
quickly well-intentioned legislation can become perverted in the hands of unreasoning bigots and other
unscrupulous persons who never hesitate to attribute the foulest crimes to those who have incurred
their personal displeasure.   Probably there were
women, and men also, in ancient days who "peeped

and muttered," and by the aid of vile incantations endeavored to bring misery upon their victims, and such there may be to-day; but wholesale condemnation of entire classes of people is always unjust and utterly irrational. Wheat and cockle grow together in all fields, and it often needs far more than average insight to discriminate between them until a time of harvest; it therefore becomes us, when reviewing ancient records, and especially when dealing with events in our own day, to give the benefit of a doubt wherever uncertainty prevails. Of one thing we may rest thoroughly assured, viz., that the universe is not regulated in so insane a manner as to permit devils to lure the unwary to destruction, while angelic ministry is beyond the reach of humanity. Whatever is true of the history of Israel is equally true of other nations, and whatever could and did occur in days of old is also possible at this moment. We only learn a moral lesson when recounting the experiences of the past, if the recital thereof inspires us to heroic resolve to devote all our energies, along all the lines of our activity, to the great threefold object worthy of all noble men and women: The discovery of truth; the diffusion of truth; the application of truth to the needs of humanity. With this spiritual amulet in our possession, we carry with us a potent magnet to attract celestial forces and an efficient safeguard against all hosts of darkness.

# CHAPTER V.

It seems scarcely necessary at this period to tell any fairly well-informed persons that the first two chapters of Genesis were never regarded as literal history by any students of esoteric doctrine, and we can readily believe the testimony of Swedenborg to the effect that records of very ancient "Churches" prove conclusively that in times of old narratives regarded as specially sacred were all believed to contain an interior meaning with which the uninitiated may have been unfamiliar, but which was the only meaning with which spiritual teachers were concerned.

The iconoclasm of Thomas Paine, Volney, Voltaire, and other famous writers of a revolutionary and reactionary period, did yeoman service in the cause of intellectual liberty, but it was no part of their mission to unfold interior meanings or call attention to the spiritual agreement which can now be traced, thanks to modern critical research, between all the Scriptures venerated by different sections of humanity. It was really not earlier than 1893, in America, and then chiefly by reason of the

Parliament of Religions held in Chicago, in connection with the World's Fair, that the masses of
the people began to take a really live interest in
Comparative Religion, and even then, during the
seventeen days of the September of that memorable
year in which the Congress assembled, there were
many pious people of fossilized convictions who
were quite shocked at the idea of "heathen" Orien-
tals being invited to proclaim their "idolatrous" doctrines on the same platforms with Christian ministers.   But, to the credit of many distinguished
representatives of the largest Christian denominations, be it recorded that they treated the Asiatic
delegates extremely well, and though it cannot be
truthfully asserted that that memorable gathering
resulted in completely breaking down all barriers of
prejudice between East and West, it is no exaggeration to aver that since that great historical event
there has been far less ignorance and bitterness displayed by opposing religious systems than before
that momentous gathering.   True it is that some few
Americans were so carried away by the picturesque-
ness of Oriental costumes and the fascinating personality of some of the Oriental Swamis, and other
speakers at the Congress, that they were received
into the Buddhistic or some other Asiatic religious
fold, but, for the most part, no proselyting was
either accomplished or attempted.   The more intimately acquainted we become with differing religious systems, the less need do we imagine for going
over from one to another, seeing that they all manifest defects as well as excellences, and we are not
likely to find all our ideals realized in any system.

The chief value of the research we are now attempting is an endeavor to pierce external crusts of mythology and arrive at some reasonable and instructive views of the universe in which we are abiding. The number seven has always been regarded as particularly sacred by all peoples of antiquity, and the reason for this is to be found in Nature, entirely apart from human fancy. The seven hues of the Rainbow, the seven notes in the Musical Scale, and many other equally universal examples may be given of the prominence of seven. The seven "Days," or, more correctly, Periods, of Creation enumerated in the first chapter of Genesis agree substantially with similar enumerations in other and older Scriptures, and when we turn to Swedenborg's "Arcana Cœlestia" for exposition, we find that he informs us that they have nothing necessarily to do with external history, and that it makes no difference what facts may be disclosed through geology, the spiritual truth conveyed in the Pentateuch remains unchallenged. This strong position was finely elucidated and upheld by the scholarly Dr. Bayley, for many years minister of the New Jerusalem Church in Kensington, which was largely attended by earnest people who clung to the spiritual meaning of the Bible, while they followed their highly gifted pastor gladly in his many and wide pulpit excursions into scientific fields. "The Divine Word Opened" is the title of Dr. Bayley's best known book, which is one of the most remarkable and thought-provoking volumes of sermons anywhere procurable. Such works as this deserve much wider reading than they usually receive, for it is certainly lamentable to note the crass ignorance of the Bible still largely prevalent among would-be expositors.

Just as it has been truly said that no one can really understand any single language without some familiarity with several tongues, so is it also true that no one can duly appreciate any Creation Legend without an outline acquaintance with several. The seven Great Ages of the Earth must be seven vast periods, agreeing far more nearly with Oriental than with Occidental chronology; but no chronological element necessarily enters into the earliest parts of Genesis. The first word in the Hebrew Torah, *berashith,* is commonly rendered in English "in the beginning," a phrase which has no necessary reference either to time or place, but is equivalent to "at the starting-point." GOD (Elohim) is said to be the author of all that is produced, and as the author is declared to be entirely good, the results of Divine activity are pronounced likewise good. "And GOD saw that it was good," is a sentence several times reepated, referring to the goodness, each in its own degree, of the various orders of existence which appeared on earth before the advent of Humanity, and no matter what opinions any one may entertain concerning the second and following chapters of Genesis, the first chapter leaves no doubt in the minds of unprejudiced readers that the original tradition narrated in the Bible concerning human origin declares men and women to be a simultaneous creation. Let any child be given the first account alone, and then questioned as to what it relates, that child is certain to say that men and women were created together. Gnostic or Theosophical commentators may undertake to discourse upon some original creation antedating the complete materialization of human frames, and such disquisitions are always interesting and thought-exciting, though to many minds they appear incapable of demonstration. Pre-existence is taught in all Bibles, and, as the venerable Dr. J. M. Peebles, and other modern Spiritualists of learning and experience have stoutly maintained, there can be no evolution of aught that is not involved. Monkeys cannot beget men, though the Simian race may have existed on this planet long before the human. Esoteric teaching is to the effect that every type which appears on earth comes from a spiritual typal germ, a doctrine far more comprehensible than the foundationless assertions of Materialists, who give us no foundation whatever for their atheistic dogmatism. Many scholars are confessedly agnostic; but agnosticism postulates nothing definitely concerning human origin.

A truly wonderful exposition of Genesis has reached us from the inspired and fertile pen of Erastus Gaffield, a gentleman of high literary attainments and social standing, who has written, under spiritual influence, several very instructive books, among which "The Past Revealed" deserves distinctive pre-eminence. In that remarkable treatise we find it stated that "Before the existence of inhabitable conditions upon the earth, there were, as now, many planets in the universe, where only rudimentary conditions of life prevailed, inhabited by beings in various stages of evolutionary progress, by multitudes who had attained only very circumscribed powers of reason, a limited control over weak and imperfectly developed mental faculties, which but partially reflected the intuitions of spirit, and which could not have been used for the investigation of the laws of cosmic creation, evolution, or other scientific facts, nor for the teaching of ethical precepts." "From such very primitive conditions, after having acquired an understanding of certain inherent principles of the Law, graduations sometimes occurred. Many aspiring, intuitive ones, having realized certain degrees of spiritual understanding, and having passed out of their physical bodies, entered into celestial states of existence where larger opportunities were afforded for acquiring knowledge of the divine principles of the Law, and for a more perfect realization of spiritual aspirations. Such needed not further experiences upon material planes. Vast multitudes, however, required and sought new experiences in physical states, and without them could have made but litle progress in the accomplishment of destiny. Therefore it may be said that the 'beginning' referred to in the first verse of Genesis relates to the molding of the plastic elements afore-existent in space, into conditions adapted to the production of such things as physical beings would require when they should appear, who, at first though manifesting only very rudimentary states of intellectual perception, would have certain natural wants, such as air to breathe, water to drink, and food to eat. The text in no way relates to the calling into existence of original elements concerning which no one can conceive a possible explanation."

The first immigrants to earth came without materialized forms, after having accomplished missions in other planets, while incarnated in bodies adapted to conditions there prevailing. They came gladly hither as to a new Golconda, where they hoped to achieve important victories over the elements and to realize spiritual and material progress when conditions should permit them to again assume material bodies." This author then goes on to inform us that those districts of the earth were first inhabited which possesed climates similar to those of the planets from which the immigrants from other worlds had come. "The regions of the far north were first inhabited by physical humanity. Here for unnumbered ages lived a race, small in stature, given to the chase, without knowledge of many refinements subsequently realized in latitudes further south, peacefully inclined, the representatives of an order or condition of life like unto that which their predecessors had evolved in other planets. It may be stated that the destruction of life-possibilities upon the moon, and the formation of inhabitable conditions upon the earth, were coeval." Much teaching regarding the "Lunar Pitris" is to be found in Theosophical literature, and it seems to be the general teaching of those who claim to know something of the immense antiquity of the human race that there was life on the moon before this earth was ready for human inhabitation. Nothing could be easier than to endorse the famous Robet Ingersoll's alleged "mistakes of Moses" did we believe that the letter of Genesis was intended to be taken altogether literally, but, judging it in the light thrown upon it by comparison with other ancient records, we regard

all such iconoclastic ridicule as undeserved and also
utterly unscholarly.  But as Ingersoll was a popular
lecturer, expected to entertain as well as to instruct,
and moreover as some kinds of ignorant theology
are quite as ridiculous as he made them out to be,
the name of Ingersoll endures as that of a champion
of the right of free thought and free enquiry, without which no arrival at truth is ever possible.

We will now direct attention to Hindu traditions
concerning the age of the world and human origin.
These appear highly extravagant to many readers,
on account of the immense periods which they designate to a year, and it seems incredible that we can
estimate the extent of ages with such complete pre-
cision.  However, it is not impossible that there
may be somewhere carefully preserved records
which largely justify even the astounding affirma-
tions of Baba Premanand Bharati in his decidedly
beautiful book, "Sree Krishna; the Lord of Love,"
in which he undertakes to present to English readers "the history of the Universe from its birth to
its dissolution."  The author says that in the course
of his treatise he has explained "the science of creation, its making and its mechanism, according to
information derived from the recorded facts in the
sacred books of the Root-Race of Mankind."  This
is declared to be the doctrine of true Hinduism.
The enthusiastic writer tells us that if we read this
record with an open mind it will grant us illumination and solve many a riddle of life and untie many
a tangle of thought.  The following quotation from
the preface clearly sets forth in highly condensed
phrase the entire substance of the Hindu Doctrine:

"The belief that our life begins with the birth of this physical body and ends with its death, is the worst superstition, because it is the worst obstacle in the way of our soul's unfoldment. This life has sprung from Eternity; it draws its breath in Eternity and is finally absorbed by Eternity, which is Absolute Love. To think that we, human beings, were never blessed with greater powers than we possess in this age is the saddest of mistakes. To believe that we were once as great and powerful as Divine beings, and that we can recover that greatness and those powers, is to believe in the actual potentialities of the human mind. This life can be made one long ecstatic song, this life can, if we take the trouble to make it, be made a source of joy to ourselves as well as to all around us forever and ever; it can even attain to the Essence of Godhood, from which it has sprung. by developing uninterruptedly God-consciousness.

"We are all idolators. Some of us worship idols of Divinity, others woship idols of Matter. Some of us worship the Spirt through suggestive signs and symbols; others worship Flesh. Since our mind wants idols for worship, just as our body wants food for sustenance, let us all worship idols of Spirit in Form. Through its concrete Form-Center we can enter into the Abstract Spirit of Love—Love which is our one object and goal in life. This Love is Krishna, and the universe, and we, its parts, are the materialized manifestaions of that Love." Baba Bharati may well tell us that when we peruse his writings we are reading a book of purely Eastern thought clothed in pure Eastern dress, for without

this explanation, we should be at a loss to understand the foregoing eulogy of idolatry; but when we
know that in the Orient the equivalent of our word
idol simply means any manifestation of life which
we can symbolize, and therefore in some measure
comprehend, as soon as we grasp the Hindu writer's
meaning we can readily sympathize with the clear
and sharp line of demarkation he has drawn between
idols of spirit and idols of flesh.   But it is with the
ages of the world that we are now particularly concerned.   These are styled Gold, Silver, Copper, and
Iron.   The Golden Age lies far back in antiquity,
and is said to have lasted 4,800 Divine years, each
of which contains 360 of our years; thus the entire
length of the Golden Age must have amounted to
1,728,000 of our years, which may well be imagined
as the extent of a geological epoch.   This, according
to Hindu tradition, was the most spiritual age, and it
is claimed that gold literally abounded during that
remote period.   Let us now remember that in the
Book of Genesis we are told of gold as abounding in
the whole land of Havilah, which is said to be
watered by the river Pison.   The word Havilah
means to bring forth and to supply strength; thus
we may readily see some striking connection between
the Oriental traditions now exhibited to our gaze by
Asiatic visitors to Europe and America and the references to remote antiquity found in the early
Hebrew legends. The Silver Age, following immediately upon the Golden, is said to have lasted for 3,000
Divine years — that is, 1,080,000 human or lunar
years.   Hindu chronology always calls Divine years
Solar, and earthly years Lunar, because we count

our months by the movements of the moon and reckon our calendar from a purely geocentric stand-point. During the Silver Age occurred the Fall of humanity mentioned in the Bible. This event is described by Hindu teachers as being due to the attraction of the Unreal. During the Golden Age it is said that humanity knew nothing but Truth, but in the Silver Age they became led astray by decep-tive appearances, and fell from original purity by confounding the illusory with the real. Our fall con-sists in the fact that we become so attached to the unreal that we cannot leave it, though we know it to be unreal. All the ages have their Twilight and their Daylight periods, suggesting very nearly the various Evenings and Mornings mentioned in the Penta-teuch. The life of the Silver Age, though not so beautiful as that of the Golden Age, was neverthe-less in many respects quite delightful, and it is not till we come to the Copper Age that we read any-thing in Hindu literature of ferocious beasts or warlike people. The length of the Copper Age is estimated at 2,000 Divine years, equal to 720,000 human years. The Iron Age carries us to the very depths of human ferocity and degradation, and out of this we are now happily emerging to a very much higher condition, as we are now rounding the curve and passing out from a Dark Age into one of much greater brilliancy.

# CHAPTER VI.

## EGYPT AND ITS WONDERS: LITERALLY AND MYSTICALLY CONSIDERED.

"Out of Egypt have I called my Son." In this highly significant and important Scripture phrase we are introduced to far more than simply an historical allusion; at the same time, the historical information suggested is of great interest and value. Though in a very special sense a land of great antiquity, Egypt is also a modern country, which is attracting ever-increasing multitudes of fascinated students, as well as tourists, who find in the Delta of the Nile almost more to excite their curiosity, and also to repay diligent research, than in any other district usually included within the itinerary of popular travel. Though there are thousands of interesting things to be seen in Egypt, the object of supremest interest is the Great Pyramid at Gizeh, which is well called a miracle in stone. Many of our readers have doubtless read that large and learned work, "Our Inheritance in the Great Pyramid," by Prof. Piazzi Smyth, for many years Astronomer Royal of Scotland, but as that work abounds with elaborate mathematical calculations, and is also written from the standpoint of a certain type of dogmatic theology, it has never served to give a broad general view of the object for which this mighty structure was erected, notwithstanding the fact that it contains a vast amount of extremely valuable information. Prof. Smyth maintains that in order to account successfully for this mighty edifice, we must attribute to it an actually divine origin, for he contends that the architect was none other than Melchisedec, by far the most mysterious character mentioned in the Bible, concerning whom it is related that he was a priest of the Most High God, also a King of Salem, and it is also stated that he had neither father nor mother, beginning of days nor end of life. Such statements cannot refer to any ordinary human being, but they do have reference to human immortality, and they also refer in some incidental sense to a mighty Order of Adepts who exist upon earth in unending succession from age to age. These highly illumined Masters were undoubtedly the great rulers in ancient times, under whose benign sway the land of Egypt was at one time the chief center of civilization upon earth, or at least one of the great head centers whence knowledge was distributed to many other lands. The Great Pyramid differs widely from all other pyramids in its interior arrangements, though it closely resembles them all in its outward construction, as all are built on a common ground plan and all may be regarded as ancient temples, in many of which the bodies of distinguished people were doubtless buried, for the practice of burying the bodies of notable men in temples of worship is of immemorial antiquity. But all the pyramids, save this most imposing one, are elaborately adorned both

within and without with all manner of emblems
and inscriptions, the Great Pyramid alone being
perfectly devoid of all embellishment. This fact in
itself very largely justifies the positive declaration
of Prof. Smyth, and many other learned men who
largely coincide with him, that this unique structure has memorialized through all succeeding centuries, a purely spiritual religion which flourished
in ancient Egypt surrounded by popular forms of
idolatry. The Great Pyramid is well regarded as
a massive Masonic Temple carrying us back to a
period in human history when the astronomical religion of the ancient world was stated and preserved
in fanes of superb architecture which were built
according to the exact principles of mathematics
and geometry, requiring no ornamentation to en-
force doctrines or to portray the ceremonies for
which these structures stood, as abiding and well-
nigh indestructible monuments. The most curiously
interesting theory which we have ever encountered
is that elaborated by Albert Ross Parsons in his extraordinary book, "New Light from the Great Pyramid," which declares that it was built to commem-
orate a great cosmic catastrophe, an idea thoroughly
familiar to the many readers of "Atlantis," by Ignatius Donnelly, who maintains that long before the
great Island-Continent was finally overwhelmed by
the ocean (between 11,000 and 12,000 years ago),
it had already entered upon its declining period, during which certain great teachers from that enlightened land went to Egypt and established there the
beginnings of a vast Atlantian Colony. Such a
theory will make the great Pyramid very much

older than the date given for its erection by Prof. Smyth, who traces it only to 2170 B. C., when Alpha Draconis was Polar Star. But as the phenomenon known as the procession of the equinoxes is accomplished every grand cycle, which occupies about 25,840 years, it is quite easy to admit that the Great Pyramid may be fully 30,000 years old. A very singular book on this intensely interesting subject was issued in California by an author named McCarthy, in which a claim is raised that this wonderful structure is between 50,000 and 60,000 years of age; but in all cases the astronomical phenomenon referred to remains the same. With the age of the Pyramid we need not greatly concern ourselves, but in the object of its construction, and the mysteries celebrated within its walls, we may well take active interest. Though there are many among modern Freemasons who place no great reliance upon very ancient traditions concerning the Masonic Craft, many other Masons, among them men of wide research and profound learning, declare that there is abundant evidence in support of the most venerable traditions. Among gifted authors who have treated of this subject in popular style. Rev. Chas. H. Vail, author of "The Ancient Mysteries and Modern Masonry," ranks conspicuously high. This very liberal-minded minister, for a long time pastor of Pullman Memorial Church, Albion, N. Y., has furnished us with an enormous amount of evidence wonderfully condensed in a portable volume issued by the Macoy Publishing and Masonic Supply Company, New York. Concerning the Egyptian mysteries he has quoted from

a number of distinguished writers, all of whom
testify to substantially the view taken in that curious book, "Art Magic," which contains a section
on the Great Pyramid which we herewith substantially reproduce in abbreviated language of our own.
The author of that singular treatise does not presume to speak dogmatically, but very modestly heads
the section "The Great Pyramid of Egypt—Its
Possible Use and Object." The chapter is headed.
with a hieroglyphic entitled "Man, the Microcosm
of the Universe." This is a double triangle with
a human figure at its center. At the left side of
the apex of the ascending triangle is the word
Macrocosmos; at the right-hand side of the apex
of the descending triangle is written Microcosmos.
At the right side of the apex of the ascending triangle is printed Dragon's Head, and on the left side
of the apex of the descending triangle Dragon's
Tail, illustrated by their well-known astrological
emblems. The letter U (the original form of the
horseshoe inverted) is represented on the left side
of the horizontal line drawn through the middle of
the figure, and the same letter inverted (making the
familiar form of the horseshoe) at the right extremity of this line. Students of astrology will
at once recognize that such a frontispiece to a
treatise on the Great Pyramid is intended to convey to every reader that the structure itself was
built to embody the sublime sciences mathematics,
geometry, astronomy and astrology, which were regarded as the very foundations of all true science,
philosophy and religion by the truly enlightened in
days of old. Those who search Egyptian records

profoundly, and thereby learn to decipher the real meaning of the Great Pyramid, can never fall into the error of supposing that it was either a granary or a tomb, but, speaking Masonically, a veritable stone rejected by modern builders but in reality "the head of the corner." The vulgar supposition, still entertained by many writers and travelers (and frequently hurled at public audiences by lecturers who entertain us with travelogues), that all the pyramids, including the greatest, were burial-places for the bodies of kings, and that the Great Pyramid contains the remains of Cheops, is probably due to the fact that that inspiring object, the lidless Sarcophagus in the Grand Gallery, resembles a tomb; this has led them through their ignorance of ancient symbolism and the rites of initiation performed in ancient temples, to mistake this emblematical and ceremonial laver of regeneration for a literal coffin in which a dead body had at one time lain, but from which it must have at some time been removed, for it is certainly not there now. Prof. Smyth has clearly shown that the body of Cheops was buried in the vicinity of the pyramid, but nobody was interred within its walls. But even had a body been buried within this mighty structure, such a fact would no more supply evidence that the building was primarily intended for a place of sepulture, and not for a mighty temple, than the fact of many interments in Westminster Abbey and many other famous churches, would prove that they were intended only as tombs because the bodies of many illustrious men repose beneath their pavements.

As a Temple to the great and glorious Central Sun of our Universe, Alcyone of the Pleiades, the Great Pyramid is comprehensible, for the only entrance being on the north side, has convinced all astronomers who have visited it that it was designed for astronomical purposes; and we must never forget that astronomy and astrology were inseparable from the religious concepts and ceremonies of the learned among all ancient nations.  The total absence of all inscriptions, both within and without, distinguish this unique pyramid from its numerous companions, of which there are over fifty in the near vicinity.  The populace in ancient Egypt, as well as in Persia, Assyria, India, and all other mighty lands renowned in ancient song and story, employed animal and vegetable forms to typify their spiritual ideas and to furnish them with appropriate aids to contemplation while engaging in religious exercises, but none of these objects were employed by those whose ideas were of the utmost sublimity and to whom the regular order of Nature, and especially the march of the constellations, not only suggested but definitely revealed the universal Cosmic Process.  To these mighty minds nothing less than a Temple erected according to the plan of the heavens, as far as they could possibly discover it, would suffice to satisfy their religious aspirations and at the same time afford them the observatory they needed, in which to carry forward their continuous and elaborate astronomical calculations.  The Spiritual Sun, not the physical orb we see, was the central object of veneration among these great Adepts of antiquity, and it is to this day among the

most enlightened Brahmins and all others, in India
and elsewhere, who have preserved intact the earliest
and purest of all the combined systems of natural
and revealed religion originally communicated to
humanity by those wise and powerful guardians of
our race who are known by various names and
titles among the different schools of Theosophists
scattered over the whole earth.   It is in the 19th
chapter of Isaiah that Bible students will find the
clearest and most copious references to the Great
Pyramid, according to the conclusions of many
learned astronomers who have also devoted much attention to Biblical testimony.   In that wonderful
chapter we are told that there is an altar to the
Lord and a pillar of witness in the land of Egypt,
and a pillar at the border thereof to the Lord (verse
19).

From Stewart's erudite work on "Solar Worship," the author of "Art Magic" culled the following intensely interesting facts: "It is important not
to lose sight of the fact that formerly the history
of the heavens, and particularly of the sun, was
written under the form of the history of men, and
that the people almost universally received it as such,
and looked upon the hero as a man.   The tombs
of the gods were shown, as if they had really existed; feasts were celebrated, the object of which
seemed to be to renew every year the grief which
had been occasioned by their loss.   Such was the
tomb of Osiris, covered under those enormous
masses known as pyramids, which the Egyptians
raised to the star which gives us light.   One of
these has its four sides facing the cardinal points

of the world.   Each of these fronts is 110 fathoms
wide at the base, and the four form as many equi-
lateral triangles.   The perpendicular height is sev-
enty-seven fathoms, according to the measurement
given by Chazelles of the (French) Academy of
Sciences.   It results from these dimensions and
the latitude under which this pyramid is erected,
that fourteen days before the Spring equinox, the
precise period at which the Persians (and others)
celebrated the revival of nature, the sun would
cease to cast a shade at midday, and would not again
cast it until fourteen days after the Autumnal
equinox.   Then the day, or the sun, would be found
in the parallel or circle of the Southern declension,
which answers to 5 deg. 15 min.; this would hap-
pen twice a year—once before the Spring and once
after the Autumnal equinox.   The sun would then
appear exactly at midday upon the summit of this
pyramid; then his majestic disc would appear for
some moments, placed upon this immense pedestal,
and seem to rest upon it, while his worshipers, on
their knees at its base, extending their view along
the inclined plane of the Northern front, would contemplate the great Osiris—as well when he descended into the darkness of the tomb as when he
arose triumphant.   The same might be said of the
full moon of the equinoxes when it takes place in
this parallel.   It would seem that the Egyptians,
always grand in their conceptions, had executed a
project (the boldest ever imagined) of giving a
pedestal to the sun and moon, or to Osiris and Isis;
at midday for one, and at midnight for the other,
when they arrived in that part of the heavens near

to which passes the line which separates the Northern from the Southern hemisphere; the empire of good from that of evil; the region of light from that of darkness.   They wished that the shade should disappear from all the fronts of the pyramid at midday, during the whole time that the sun sojourned in the luminous hemisphere; and that the Northern front should be again covered with shade when night began to assert supremacy in our hemisphere—i.e., at the moment when Osiris descended into hell.   The tomb of Osiris was covered with shade nearly six months, after which light surrounded it entirely at midday, as soon as he, returning from hell, regained his empire in passing into the luminous hemisphere.   Then he had returned to Isis and to the God of Spring, Horus, who had at length conquered the genius of darkness and winter.   What a sublime idea!"

Prof. Smyth has made a great deal of the perfect standard for weights and measures which is found in the Great Pyramid, and he draws particular attention to the Sacred Cubit which measures exactly twenty-five inches, in contradistinction from the "profane" cubit in common use among the Egyptians, which measures a fraction over twenty-six inches.   This fact of only the "sacred" cubit being employed throughout the Great Pyramid goes far to prove that it is not actually an Egyptian, but a truly universal structure, designed to perpetuate those profound mysteries which, though they have been celebrated in Egypt, were never confined to any special country.   Though it is quite rational to insist that literal commercial transactions can be equitably balanced only by the adoption of a world-wide standard of perfectly accurate weights and measures, these external business matters are entirely subservient to the sublime spiritual purpose for which the lidless sarcophagus in the Grand Gallery was designed.   Here again a quotation from "Art Magic" will prove illuminating: ".A better understanding of the profound heights of metaphysical speculation in which the Oriental mind employed itself would have shown......that this vast edifice was designed as a sky and earth metre, and that the huge problem of scientific discoverers, the mystic, lidless, wholly unornamented, uninscribed coffer, in the midst of the vast unornamented and uninscribed chamber, was not intended as a model for all generations of succeeding corn and seedsmen, but as a sarcophagus for living men, for those Initiates who were there taught the solemn problems of life and death, and through the instrumentality of that very coffer attained to that glorious birth of the Spirit—that second birth so significantly described by the great Hierophant of Nazareth when he answered those who came to enquire of him by night, saying: 'Except a man be born again, he cannot see the kingdom of God.'   The time was when Egypt, the young untutored child of the desert, was not the queen of arts and sciences who sat enthroned over the intellectual world.   Then did she become the prey of the spoiler.   She was invaded and conquered by the 'Pali' — Shepherd Kings, or 'Hyksos,' who, according to Manetho, overran the land, put the inhabitants to chains and tributary service, and became for awhile the rulers

of Egypt.   What this country was before the advent of these Shepherd Kings we can hardly conjecture, but after their rule, every monument, pyramid and inscription bore the stamp of Oriental
ideality.   It needs not that we particularize the
details of these revolutionary changes; we only al-
lude to them to account for the wonderful parity
which exists between the religious opinions which we
have enlarged upon in our descriptions of Hindu
worship, and those which reappear in Egyptian
Theogony.   Let us, as Solomon says, consider the
conclusion of the whole matter.   Cheops, a monarch
of the invading line, caused a temple to be erected
in conformance with those strict rules of science,
revealed to the ancient Hindu metaphysicians, as the
mode in which God worked."

Remembering that the book from which the
above quotations are taken was published in 1876,
since which time much added light has been thrown
on the close similarity between Central American
and Egyptian monuments, especially through the
indefatigable explorations conducted by Prof. and
Mme. Le Plongeon, it seems quite reasonable to refer to an Atlantian as well as to a Hindu origin, for
an adequate explanation of the building of the
Great Pyramid.   But it matters not who built it or
in what age it was erected, for as a temple of the
immemorial mystery of human life, fashioned in
accordance with the plan of the Solar System, it
stands pre-eminent, and it is therefore to universal
esoteric Co-Masonry that we must turn for a complete elucidation of its abiding as well as original
significance.

There is one more mighty wonder in Egypt of world-wide celebrity—the majestic Sphinx—which ranks second only to the Great Pyramid in symbolical expressiveness. The special feature of this mysterious stone preacher is its emphatic protest against the animal worship outpictured in all common Egyptian architectural productions. We are all familiar with representations of Anubis, the dog-headed divinity, and with many other works of popular art which equally exalt animal forms above the human level. In the massive Sphinx, propounding its agelong riddle to every passer-by, we see the exactly contradictory concept, for here is a lion's body surmounted with a human head. In this portrayal we can clearly trace the work of some truly enlightened cult, erecting its silent age-enduring protest against animal-worship, and displaying unmistakably the exaltation of the distinctively human, and the consequent rightful subordination of the animal. This is truly the problem which all humanity is called upon to solve. Neither the worship nor the extirpation of the animal is our goal, but the perfect ascendancy of the human over the animal, so that the human may jutsly reign and the animal as justly serve. Let Egypt reveal her message to the modern world as she revealed it in remote antiquity, prior to her decadence, and we shall understand aright the double meaning of the passage: "Out of Egypt have I called my son."

# CHAPTER VII.

## THE PHILOSOPHY OF ANCIENT GREECE—THE SCHOOL OF PYTHAGORAS—THE DELPHIC MYSTERIES.

We have all heard the famous inscription on the Temple of Delphi, "Know thyself and thou wilt know the universe and the gods." On the basis of this maxim the entire theosophical system of the ancient Greeks was based. The three leading propositions of all the Esoteric Schools are summed up in the sentence frequently quoted as the gist of the teaching of Pythagoras: "Evolution is the law of life; number is the law of the universe; unity is the law of God."

The wonderful character known as Orpheus is no mythical personage, but a genuine adept of antiquity around whose wonderful career, as in all similar cases, multitudes of fairy tales have gathered. The work of Orpheus, like that of all other great spiritual teachers, did not consist in establishing a sect or party, but in disseminating truths of universal import which gradually percolated through many existing systems, constituting an inner body of doctrine of which simply literalists were always ignorant. Pythagoras, the Sage of Samos, though his period was not earlier than 600 B. C., is regarded as quite a legendary character by many who have not deeply studied the history of that epoch, and as in the case of so many other great leaders who worked from a spiritual standpoint, fierce persecution assailed this renowned Initiate and all who had the hardihood to publicly espouse his doctrines and remain faithful to his cause. The more we study history, the more convinced must we become that the persecuting spirit, which has relentlessly attacked all the world's great reformers, is excited not by religious conviction in any case originally, but by scheming demagogues, whose tyrannical authority, whether in Church or State, is always threatened by the spread of knowledge, and particularly by a real understanding of the Mysteries. In the case of Pythagoras and his followers, this persecution took place in Sicily, from which island many of the instructed fled to Greece, which furnished them a safe asylum. It is to Plato that we owe almost all our information concerning Pythagoras and his teachings; for, like other great spiritual enlighteners, this noble master gave instruction orally and never transferred his esoteric teachings to writing except under cover of symbolical signs, which only his disciples were able to interpret. It appears that all masters have adopted the two-fold method of giving moral instruction freely to multitudes, but confiding the deeper meaning of their teaching exclusively to those disciples who had prepared themselves to profit by more interior instruction. No sensible or thoughtful person can fail to see the wisdom and complete justice of this course, for no one was excluded from the deeper teaching who was prepared to receive it, and preparation con-

sisted in thoroughly digesting and practically applying the general teaching given openly to the multitudes.    All sorts of curious names have been given
to this inner teaching by those who referred to it
metaphorically.    In India the curious title of "Boar's
flesh" has been sometimes applied to an inner philosophy which was concealed from the masses, a similitude which has led to the ludicrous mistake entertained by some shallow critics that one of the Buddhas died from gourmandizing on flesh, when it is
well known in the East that those who occupy high
spiritual stations are always vegetarians.    In the
School of Pythagoras, great stress was laid on simple
diet, as one means for purifying the body of a candidate seeking admission into the inner circle of
disciples, for it was stoutly contended that no one
could become thoroughly clairvoyant, in the higher
acceptance of the term, who partook of animal food,
or who used any stimulants or narcotics.    The Sage
of Samos was not an ordinary theurgist or worker
of miracles, serving merely to create transitory sensational interest, his avowed mission being to assist
humanity in the work of such complete regeneration
that strife should cease upon the earth, both in the
inward lives of his disciples and in the outer world
also, so far as their influence extended.    The essence of the Pythagorean Doctrine has come down
to us in the Golden Verses of Lysis, in the commentary of Hierocles, and especially in the Timaeus
of Plato, which contains a perfect system of cosmogony.    All the great writers of ancient Greece radi-
ate the spirit of Pythagoras, whom they admired
so greatly that they never tire of relating anecdotes

depicting the wisdom and beauty of his teaching and his marvelous power over all with whom he came in contact. He is quoted as an authority by the Gnostics of the early Christian Church as well as by the Neoplatonists of Alexandria. This teaching constitutes a magnificent whole, and serves greatly to simplify the mysterious symbolism of India and Egypt, which often requires a clear Hellenic mind to portray it in intelligible language consistently with rational and ennobling ideas of human liberty. That wonderful period which witnessed the life and work of Pythagoras was also the age of Lao-Tse in China, and of Buddha Sakya-Muni in India. Pythagoras was a great traveler; he is said to have crossed the whole of the ancient world before delivering his message in Greece, to which country he brought the ripe fruits of a thoroughly matured philosophy. A fascinating account of this wonderful teacher is given by the gifted French author, Edouard Schuré, who enters with much picturesque detail into an account of the early years and extended travels of this brilliant yet calm philosopher, who was the son of noble-minded parents. His father was a wealthy jeweler of Samos; his mother a woman of much refinement. It is said that the Pythoness of Delphi, when consulted by these good people shortly after their marriage, promised them a son who would be useful to all men throughout all times. The oracle directed them to Sidon in Phoenicia, where the child could be born far from the disturbing influences which then ruled in their native land. Before his birth Pythagoras was fervently consecrated to Apollo, the God of Light.

When the child was only a year old, acting on advice received from a priest of Delphi, his mother took him to an Israelitish temple in a valley of Lebanon where the high priest gave the infant a special blessing.   Parthenis, the mother of this wondrous babe, is reported to have been a singularly beautiful and gentle woman, highly intellectual and of a very gracious temper.   As the boy grew toward manhood, his parents encouraged him in that pursuit of wisdom in which he took a most keen delight, and so earnest a student was he that when only eighteen years of age he had studied in classes composed almost exclusively of thoroughly mature and particularly able men.   But though, when at the age of twenty-three, he had enjoyed conference with Thales and Anazimander at Miletus, and others of the greatest among philosophers, none of these distinguished teachers had satisfied his yearning for the knowledge of perfect truth.   Their teachings seemed to him contradictory, and he was ever searching for a grand synthesis.   We translate freely the following paragraphs from the french of Edouard Schurè describing the hour when this marvelous genius seemed to attain his first complete glimpse of the great mission which lay before him: "Through the length of a glorious night Pythagoras directed his gaze now to the earth, now to the temple, and now to the starlit skies. Demeter, the Earth-Mother, that Nature whose secrets he sought to penetrate. was there outspread beneath him and around.   He imbibed her potent exhalations and felt the invincible attraction uniting him, a thinking atom, to her bosom, an inseparable portion of herself.   The

Sages whom he had consulted had told him that it was from her that all things spring. From nothing comes nothing. The soul proceeds from water and from fire, but this subtle emanation of the primal element issues from them only to revert. Nature, said they, is sightless and inflexible; resign thyself to her unchanging laws. The sole merit thou canst have consists in this, that thou knowest them and art resigned to them. Then he gazed upon the firmament and sought to decipher the letters of flame formed by the Constellations in the fathomless depths of space. These signs, said he, must have a meaning, for if the infinitesimal, the motion of atoms, has its reason for existence, surely then also the immeasurably great, the wide-extended stars whose constellations represent a body of the universe! Verily each of these worlds must have its law, for all move unitedly according to number and in perfect harmony. But who will decipher this starry alphabet? The priests of Juno had told him this universe is the abode of the gods which existed before the earth. 'Thy soul cometh' (said they) 'from thence. Pray to the gods that it may remount to heaven.' Then we are told that his meditations were interrupted, first by the chants of the Lesbian women and the Bacchic airs chanted by the youths, but these melodious sounds were soon interrupted by piercing mournful cries issuing from men who were to be sold as slaves and were being cruelly struck by those who were compelling them to embark for Asia. Then it was that a painful thrill ran through his frame, for a mighty problem presented itself before him, as he con-

trasted vividly the different estates of the various
classes of human beings who were thus brought before his notice.   Whatever others might say and
whatever appearances might indicate, the young
Pythagoras cried out for liberty, liberty from all
the pain, slavery and madness so abundantly spread
around him.   Who were right? he asked.   The
Sages who taught a doctrine of blind fatality, the
priests who attributed everything to Divine Providence, or the great mass of humanity who stood
between the two with no well-defined philosophy?
All voices, he decided, declared some aspect of
truth, but none gave to him the true solution of the
problem.   The three worlds, elaborately described
in ancient cosmology, undoubtedly existed, and it
was in the law of their equilibrium that the secret
of the Kosmos lay.   Having given utterance to this
discovery, he rose to his feet, his glance fixed on
the majestic temple which seemed transfigured in
the moonbeams.   In that magnificent temple he believed he saw an ideal image of the universe.   The
Kosmos guided and penetrated by God formed the
sacred Quaternion, which is the source of Nature
whose cause is eternal.   Concealed in the geometri-
cal lines of the Delphic Temple, he thought he found
the key of the universe.   The base, columns, archi-
trave and triangular pediment represented to his
view the three-fold nature of humanity and the
universe: of the Microcosm and the Macrocosm
crowned by divine unity, itself a trinity.   The
three worlds natural, human and divine, sustaining
one another and performing a universal drama in
an ascending and descending movement signified to

him the balance of earth and heaven, of which human liberty holds control. It was then that he conceived of human purification and liberation by triple initiation. But he must prove by reason what his simple intelligence had received from the Absolute. This needs a human life; this is the task of Hercules. But where could he find the necessary knowledge to conduct this mighty labor? Nowhere but in his own soul. It was then that he forsook all allegiance to existing schools, and began the great task of working out for himself that wonderfully complete and simple, though seemingly intricate system, which we have learned to venerate as Pythagorean philosophy."

Modern natural philosophy has always been compelled to acknowledge an imponderable universal agent, and has, therefore, sometimes quite unconsciously, fallen largely into line with the ideas of both ancient and modern Theosophists.

In the ancient Greek thought, Cybele-Maia reigns everywhere; for this is the name given to the soul of the world, that plastic, vibrating substance through which creative spirit acts. Oceans of ether unite all worlds, and this mysterious element is called the great mediator between invisible and visible, between spirit and matter, between the interior and exterior of the universe. The modern Theosophical doctrine of the "astral light" is practically identical with the doctrine of the Logos and its many manifestations, as held in ancient Greece as well as all over the Orient. With these ancient concepts the philosophy of Pythagoras is very largely in accord; but when he visited the

temple of Delphi and infused new life into the doctrines taught there, he gave to his disciples a very
much loftier idea of the universe and of humanity
than was then popularly known among the fre-
quenters of that world-famous shrine. Pythagoras
visited Delphi after visiting all the other Grecian
temples, and at a time when its art of divination
had somewhat deteriorated. His mission everywhere was both to restore and to infuse new light.
In that wonderful temple he found Theoclea, a
priestess of Apollo, who belonged to one of the
leading hereditary priestly families. This remarkable girl positively disliked most things which attracted others, and she was of so deeply spiritual
a nature that she seemed to require none of those
accessories to devotion, or aids to mystic development, which seem usually necessary. She is reported to have heard spiritual voices in open daylight, and on exposing herself to the rays of the
rising sun, their mystical vibration developed in
her a true ecstasy, during which she listened to the
singing of choirs celestial. Feeling herself attracted
to some higher world than earth, to which she had
not yet found the key, she was at once attracted by
that much deeper teaching, and by the far nobler influence exerted by Pythagoras than she was able
to obtain from the priests of the Delphic temple,
whose instructions and ceremonies by no means satisfied her inmost spirit. It is said that he and she
recognized each other immediately as kindred souls,
who must work together for the elevation of humanity. Pythagoras at that time was in his prime;
his eloquence was amazing, and his presence so en-

chanting that the very atmosphere became lighter, and the intelligence of those around him awakened to an extent far beyond the usual.  From this time on the work of this mighty Sage made an impression in Greece far greater than that of any other teacher, and his school was at once renowned for the extreme purity of its philosophy and its astounding depth of insight into the profoundest mysteries of the universe.  Pythagoras and Theoclea worked together for a full year at Delphi in complete spiritual concert, and before he took his departure he had fully prepared her to carry on a ministry virtually identical with his own; thus did he demonstrate the underlying principle of ancient Co-Masonry which always assigns to woman an equal place with man in the celebration of all mysteries, wisely drawing a horizontal line between classes of individuals solely on account of qualification, never an absurd perpendicular line based on sex-differentiation.

After leaving Delphi, Pythagoras worked in Croton, where the famous Pythagorean Institute arose, which was a college and a model city under the direction of this great Initiate.  Through a wise combination of art and science, that magical harmony of soul and intellect which Pythagoreans regarded as the arcanum of philosophy was established.  Science and religion were entirely at one, and it would be well indeed for many in this modern world, who are vainly endeavoring to reconcile false notions of religion with partly comprehended facts of science, to quaff a deep draft of inspiration from the Pythagorean synthesis.

Edouard Schurè gives us a fascinating narrative descriptive of the white dwelling of the Pythagorean Initiates situated on a hill encircled by olive and cypress trees.   The following is a free translation from the exquisite french of this delightful author: "On ascending the hill, the porticos, gardens and gymnasium were distinctly seen.   The Temple of the Muses, with its circular colonnade, light and elegant, towered above the two wings of the building.   The terrace of the surrounding gardens overlooked the town and its harbor.   In the far distance stretched the gulf, between sharp, rugged portions of the coast, as though in a frame of agate, while the Ionian Sea enclosed the horizon with a line of azure.   One might often see women dressed in many-colored costumes making their way on the left side of the hill down to the sea through an alley of cypresses.   These were on their way to worship in the temple of Ceres.   On the right side men were often seen mounting in white robes to the temple of Apollo.   It was a great attraction to the keen imagination of youth to realize that the school of Initiates was under the protection of these divinities, one of whom (Ceres) held the profound mysteries of Woman and of Earth, while the other (Apollo) revealed those of Man and of Heaven."

Pythagoras soon sustained a reputation for sternness in discipline by refusing to admit unworthy novices, for he said that "not every kind of wood was suitable for the making of a Mercury."   Young men who desired to enter the association must undergo severe tests.   When introduced by their parents or one of the masters, they were first allowed

to enter the gymnasium in which the youths played
games appropriate to their age; but every new-
comer noticed at once that this was a gymnasium
of a very peculiar sort, quite unlike those of the
Grecian towns in which were heard the violent cries
of clamorous groups boasting of their strength, challenging each other and proudly exhibiting their
muscles.   Here were only groups of well-behaved
and singularly fine-looking young men walking in
couples beneath the porticos or playing rationally
in the arena.   They always invited a stranger to
join them with kind simplicity, making him feel at
once at home among them and never subjecting him
to any annoyance or humiliation, a lesson which
modern colleges in Europe and America need to
mark, learn and inwardly digest until the disgrace-
ful practice of hazing and similar abominations are
once for all eliminated root and branch from all
educational institutions claiming respectability and
seeking the patronage of an enlightened public.

Before we can reasonably hope to make any real
progress in spiritual or ethical directions we must
lay a firm foundation in physical and mental culture.
The gymnasium, according to Pythagorean philosophy, is a valuable vestibule to the inner temple
in which profound instruction is given pertaining
to mind and spirit; but as during a soul's terrestrial
embodiment it needs to operate through a physical
instrument, the part of reason is to provide as perfect an instrument as possible, and keep that vehicle
in excellent working order.   In the system of Pythagoras there is consistently maintained, from first to
last, the idea of perfect equilibrium.   Here is to be

found neither voluptuous indulgence nor harsh asceticism.   The body is not treated as though it were the foe of the spirit, but it is never allowed to usurp any throne of mastery.

In this matchless school of ancient Greece every principle of virtue and nobility was inculcated and exemplified which the foremost educators of to-day are endeavoring to impress upon the gradually awakening consciousness of colleges and churches, and it must prove somewhat humiliating to the haughty heads of Christian seats of learning to find that a "Pagan" philosopher, several centuries before the Christian era, had carried out successfully a scheme of discipline which excluded all objectionable features, such as stupid, and often brutal, wrestling, while it afforded vigorous young athletes ample opportunity and encouragement to cultivate their muscles to the utmost within the reasonable bounds of healthy exercise and good behaviour.   On the question of friendly feelings between fellow students, Pythagoras took uncomprising ground.   True friendship can never exist in company with brutality, nor can real courage be developed by cultivating envy or catering to unrighteous pride. Hatred makes us inferior to those we hate, precisely as terror puts us in the power of what we dread.   Heroes are developed in schools where honest mutual esteem is cultivated to the utmost, and should it ever be necessary for a hero to fight he could do so with great courage and ability, but without a shade of fury.   The Pythagorean method was both simple and conclusive.   Fresh arrivals at the college were encouraged to express their own views freely among their new acquaintances, and as no restriction was placed upon the expression of their sentiments, they soon registered themselves as suitable or unsuitable for admission into the classes.   If any new applicant proved himself intelligently appreciative of the high standard in vogue among the Initiates, he was cordially welcomed; but if he evinced a preference for the cruder standard of the popular gymnasia of the towns, he properly drifted thither.   While a new candidate was expressing his sentiments without restraint, the teachers were taking note of all he said, and it never took them long to ascertain whether he showed fitness for admission or otherwise.   Pythagoras himself would often appear unexpectedly in the presence of the stranger, and study his words and gestures, in estimating which he was never at fault; he paid particular attention to gait and laughter, which are always faithful indexes of character; he had also made so profound a study of the human face that he read dispositions at a glance.   Pythagoras introduced some of the Egyptian tests into his system, but the severer among these he wisely modified. After a few months of preliminary training, the candidate was submitted to an ordeal intended to test his bravery and prove his spirit.

One of these tests consisted in spending a night in a cave which had the reputation of being haunted with mysterious elementals who appeared to the aspirant in gruesome shapes.   If his courage withstood this ordeal, he was accounted worthy to pass on to higher initiations, but if he shrank in terror from this external test he was considered too irresolute to be eligible for advancement.   Being accepted for the preliminary degree, it was usually not long before the candidate was put through moral trials accompanied by severe tests of intellectual character.   Among these the ready solution of intricate mathematical problems held prominent place.   For example, a teacher would call upon a student without warning to explain the meaning of a triangle within a circle, or to answer such a question as, Why is the dodecahedron, contained within a sphere, the symbol of the universe?   When passing these tests, the student was required to spend twelve consecutive hours in his cell, during which time he might partake of bread and water, but no other food was allowed him.   To young men of sybaritic temperament, such discipline might seem excessively severe, but to those of frugal tastes and sincerely bent on study, this was only healthy mental exercise. When these twelve hours were ended the youth was taken into a company of assembled novices, who were allowed to ridicule him to test his metal; if he withstood all jibes and sneers complacently, he was regarded by the teachers as truly an embryonic philosopher, but if he became angry and resentful, Pythagoras would inform him that such lack of self-control demonstrated ineligibility for advancement.

It was only in extreme cases of misconduct, however, that this thoroughly equitable master expelled students from his school, and when he did so he always addressed them calmly and graciously, explaining to them that it could be of no use to them to attempt to continue their studies when they were quite out of harmony with the requirements and discipline of the college. These tests of temper proved conclusively the degree of self-control already attained by the young men who wished to become renowned in future as philosophers. Rejected candidates would sometimes inveigh bitterly against the college and its head; among these was the fanatical Cylon, who never forgave the college for his dismissal, and finally excited the populace to bring about its downfall. Those who bore everything with firmness were welcomed into the novitiate and received enthusiastic congratulations from their new companions.

The First Degree was called Preparation. This lasted from two to five years. Novices were called Listeners; during lessons they were subject to the rule of complete silence. They were not permitted to offer objections or to enter into discussions, for they must absorb the teaching before they could be prepared to discuss it intelligently. The Second Degree was called Purification. During this process of study the novice was welcomed into the house of Pythagoras and numbered among his disciples; real initiation now began. A rational exposition of occult doctrine was now given, which consisted especially in a study of the Science of Numbers, the esoteric meaning of which was concealed from the people at large, and only communicated to students who had proven their worth. A great distinction was made between sacred and secular mathematics; the latter alone are known to European *savants*, but the knowledge of the former has always been carefully preserved in the East.

' The number One necessarily is all-including, as

perfect white contains all colors; but as we cannot conceive of the Absolute Unmanifest with our finite intellects, all expressions of Divinity must be dual, consequently the Dyad reveals the Monad. Here we find another link between the Pythagorean and the Jewish conception of Divinity, as set forth in the opening chapters of the Pentateuch. Man and Woman hold equal rank in all ancient philosophies, but the feminine is always regarded as interior, while the masculine is external; therefore it often happens that short-sighted or unreflecting students imagine that the masculine is more sacred than the feminine, according to the teaching of ancient and Oriental philosophies. During the training of the Initiate in the Second Degree, the student was instructed in a doctrine very similar to much of the teaching with which we are familiar through the epistles of S. Paul, who was undoubtedly familiar with Greek philosophy as well as with Hebrew and Roman law. In the scheme of Pythagoras the number 7 (compound of square and triangle) signifies the union of Man and Divinity. It is the figure of all great Initiates, who understand that there are 7 degrees in involution and evolution. The number 10 represented completeness; it is called the perfect number in the highest sense, for it represents all principles of divinity evolved and reunited in a new unity. We have all heard of the 9 Muses personifying the sciences, grouped 3 by 3, presiding over the triple ternary evolved in 9 worlds, which together with Hestia, Guardian of the Primordial Fire, constitute the sacred Decad.

The Third Degree was called Perfection, as

among the Essenes.   In this degree psychology and
cosmogony were the leading studies.   While the lessons in the earlier degrees were given in daylight,
often in the full blaze of the outdoor sun, these
deeper teachings were usually given during the night
season in the open air by the seaside, or sometimes
in the crypts of the temple which were gently illuminated by lamps of naphtha.   It was at these times
that clairvoyance asserted itself, and the inner faculties of the students began to enable them to personally verify by their own experience that which
the teachers taught.   It cannot be doubted by any
who have studied deeply the records of ancient esoteric teaching that the old astronomical glyph, which
everywhere presents itself, was chiefly a veil thrown
over the secret teaching, which related far more
to the evolution of the human soul than to the movements of the literal planets.   Ancient astrology was
something very different from the misguided substitute with which in these days we are often made
disagreeably familiar.   In sacred astrology there
are no "malific" planets or "evil" aspects, though
it is very clearly taught that one star does indeed
differ greatly from another; but as members of
one family may be persons of widely different temperament, occupation and appearance, and yet all
be good and useful, so in a family of worlds like
our solar system the different planets may be spoken
of as brothers and sisters, the sun being the parent
of them all.   We can only understand the famous
saying quoted by present-day astrologers of the better type, "The wise man rules his stars, the fool
obeys them," when we contemplate the significance

of the personal pronoun in the sentence, for no man, however wise, can regulate the motions of the stars, but we can learn to regulate their correspondences within his own nature. Pythagorean astrology is founded upon the acknowledgment of universally diffused intelligence, which is now coming to be largely recognized by Western as well as Eastern philosophers, and indeed the whole scientific world of to-day is coming very near to an acceptance of that ancient esoteric teaching which alone accounts intelligently for the behaviour of all forms of existence observable under the microscope. The celestial history of Psyche formed the ·climax of the instruction given by Pythagoras to his disciples. What is the human soul? he asked. "A portion of the mighty soul of the world, a spark of Divine Spirit, an immortal Monad. Still, through its possible future opens out into the unfathomable splendors of Divine consciousness, its mysterious dawn dates back to the origin of organized matter. To become what it is in present-day humanity, it must have passed through all the reigns of nature, the whole scale of beings gradually developing through a series of innumerable existences. The spirit which fashions the worlds and condenses cosmic matter into enormous masses manifests itself with varying intensity and an ever greater concentration in the successive reigns of nature. A blind and confused force in the mineral, individualized in the plant, polarized in the sensation and instincts of animals, it stretches towards the conscious monad in this slow elaboration; and the elementary monad is visible in the most inferior of animals.

The animal and spiritual element accordingly exists in every kingdom, though only in infinitesimal quantities in the lower kingdoms. The souls which exist in the state of germs in the lower kingdoms stay there without moving away for immense periods of time, and it is only after great cosmic revolutions that, in changing planets, they pass to a higher reign. All they can do during a planet's period of life is to mount a few degrees. Where does the Monad begin? As well ask at what hour a nebula was formed or a sun shone for the first time. Anyhow, what constitutes the essence of any man must have evolved for millions of years through a chain of lower planets and kingdoms, keeping through all these existences an individual principle which follows it everywhere. This obscure but indestructible individuality constitutes the Divine seal of the Monad in which God wills to manifest Himself through consciousness.

The higher one ascends in the series of organisms, the more the Monad develops the principles latent in it. Polarized force becomes capable of sensation, capacity of sensation becomes instinct, and instinct becomes intelligence. In proportion as the flickering flame of consciousness is lit, this soul becomes more independent of the body, more capable of existing freely. The fluid, non-polarized soul of minerals and vegetables is bound to the elements of earth. That of animals, strongly attracted by terrestrial fire, stays there for some time after living in the body, and then returns to the surface of the globe to reincarnate in its species without ever having the possibility of leaving the lower layers of the air. These are peopled with elementals or animal souls which play their part in atmospheric life and have a great occult influence over man. The human soul alone comes from the sky and returns there after death. At what period of its long cosmic existence has the elementary become the human soul? Through what incandescent crucible, what ethereal flame has it passed? The transformation has been possible in an interplanetary period only by the meeting of human souls already fully formed which have developed in the elementary soul, its spiritual principle, and have impressed their Divine prototype like a seal of fire in its plastic substance." (Quoted from J. Rothwell's Translation.) According to the esoteric traditions of India and Egypt, we began our human existence on other planets where matter is far less dense than here. Human bodies were then almost vaporous, and it was quite easy for the soul to accomplish incarnation. Here we note a close resemblance between the teaching of Pythagoras and that profound Oriental doctrine which we have summarized in the section of this volume dealing especially with Hindu doctrine and tradition. We must refer our readers to the fine work of Edouard Schurè, from which we have already quoted freely, for further dissertation on this exhaustless theme, and pass on to a mere mention of the teaching of the Fourth Degree, called Epiphany, meaning vision from above. The initiation of intelligence must be followed by that of will, the most difficult of all. The disciple must become deeply imbued with truth in his inmost being, and must put the high teachings into practice in daily

life.    To attain this ideal, one must unite three kinds
of perfection, called respectively realization of truth
in intellect; virtue in soul; purity in body.    The
astral body participates in all the acts of the physical; it does indeed give effect to them.    A doctrine of regeneration, which Pythagoras expounded
very clearly, teaches how a second nature must re-
place the first, and finally the intellect must reach
wisdom beyond mere knowledge till it can distinguish good from evil in every department of existence, and behold a revelation of God in the smallest
of creatures, as well as in universal immensities.

On reaching this altitude, man becomes an adept,
and enters into conscious possession of new faculties and powers; the inner senses of the soul expand
and the physical senses are dominated by radiant
will.    Bodily magnetism, penetrated by the potency
of the astral soul, electrified by will, acquires force
apparently miraculous.    Among the accepted Initiates, many healed the sick by their simple presence,
though others resorted to the laying on of hands.
Clairvoyance, like that of Apollonius of Tyana in
one age and of Swedenborg in another, was frequently exhibited; indeed, all the wonders recorded
of saints and seers throughout the literature of the
ages seem to have been demonstrated in the school
of this mighty master whose name to-day is being
pronounced with ever-increasing reverence.    The
Christian doctrine of the Trinity, so much misunderstood, because so deeply veiled in mystery, was rendered far more intelligible by Pythagoras six hundred years before the beginning of the Christian era
than by those controversial Fathers of the Church

who rejected the Divine Feminine, and therefore
made quite unintelligible the original doctrine of the
procession of the Logos.   Father, Mother and Child
we can understand; but Father, Son and Holy Spirit
is an unintelligible phrase until we know that the
Holy Spirit originally stood for the Divine Feminine.   The Pythagorean Trinity is described as
Spirit, Soul, and Heart of the Living Universe. The
life of Pythagoras was extremely beautiful, and
in the truest sense both spiritual and natural.   When
sixty years of age he married one of his pupils, a
maiden of great beauty and singular intelligence.
This noble woman, Theano, entered so thoroughly
into her husband's thought and life that after he had
passed from earth she became the centre of the
Pythagorean Order.   Two sons and one daughter
were the result of this union, and the whole family
offered a high model for all other families to follow.
On all political questions Pythagoras was as highly
enlightened as in the transcendent domain of directly spiritual philosophy, for he was a reformer
in the widest and highest acceptance of the term.
The system of government which he advocated
united the best elements of democracy and aristoc-
racy, and it will be well indeed if those who are
wrestling with modern legislative problems investigate more deeply the wise teachings of those true
Initiates of old, who, while loving the whole people
devotedly, and desiring in every way to promote the
common interest, wisely realized that only the most
intelligent and in every way enlightened among the
people were competent to represent the multitudes as
governors or legislators.

Cylon, the inveterate persecutor of the Pythagorean school, from which he had been expelled, was a fair sample of the unscrupulous modern demagogue.    Tradition asserts that one evening, when forty of the principal members of the Order had assembled, this outrageous man, who was then a tribune, surrounded the house with an enraged crowd and set fire to the buildings.    Thirty-eight of the disciples, together with Pythagoras himself, were either burned to death or massacred by their assailants, but the Order did not die; it was only dispersed, and continued for two hundred and fifty years to exert a benign, regenerating influence wherever it was established.    Many of the predictions of Pythagoras were literally fulfilled, and this fact in itself inclined many to investigate the sublime doctrines of an Order which had had for its founder a sage and seer of such wonderful graces and lucidity.    Truly has it been said that Pythagoras was an Adept and Initiate of the highest type; he enjoyed a direct spiritual vision, and had found the key to the occult sciences and to the spiritual world.    He drew supplies of knowledge from the primal fount of truth, and united with a wondrous intellect a high moral nature, which commanded the respect and love of all capable of appreciating real nobility. The philosophic edifice he reared was never destroyed.    Plato took from Pythagoras his entire system of metaphysics.    The closing words of Edouard Schurè's magnificent french treatise amy be translated thus: "The school of Alexandria occupied the upper stories of the edifice, while modern science

has possessed itself of the ground floor and strength-
ened its foundations.   Many philosophical schools
and mystical or religious sects have dwelt within its
numerous chambers.   No philosophy, however, has
yet embraced it in its harmonious entirety."

# CHAPTER VIII.

## APOLLONIUS OF TYANA.

One of the ablest followers of Pythagoras was Apollonius of Tyana, who was so great a wonder-worker that the Emperor Antonius Caracalla worshipped him as divine, while Alexander Severus and other emperors showered upon him great honors, and regarded him with high esteem. During a terrible plague at Epathuses, it is recorded that he caused it to cease immediately on his arrival there, having been summoned thither by men in high authority, who firmly believed in his miraculous healing power. Concerning his many works of healing, we are told that sometimes he was present with his patients and even laid his hands upon them, but in many instances he performed marvelous cures at a distance; he is indeed reported to have done as many mighty works as any of the great prophets or apostles of whom Holy Writ makes any mention. Like all other truly learned and holy men, Apollonius made a clear distinction between righteous magic and unholy sorcery. By true magic he understood that mysterious power which acts through sacred ceremonies performed with good intent by honorable persons, while under the term sorcery he included all acts which, however performed, pro-

ceeded from malicious motives and were worked
with the intention of inflicting injury.    Here we
have one more illustrious tribute paid to a noble
universal idea, one that, though it has long been
eclipsed, is now shining forth again in all its native
brilliancy, inspiring men and women in this day in
many lands to perform many benevolent works similar to those which wrought so much benefit in by-
gone time in ancient countries.    The leading doctrines of Apollonius were so similar to those of
many other great teachers that his personal identity
does not always stand out very clearly; he has been
many times confounded with other illustrious spiritual teachers and mighty wonder-workers, but there
seems good historical evidence that he was a very
real and influential personage, and one moreover
who wrought great blessings in his own day and
handed on a far-reachng benign influence to pos-
terity.    Speaking for himself, his biographers make
him declare that his mode of life was very unlike
that of the bulk of the people among whom he
mingled; he took very little food, but gained much
nourishment from an extremely simple diet; he
seems to have been entirely free from ostentation,
and simply went about doing good to the fullest
extent of his opportunity.    As a seer he takes exceptionally high rank, for he evidently possessed
ability to foresee and foretell many important events
as well as to heal many diseases and quell many riots
by the exercise of a power entirely super-physical.
Apollonius lived at a time when faith in the gods
and goddesses of the classic world had greatly
waned, and when the priests and priestesses of once

glorious temples had largely declined from their former high estate, and it was his earnest mission to seek not only to restore the ancient glories but to enkindle a new flame and fervor in his own generation surpassing in brightness and purity that of departed days. Like all other great teachers who undertook to enlighten the world, he was withstood and persecuted by many classes of opponents, but he always showed himself able to so thoroughly defend his doctrine and practices whenever they were attacked that he made hosts of friends from the ranks of the opposition, and surrounded himself with companies of faithful disciples who were loyal and devoted even unto death. This great teacher laid no stress on sacrifices, and paid little heed to any ritual observances; a pure life and a philanthropic temper he extolled far above all ceremonies, for moral excellencies he regarded as the only great essentials for spiritual attainment. Magical powers he looked upon as belonging by right to those who lived on a higher plane than the majority, and like all really spiritually-minded teachers he expected higher human faculties to unfold normally when the right life was lived conducive to their development, without recourse to any artificial means for stimulating them. Philostratus, in a minute description of the life of Apollonius, says that he visited the temple of Aesculapius at Aegea, the Oracles of Anphiaraus, Delphi, and Dodona; the Magi of Nineveh and Babylon; the Brahmins of India; he also visited Egypt, Ethiopia, Crete, Sicily and Rome. In his later years he resided for some time at Smyrna, Ephesus and Tyana; the date of his death is given as 96 C. E., at the age of about 100 years. Wherever he went he urged the people to a life of the strictest morality accompanied by works of piety and prayer. He is said to have cured every kind of malady, including the most dangerous and fatal diseases, and many of his predictions were accurately fulfilled. We can gather much from these recorded incidents that will throw bright light upon the early years of the Christian era, for at that period it seems impossible to doubt that a mighty spiritual wave was sweeping over this planet and manifesting its potency through the agency of a great number of contemporary wonder-workers, many of whom were unmistakably men and women of the noblest character devoted to the highest imaginable ideals. It would be a vain and useless task to attempt to disentangle the exact deeds of this one man from those of all the rest, and it is surely only necessary to consider the works themselves if our aim is to prove the reality of inspiration and its continuous flow through all the ages. Apollonius was one bright light shining with far more than ordinary brilliance, but he was not a solitary figure, nor did he claim to be an only master. We greatly need in our own day to take a far more intelligent and comprehensive view of so-called magic and all pertaining to it than can ever be taken by any who wish to prove too much for one teacher and equally too little for all the rest. We might easily cite examples from an enormous array of testimony to similar works accomplished in all parts of the world and under many widely different auspices, but enough has been said to put our readers in the way of considering the claims of ancient and modern mystery and revelation, to the end that they may search the records for themselves with renewed interest and vigor, and we trust always with the sole desire of discovering truth and weighing evidence impartially. The study of history is beneficial only in so far as it spurs us on to seek to duplicate, if not transcend, the good deeds that have been wrought by those who have blazed the path of human progress before our day. Century after century and millennium after millennium the same great problems are presented to humanity for solution, for similar needs arise continually for the exercise of that marvelous power to teach and heal which is the one indisputable credential of the true prophet and the pure white magician. It will be indeed well for us all if, considering the great interest now everywhere displayed in psychic marvels, we learn to tread the consecrated way which leads to that true adepthood which, in its last analysis, is the supreme triumph of the spirit over all that would fetter its radiant activity in individual and in communal life. There is much deep significance in the following extraordinary testimony to what Apollonius conceived to be a mode of life and course of action conducive to the most beneficial results. He says of himself: "I wear a robe of linen which as well as being conducive to cleanliness also produces more truthful dreams. Between God and man exists a bond of relationship, and by this is man in some measure a participator in the Divine nature. All are convinced that the powers of the mind and the soul are derived from God, and that those are the nearest to God who are most highly endowed with them. The Indian wisdom, to which the Egyptian is related, says that God created all, and the cause of Creation was the goodness of God. If God is therefore good, we may consider a good man as participating in the spirit of God. To what this leads he shall know who is acquainted with the philosophy of Eclectics." (Quoted from Enne-moser's "History of Magic.")

This philosophy is a combination of the purely Platonic and Pythagorean schools, which are indeed essentially at one. As the dialogues of Plato are so easily accessible and so well known to scholars, we need not proceed to dilate upon the leading tenets of that glorious Grecian school. Suffice it to say that a sense of harmony with all creation is the one great aim and object of all true philosophic doctrine. The road to this attainment is through following out in all cases the innermost dictates of one's own highest consciousness.

# CHAPTER IX.

There are five kinds of Yoga, termed in Sanscrit
Karma Yoga, pertaining to Divine Union through
unselfish performance of duty; Hatha Yoga, treating of Mental and Physical Attainment through exterior disciplinary exercises; Raja Yoga, dealing
with Internal Realization of Truth; Bakti Yoga, intended to cultivate conscious union with Divinity
through performance of Works of Devotion; Jnana
Yoga, the object of which is to accomplish perfect
knowledge of Divine Nature.

The simplest English equivalent of Yoga is
Union. There are three special kinds of union to
be effected before any of us have become Yogis.
First, we must seek to realize something of the
mighty truth involved in the matchless phrase, Divine Unity. Far transcending all limited views of
Deity is the magnificent thought of an all-pervading
as well as all-transcending Deity. According to the
teachings of genuine Yogis, no idea of God can be
altogether false, neither can any finite concept be
entirely true, as no finite intellect can possibly encircle Infinity. We all entertain just those ideas of
the Supreme Being which register accurately our

stage of development, and when this is clearly understood, all difficulties vanish regarding the many
discrepancies which abound in Sacred Literature.
Yogis are they who have so far outgrown depend-
ence upon outward aids to devotion that they can
realize God everywhere and through everything; to
them, therefore, all manifestations of life are sacred.
This mighty truth, sublime as it is, like all other
universal verities, is easily liable to misapprehension;
we need not then be in the least surprised to encounter ignorant fanaticism associated with prevalent ideas of Yoga entertained in India to-day.   It
is a very common mistake made by Western admirers of Hindu philosophy to take as true expositions thereof whatever doctrines may be promulgated by any native teachers from India who may
be visiting our shores.   This attitude of undiscriminating acceptance of widely divergent teachings has
led to much mental confusion, and it certainly be-
hooves us to compare thoughtfully one Oriental doctrine with another, precisely as we need to judge
between different theories promulgated in the West.
Between Yogis and Fakirs there is an enormous difference, though the two are often mischievously
confounded.   Fakirs are ascetics who work marvels
which greatly astonish multitudes of wondering
spectators, but they are in no sense Yogis, for such
as truly practise Yoga are in no sense sensational
wonder-workers, but profound practical students
of the Law of the Universe.   Hatha Yoga, which
has been much exploited in America of late, needs
to be comprehended, at least in outline, before we
proceed to discuss the other and more spiritual vari-

cties, as this deals very practically with training body
and mind together, so as to produce a healthy vehicle through which the spirit can act during incarnation.

The topic of rhythmic breathing is always one of
extreme interest, as it lies at the very foundation of
all health exercises; but it is often claimed that
methods in vogue in India may be injurious to
Americans and Europeans, owing to wide differences
in temperament and general habits of living.   This
is probably true to a certain limited extent, but by
no means so far as many people seem to imagine, for
though heredity and early training count for a good
deal everywhere, it can never be injurious, but, on
the contrary, highly beneficial, to cultivate the excellent habit of deep, regular breathing.   True it is
that if we live naturally from childhood we shall not
need to practise formal breathing exercises, just
as we shall not need to exercise in a gymnasium if
we accustom ourselves to taking regular outdoor
exercise sufficient to keep all our limbs and muscles
normally active.   We cannot on that account declare that gymnastic exercises are dangerous or
harmful, nor should we allow ourselves to discountenance them because when injudiciously taken they
often prove highly injurious to the muscles, which
are thereby overstrained.   Hatha Yoga is the most
popular and at the same time the most nearly dangerous of all varieties of Yoga, when undertaken
in the Western world.   In India, the original home
of Yoga practices, the native population, by reason
of a long line of suitable heredity, and also in consequence of appropriate diet and dress, are able to

take many exercises with impunity, and even with decided benefit, which would soon prove disastrous to those Europeans and Americans who persist in adhering to a flesh diet and to the wearing of garments which restrict the normal activity of vital sections of the body.  Without insisting immediately upon the adoption of a strictly vegetarian diet, it is essential for all who make flesh a staple article of food to at once greatly diminish the quantity they eat and cultivate a wholesome taste for nutritious grains, luscious fruits and succulent vegetables which, when wisely selected and rightfully prepared, supply all the nourishment obtainable from meat, without its over-heating and other injurious tendencies.  Clothing also needs to be greatly simplified, and this can readily be accomplished by following excellent suggestions given by Greek as well as Hindu costume.  The love of beauty is natural and needs to be encouraged; so does an appreciation of delicate and delicious flavors; but there is no beauty in unwholesome garments, and no delicious flavor in improper food.  Simple white robes should always be worn when taking breathing exercises; these can be ornamented to suit the wearer's taste, or worn quite undecorated.  In either case they are thoroughly hygienic.  Fruits, vegetables and cereals can be eaten cooked or uncooked; but as all garments must be cleanly, so must all food be fresh. Rooms in which a student or company of students breath rhythmically must be kept well ventilated, and the atmosphere must be solarized as much as possible.  This is a very important matter, but one that is greatly overlooked.  Very many of the unpleasant results of sitting in Spiritualistic séances are due far more to imperfect physical ventilation than to any alleged evil influences in the spiritual universe, though it may be reasonably declared that undesirable visitors from unseen states may find foul air a congenial habitat. The law of correspondences works so universally and so completely that it manifests its unceasing operation wherever we may turn; therefore we cannot logically deny that foul thoughts and bad air are in close affinity, while pure thoughts and fresh air are equally near neighbors. But when the general habits and customs of life are rational, and even beautiful, a word of caution may still be needed for the over-zealous, who in their intense desire to make rapid progress, often throw aside discretion. We cannot remodel our sub-conscious habits instantly, even though we may very rapidly transform our outward customs, and it is the sub-conscious plane of our activities which is the chief seat of those indispositions which regular, systematic breathing is intended to correct It is usually unwise to assign the first or highest place to Hatha Yoga; other forms of Yoga had better be considered and practised at first by a large majority of persons, in order to counteract a pernicious tendency to put the welfare of the flesh higher in our esteem than the concerns of the spirit. Nevertheless, it must be admitted that many spiritually-minded people are far from healthy physically, and this is chiefly due to the mistaken notion that the care of the outer body is a work which can be left entirely to those in whom spiritual consciousness is not yet awakened.

Rightly and fully comprehended, spirituality is fulness of breath; the very etymology of the word is sufficient to make this entirely clear, for our english word spirit is only the latin spiritus (breath), abbreviated. Spirit and breath originally mean exactly the same. A Master breathes on his disciples, and they receive the holy breath, or spirit. Physical breath may be rightly regarded as a vehicle through which inner breath or prana is conveyed; therefore the connection between our inward and our outward living is far more intimate than we usually suppose. During physical embodiment we cannot ever attempt to separate the interests of the Ego from those of its most exterior personal sheaths, without working havoc in our philosophy and injuring the integrity of our general mode of life. One plane of expression is indeed higher and more enduring than another, but all must duly synchronize. The greatest benefits we can possibly derive from any useful mental and physical practices must be to bring our minds and bodies into such complete accord that one never acts at variance with the other. The good old saying, "A pure mind in a pure body is health," is completely true, and by pure must be meant free from confusion as well as from pollution. When we protest against adulteration in food or clothing, we are often inveighing against an admixture which is unwholesome and unlawful, though no single ingredient introduced is objectionable in itself. Sand in sugar and cotton mixed with wool may be cited as well-known examples, for when a grocer professes to sell pure sugar or a tailor declares a piece of cloth to be pure wool, he uses the

word to signify simple—i.e., free from any extraneous element. Pure breath is simply fresh air
vitalized with Prana circulating uninterruptedly
throughout an entire body; therefore we read in
treatises on Yoga that we can breathe through our
bones as well as through our skin, a statement which
harmonizes completely with all we know of the
constitution of matter, which is made up of innumerable infinitesimal particles, no two of which
ever really touch. We are now beginning to see the
wisdom and the rational application of many strange
old sayings and practices which are often discarded
by modern critics as outworn superstitions. Take,
for example, the Biblical precept, "Remove thy san-
dals from thy feet, for the place whereon thou stand-
est is holy ground." Consecrated temples were not
only dedicated to sacred uses, they were also charged
with a peculiar atmosphere, particularly beneficial
to all who deliberately opened themselves to receive
it. In the temples of Greece, many sick people were
healed by simply resting in those beautiful sanctuaries, though at other times specific treatment was
administered by the officiating Therapeutae. In
Christian churches much benefit is often derived by
those who respond to a frequent invitation to quietly
rest and meditate, as well as pray. We all know
how greatly sensitive people are affected by an unseen atmosphere without knowing what it is that
affects them. A scientific study of Occultism inter-
prets this riddle by introducing to our notice subtle
ethers and atmospheres with which the ordinary un-
trained mind is technically unacquainted, but this
ignorance does not prevent us from feeling the

effects of some mysterious element which plays upon us without our knowledge. Nothing is more common than to exclaim, "I cannot tell how I caught that cold," or, "I don't know what makes me feel so nervous." On the other hand, we are often most pleasantly affected by some mysterious agent with which we are unacquainted, but whose acquaintance we could easily make were we to spend more time than we usually do spend in quiet meditation, and busy ourselves to some extent with the study of unseen forces. Highly sensitive people usually thrive far better in the open country or by the sea-shore than in crowded cities, because there is far more Prana where nature is comparatively unmolested than in the bewildering hives of excited human industry. Nature has her holy places where we can often derive even greater benefit than in the finest temples ever built by human hands; thus it follows that to go barefooted in the country or on any grassy slope or well-kept lawn, or at the sea-shore, when the sand is inviting, is a highly beneficial exercise, and one which often serves to remove from the body many impurities which are the causes of those distressing congestions which only proper breathing can permanently prevent. It has often been said during recent years that breathing exercises patterned after Oriental models have developed hysteria and many other distressing maladies, particularly in delicate American women who have taken the exercises without the guidance of a competent instructor. This may be the case, but if it be so, it only serves to illustrate the extreme unwisdom of neglecting necessary preliminary caution, for these

misguided women have generally worn tight shoes
and gloves, as well as other unwholesome garments,
while attempting to take the exercises, and they have
also unduly strained themselves by endeavoring to
take too advanced exercises at the beginning of their
practice.  There is not the slightest reason why women should not breathe quite as deeply and steadily
as men, and they do so breathe when they wear
proper clothing and place the body in natural position.  Whoever attempts Yoga breathing should
concentrate completely upon some great idea which
can be readily expressed in a single expressive word,
such, for instance, as courage, rest, truth, or any
other which embodies the particular virtue one now
desires especially to cultivate.  We should make a
mental pitcure of the Solar Plexus, imagining it as a
miniature sun at the center of the organism, it being
the great central ganglion behind the abdomen.  This
center is electro-magnetically connected with the
pineal gland, which Descartes and other philosophers
have truly declared to be the vital center in the
brain whence the soul operates by means of influx
into all sections of the body.  When perfect harmony is obtained between the brain center and the
abdominal center, there can be no disease in the
system, because all functions are properly dis-
charged, and the whole body is completely vitalized
and ventilated.  The Yogis of India must never
be confounded with the Fakirs, for the latter do
themselves physical injury in their attempt to develop abnormal powers, and though they often succeed in performing wonderful feats of magic, they
do not perform works of healing, nor do they really

add anything to the useful knowledge of those who witness their weird exhibitions.   The Yogis, on the other hand, are both teachers and healers, and set before their students high examples of noble living, for they have gained complete control over all their appetites, and are in every sense truly exemplary in conduct.   When we come to consider, one by one, the several varieties of Yoga practice already enumerated, we shall soon discover that they may be compared with five digits of a single hand, or five branches of a tree, all growing out of one palm or ramifying from a single trunk.   Karma Yoga is the Sanscrit name for the unselfish performance of one's constant duty, regardless of the varying forms that duty may from time to time assume.   This is the work of the householder, and of the man of affairs, and has nothing to do with those peculiar practices which belong to the work and training of those who virtually retire from the world to devote themselves to a solitary contemplative life, in which most of us can take no part.   The word duty, though a very common word, is not always easy to define, seeing that it is not properly applied to all those numerous performances which people go through with at the behest of foolish customs, or to gratify the caprices of members of their families.   Many a man and many a woman is sacrificed unsparingly to false ideas of duty, and instead of receiving the blessing of gratitude from others, or the inward approval of one's own conscience, nothing but ingratitude from without and discontent within repays his or her mistaken efforts.   Duty is always reasonable, and its performance must conduce in some way to the en-

largement and ennoblement of life; it must have
a tendency to raise the moral, intellectual and physical condition of all who are influenced by it; it
cannot therefore be reasonably associated with a
ceaseless round of occupations which bring no benefit
to those who undertake them or to any who are directly affected by them.   Strange as the phrase may
sound, we often have to neglect one duty to dis-
charge another; but this is, of course, never the
case except in seeming, for real duties do not and
cannot conflict.   It can never be anyone's duty to
be in two places at once, so long as it remains impossible, but it often appears as though one ought to
be there.   Now the particular use of right meditation is to put us on the track which will enable us
to clearly perceive what is the one thing we really
ought to do just now, and where is the identical
place in which we ought to do it.   Interior illumination may show us this, and we can then set to work
at once to perform the definite duty pertaining to a
particular moment.

When we feel inwardly thoroughly convinced
that something is our duty then we must meet and
conquer whatever obstacle, inducement or temptation would lead us off in some other direction; and
though at first we may find it difficult to silence all
conflicting voices and learn to pay no heed to any
distracting solicitations, a little regular practice
faithfully persisted in will soon develop within us
such a mental habit that we almost spontaneously
do the very things which aforetime seemed her-
culean tasks almost beyond our strength to accomplish.   The sub-self or sub-conscious mind soon

gets into a good habit if we persist in educating it, and when we have once formed a good habit we need never loosen our hold upon it, because indulgence in it can only redound to our own benefit and to the welfare of all with whom we are associated. It is always at the very outset of a practice that we encounter the greatest difficulties; that is why we so often abandon the race when, if we did but persist in running it, we should be abundantly repaid for all our arduous efforts. In the practice of Yoga we need only to cultivate dispositions and methods necessary to success in every conceivable line of human enterprise. Diligence in well-doing is the only road to victory. Another phase of Yoga, Bakti-Yoga, concerns the performance of certain works of devotion which have for their object bringing the student into ever fuller realization of the oneness of all lives. These works are sometimes of a definitely regulated and even stereotyped nature, closely resembling the formal ritualistic exercises of many types of Christians who find it beneficial to perform particular acts of devotion at stated intervals and in an unvarying manner, such for instance as the Roman Catholic recitation of the Rosary. Others again consider such mechanical religious performances as hindrances rather than helps to real devotion; but these people are by no means undevout, they are simply of such temperament that nothing helps them which is not spontaneous. Very great wisdom is displayed in the Epistles of St. Paul where the subject of ceremonial devotion is quite elaborately discussed, for the apostle sums up all his advice in the memorable

admonition, "Let every man be fully persuaded in his
own mind." We are very much mistaken if we
imagine that Hindoos or any other type of Asiatics
are all possessed of the same turn of mind, or that
all find it profitable to seek spiritual enlightenment
along a single pathway, for we can find fully as
much variety among the native populations in Asia
as among Europeans or Americans, some of whom
naturally incline to the rigid simplicity of the
Quaker, while others are drawn to the most elaborate pomp and ceremony. There, is nothing surprising in this when we look at external nature, which
presents to us an unending variety of types and
phenomena, and just as every kind of animal has
its own peculiar needs which must be appropriately
met if that creature is to thrive truly, so is it that
in human life varieties of disposition and require-
ment are even more numerous and widely diversified, so that what is highly beneficial for some, is
positively detrimental to others. Works of devotion cannot always be clearly separated from the
performance of common duties, for one melts
imperceptibly into the other. The apostolic injunc-
tions, "Pray without ceasing," and "In everything
give thanks," would have no meaning were it not
possible to carry the spirit of devotion into every
ordinary exercise, and certainly if this were not so
such words as "Whether you eat, drink, or whatsoever you do, do all to the glory of God," would
be utterly incomprehensible. We are now again
tracing a vivid parallel between Oriental philosophy
and primitive Christianity, which when rightly
studied causes us to treat with utter contempt those

absurd denunciations of Oriental religions which
still disfigure Christian hymnbooks and lead many
advocates of Foreign Missions to make such ignorant and misleading statements that the good work
they are endeavoring to accomplish must of necessity be very greatly handicapped by the total failure
of these self-appointed missionaries to understand
the people among whom they endeavor to accomplish their work of proselytizing.  "The heathen in
his blindness bows down to wood and stone" is a
stupid falsehood found in the very heart of an
extremely popular hymn.  What good congregations
expect to accomplish by singing such trash is
difficult to understand, for it cannot lift the minds
of the singers to any high appreciation of divine
wisdom when they declare in a preceding sentence,
"In vain with lavish kindness the gifts of God are
strewn."  The reverential Hindoo has far too deep
a sense of the wisdom of Deity to believe that God
does anything in vain, and every enlightened
Oriental is far too intelligent, and also far too
kindly, to utter such misleading nonsense concerning well-meaning people who do not speak his language or profess his creed, but who do engage in
works of devotion very similar to his own. The more
we study Oriental philosophy the more do we feel
inclined to advocate the formation of a "Mind Your
Own Business Society" to offset the pernicious
influence of those mistaken missionary endeavors
which are no doubt founded in good motive, but
display total ignorance of the work which needs to
be done in so-called heathen countries, where it
certainly is desirable to stimulate a large percentage

of the natives to loftier practices than those they now indulge, and to induce them to give up many degrading superstitions. But as we are also superstitious to some extent in many directions, we can all learn from each other what to cultivate and what to avoid, seeing that we are all, properly speaking, pupil-teachers rather than altogether pupils or altogether teachers in the school of life. Many a Protestant regards a great part of Roman Catholic devotion as unadulterated idolatry, and many a Roman Catholic takes exactly the same view of the means of devotion employed in Oriental countries, though the outward forms are so nearly identical that an impartial observer would regard one exactly as he would look upon the other. Now these monotonous repetitions of words and movements may mean very much to some people, while they mean nothing at all to others, therefore it is only fair that we should let those people enjoy them who receive benefit from their use, without adopting them ourselves unless we honestly feel that we could derive help from them, in which case we have a perfect right to use them. We are usually inclined to sneer at the practices of others when they appear to us ridiculous, though we are very apt indeed to become hurt or resentful when others laugh at our peculiarities. This is a certain mark of foolish self-conceit coupled with less than due regard for the rights of others. Works of devotion are, however, by no means confined to ritual observances even in India or Ceylon, though in that part of the world the practice of religious ceremonial enters quite as largely into the daily life of the people as it does

into the life of the extremely orthodox Oriental
Jew who counts it a great delight to observe punctil-
iously the 613 precepts of the Torah, many of
which appear useless and antiquated to the modern
Israelites of Europe and America.   A work of
devotion is, properly speaking, any work undertaken
in a devout spirit and performed in reverent frame
of mind, but as objects of devotion are very varied,
we cannot classify all devout actions under a single
heading.   We often speak correctly of devotion to
one's country, to an honored cause, to the welfare
of one's family, and also to art, science, and business.   The kind of work in which we engage receives its spiritual quality from the motive which
prompts it, and the disposition which pervades it,
therefore we are very likely to fall into serious
error if we ever attempt to call certain definite external acts works of devotion in any exclusive sense.
Writing a letter may be a thoroughly devout act,
and it may accomplish untold benefit and bring a
great blessing upon the writer, or the letter written
may be merely frivolous, and so nearly unimportant
that we can trace no definite result from its production, or again it may be written with a malicious
motive and work great havoc.   In these three instances exactly the same writing materials may have
been employed in all cases, each letter might contain
the same number of words in the same language,
and all three be sent at the same time to the same
city at the same rate of postage.   Now, could anything be more ridiculous than to attempt to discourse upon the morality or immorality of writing
an epistle of a certain length with a particular kind

of ink on a certain grade of paper, and after having written it send it to a particular destination?    But such a discourse would be no more unreasonable than one which undertakes to measure or determine the value or demerit of any outward action without taking into account the object of its performance and the mental state of the performer.    Yoga, then, cannot be reduced to the level of mechanism, though we may use mechanical means in its performance, just as we all employ writing materials equally when we are engaged in epistolary correspondence of the highest merit and quite the reverse.    We have now entered a field of thought in which we can glean many profitable harvests, if we carry steadily with us the one all-important feeling that we can obtain blessing, no matter what we are doing, or how we may be circumstanced, provided we invariably determine to infuse into all our words and actions a benefic spirit of resolute determination to bless humanity through all our undertakings.

# CHAPTER X.

EZEKIEL'S WHEEL—WHAT IT SIGNIFIES.—ASTROL-
OLOGY IN PROPHECY.

Among the many remarkable chapters in the
amazingly symbolic book of the Prophet Ezekiel,
the Tenth is in some respects the most highly emblematical of all, and, unless it is clearly understood
that it describes a vivid vision and is in no sense
intended to be taken literally, it must certainly
appear entirely incomprehensible. But let us make
an endeavor to interpret, in some degree at least,
its marvellous imagery, and as we peer below the
depths of its astounding letter we shall soon begin
to catch some glimpses of its many deeper aspects.
Were we to attempt to exhaust the meaning of the
vision by any single attempt at interpretation we
should defeat the very end we have in view, which
is only to suggest some few thoughts which may
be helpful to students who are seeking a key to the
inner sanctuary of symbolic literature which is now
beginning to be widely dealt with in an entirely
superhistorical manner. Prophetical imagery may
have both a local and a superlocal significance, by
which we mean that certain events symbolically
described or foretold may have particular reference
to a special age and people in an immediate sense,

and at the same time be susceptible of much wider
application.   The writers of headings of pages in
the King James version of the English Bible took
amazing, and often entirely unwarranted, liberties
with their often very poor translation of the
Hebrew text, and it is these chapter-headings which
have led to a vast amount of the misapprehension
which extensively prevails as to the real meaning
of the original.   In the case of the chapter now
before us this annoyance is not encountered, for
the headings are simply descriptive, viz., "Vision
of the coals of fire and of the Cherubim."   The
man clothed with linen, who is a very prominent
character in many of Ezekiel's visions, may fairly
be considered as one of those many angelic messengers of whom we read continually, all of whom
are described as clad in pure white raiment, for at
least two reasons: First, because all ambassadors
sent forth by esoteric confraternities are invariably
clad in white garments, and, secondly, because clairvoyant vision in all ages has enabled seers to behold
the luminous white aura which radiates from all
celestial messengers whether in the incarnate or
excarnate state.   The cherubs, who also play an
important part among the characters in the vision,
represented in olden times souls not yet terrestrially
embodied, but awaiting incarnation, for, the seers
of every age and country have testified unanimously
to spiritual pre-existence.   The resemblance traced
between a sapphire and a celestial throne suggests
immediately the time-honored significance of that
extremely beauteous gem, always a type of wisdom, sincerity, and constancy   Obtaining fire from

heaven and scattering it over the earth is a symbol
to be met with throughout almost the entire range
of classic literature, the well-known story of Pro-
metheus being a highly typical example.  Fire has
occupied a place of singular honor among all
nations, and as a religious emblem it has always
held the center of the stage, and deservedly so when
we consider its three leading and distinctive properties, which are to enlighten, to purify, and to warm.
Heat, light and purification are instantly suggested
with the thought of fire, and therefore the great
alchemical work of transmutation is symbolized
thereby.  Much that refers to profound and awe-
inspiring initiatory rites is conveyed by this far-
reaching symbol.  The man in white raiment going
in and out of the mystic flame represents a thoroughly developed hierophant, one who has truly
passed through the mystic death and attained to
the glorious freedom of the new life of the risen
and regenerate.  The wings of the cherubim denote
ability to pass through air or ether as easily as
birds can fly and fishes swim, and doubtless with far
greater rapidity.  A comparison of the sound made
by the motion of the wings of the cherubim to the
voice of the Almighty when speaking, is a clear
reference to the very ancient and wide-spread idea
that GOD speaks to humanity on earth through the
agency of angels.  All revelations must of necessity
be accommodated to the state of receptivity of those
to whom they are addressed, for where there is no
comprehension there can be no revelation, a revelation necessitating a comprehender as well as a
revelator.  According to some commentators the

wheels among which the man in white raiment stands have an astrological significance, and in that curious book, "Art Magic," which gives much information of an unusual character, we find an illustration of Ezekiel's Wheel intended to set forth the astrological idea of ascending Macrocosmos and descending Microcosmos.  Six signs of the Zodiac, Aries, Taurus, Gemini, Cancer, Leo, Virgo, are on the line of ascent.  Libra, the seventh sign, is the turning-point or balance of the scale.  Scorpio, Sagittarius, Capricorn, Aquarius, Pisces, are on the descending line.  The wheels within wheels according to this rendering refer plainly to the different Houses of the Sun, as the twelve signs of the Zodiac are termed.  In each of these Houses humanity accomplishes some special work, and during each Grand Cycle of 25,840 years our Sun passes through these twelve Houses, just as our little earth goes through them in a trifle over 365 days.

The four special signs described as having respectively the face of a cherub, a man, a lion, and an eagle, are the four so-called Fixed Signs of the Zodiac.  These are Aquarius, Scorpio, Leo, Taurus. Aquarius is familiar to all of us as the man with the watering-pot; Leo is the lion, Taurus is the winged cherub as frequently represented in ancient symbolic art; Scorpio is the eagle and has been so represented as to its spiritual significance from ages immemorial.  Christian art has employed these symbols to characterize the four Evangelists, that is why we so frequently behold an eagle lectern in a Christian church; though its more ancient and universal significance is rarely mentioned except by students of astrology, who naturally wish to prove the relationship between their own modern teaching and the wisdom of the ancient prophets. Astrology must always be to some extent under a ban until its professors everywhere disclaim all connection with fatalism and with pessimism, for these twin errors rob astrology of all the good it might otherwise accomplish. Idle curiosity may prompt many people to pry into the future without any belief that they can profitably utilize the knowledge they obtain, but the serious-minded, who are ever seeking for profitable instruction, can never take interest in any predictions which do not serve to encourage those who listen to them to buckle on their spiritual armor and conquer whatever conditions would prove adverse did we allow them to triumph over us when it is our mission and prerogative to rise above them, by meeting these seeming adversaries not as foes to be exterminated but as necessary material for purposes of eventual transmutation into forms as unlike the original as an eagle is unlike a scorpion. These four very extraordinary Living Creatures mentioned in Ezekiel reappear in the Apocalypse, which is a most significant illustration of the widespread use of an identical symbology. These are Masonic as well as Astrologic emblems and are doubtless well comprehended by those comparatively few really distinguished Masons who peer into the esoteric meaning of Masonic rites and are far from satisfied with bare initiation into the outer fringe of the Masonic garment. But however deeply versed in Masonic lore the ancient prophets may have been, they were before and above all else exhorters of the people unto civic as well as private righteousness.

The highly important significance of the transformation of Scorpio into Aquilla (the Eagle) has always been regarded as the accomplishment of the Magnum Opus of the Alchemists, who were always accustomed to veil their profound esoteric teachings concerning human regeneration under a general symbolism pertaining to the literal transmutation of metals, a feat which doubtless was, to some extent, actually accomplished by those well versed in mystic chemistry.   But as the noblest and most trustworthy Rosicrucians, and all other students of genuine alchemy, invariably declared that no one could become a true White Magician until he had overcome all cupidity, the literal production of material gold was a decidedly unimportant work in the estimation of those great Magicians who made the regeneration of humanity, individually and collectively, the one supreme object of their indefatigable exertions.   Earth, Air, Fire, Water, like North, South, East, West, are employed in mystical writings as significant of the four chief divisions of human life in all directions.   The four typical rivers watering the Garden of Eden are, alchemically considered, the four great arteries which are the river-courses of the blood.   The four rivers enumerated in Genesis may well be thought to have some connection with the four Living Creatures mentioned elsewhere in the Bible.   Pison stands for the innominate artery which supplies blood to the right side of the head and to the right arm and hand. Gihon represents the second great artery at the arch

of the aorta—the left common carotid—which supplies the left side of the head and, through the
"Circle of Willis," can also supply the right side of
the brain.   Hiddekel refers to that which furnishes
blood to the upper portion of the left hand.
Euphrates stands for the descending aorta, which
supplies the lungs and all organs below them, including the major sections of the chest and stomach.
Keeping in constant remembrance the relation between Macrocosm and Microcosm we shall experience little, if any, difficulty in tracing the vital unity
of these several correspondences, for though at first
there may appear but a very slight and chiefly fanciful connection between the Signs of the Zodiac and
the different sections of the human body, no sooner
have we grasped something of the inevitable implications of the microcosmical idea than we see at
once that the constellations and all they signify are
not only without, but also most verily within every
one of us.   At the very outset of any practical instruction in astrology it is highly essential that the
teacher should seek to remove the prevailing fallacy
that when we are treating of planetary influences we
are alluding only to such as are exerted over us by
bodies distant many millions of miles from this
earth.

Every influence exerted upon us from without
must have its correspondence within, otherwise we
could not be affected by it.   It is because we are
universes in minimum that we can know and feel
something of the greater Universe outside.   Hermetic Philosophy is the only adequate reconciler of
physics with metaphysics and of idealistic with real-

istic philosophy, for in the light of Hermetism we can readily comprehend how our bodily senses can be entirely trustworthy, so far as their testimony extends, and at the same time agree with the idealist who insists that all that we perceive is within the consciousness of the percipient, for it is within us and without us at the same instant, precisely as there is air in our bodies at the same time there must ever be a far greater volume of atmosphere outside. Prophetic visions always introduce us to that universal sign and symbol language in which we usually dream, and which generally greatly baffles us until we have found a key to its interpretation.

# CHAPTER XI.

Whatever estimate we may seek to place upon
some of the doctrines of the great Swedish philosopher and seer, Emanuel Swedenborg, it is impossible to overlook fairly his enormous contribution
to spiritual and liberal religious and philosophic
thought, for though many of his followers are extremely conservative,—and apparently intolerant of
all claims to modern illumination after the time of
Swedenborg,—no narrowness on the part of sub-
sequent generations can remove any lustre from the
career of the highly learned and truly marvellous
man to whom we are all very deeply indebted for
calling renewed attention to very ancient ideas concerning Holy Scriptures quite at variance with the
conventional orthodoxy of his period. As a distinguished man of science and of letters, also as a
marvellous clairvoyant, Swedenborg shines forth
brilliantly in contrast with the general dulness and
deadness of his age. The 18th century was
remarkable for the prevalence of cold religious
formalism and much looseness in morality, and to
counteract both these depressing tendencies Swedenborg worked with skill and energy truly marvellous.

The literary output of this amazing writer would be wonderful if judged from the superficial standpoint of voluminousness alone, but when we take into account the extreme excellence of this enormous mass of literary material we cannot feel other than convinced that we are in the presence of a mind trained and cultured far beyond the ordinary. As the religious denomination known as Swedenborgian has for a great many years been industriously circulating many of Swedenborg's theological writings, either gratuitously or at merely nominal cost, the reading public is fairly well acquainted with "Heaven and Hell;" "Divine Providence"; "Divine Love and Wisdom," and several other of the smaller books, but we doubt if very many, apart from special students, have waded through "Arcana Cœlestia," "Apocalypse Unveiled;" or even "The True Christian Religion;" all of which are decidedly bulky volumes and written in that precise, leisurely, scholarly style which shows their author to have been a singularly careful, and evidently unhasting, though wonderfully fertile writer. To appreciate in any due degree the revolutionary character of Swedenborg's method of dealing with the accepted Bible of his day and country, we must remember that though he strenuously insists that there are two interior senses— Spiritual and Celestial—within the literal, which he calls the Natural sense of those portions of the Bible which he says are verily the Divine Word, he by no means allows that the entire 66 documents which constitute the Holy Bible of Protestant Christendom are to be regarded as an absolutely divine revelation.  On the contrary, he places them just about where the Church of England places the Apocrypha, which it recommends for reading, even in church services, but to which it assigns no such authority as to the Old and New Testaments.

The Pentateuch, or Torah, according to Swedenborg, is indeed a divine revelation, but not externally as touching literal history, sacrifices, and various ceremonial observances, but as to an interior meaning which has to do, primarily, not with man's outer formation, but with the 7 stages of human regeneration, which are spiritually set forth in the opening chapter of Genesis.  It is quite easy to see how complacently Swedenborgians smiled at that revolutionary Darwinism which convulsed the religious, as well as the scientific, world during the middle of the 19th Century, for the doctrine of correspondences could not be adversely affected if it were proved that man had been on earth millions of years instead of only 6,000.  It is extremely interesting to look up interior meanings in Swedenborg's "Dictionary of Correspondences," for there we are told that Balaam's ass represented his natural affection for good, and that saved him from destruction when the direful consequences of his disobedience to Divine direction were ready to overwhelm him.  To many minds such a mode of exegesis must appear arbitrary and far-fetched in the extreme, but such is not necessarily the case if we take into consideration the Hermetic method of teaching, which virtually all Mystics, alike of ancient and modern periods, have insisted upon as the only really important aspect of any edifying and spiritually enlightening literature.   It cannot be seriously admitted by thoughtful minds that a record of merely exterior events in human history is specially revealed from Heaven, but it is conceivable that outward narratives have been used illustratively and allegorically to enshrine teachings of the utmost value through all succeeding generations.

As there can be no completer summary of Swedenborg's teaching, as to its foundations, than his dissertation concerning the interior meaning of the seven "days" of Genesis, we append his interpretations translated from the original Latin (the language in which he always wrote) contained in that intensely interesting work "The Life and Mission of Emanuel Swedenborg" by Benjamin Worcester. The six days, or times, which are so many successive states of man's regeneration, are in general as follows: The First state is that which precedes, both from infancy and immediately before regeneration, and it is called a void, emptiness and thick-darkness.   And the first movement, which is the mercy of the Lord, is the spirit of God moving itself upon the face of the waters.

The Second state is when distinction is made between the things which are the Lord's and those which are man's own; those which are the Lord's are called in the Word 'remains,' and are here especially the knowledges of faith which man has acquired from infancy, which are stored up and are not manifest before he comes into this state.   This state seldom exists at the present day without temptation, misfortune or grief, which cause the things of the body and the world, or his own, to become quiet and, as it were, to die. Then the things of the external man are separated from those of the internal; in the internal are the remains stored up by the Lord for this time and this use.

The Third state is that of repentance, in which from the internal man he speaks piously and devoutly, and brings forth good things, as the works of charity, but which are nevertheless inanimate because he regards them as from himself. These are called the tender grass, then the herb yielding seed, and afterwards the tree yielding fruit.

The Fourth state is when he is affected by love and illumined by faith; he before indeed spoke pious things and brought forth good things, but from a state of temptation and distress, not from faith and charity. These, therefore, love and faith, are now enkindled in the internal man and are called the two great lights.

The Fifth state is that he speaks from faith and thereby confirms himself in truth and good; the things which he then brings forth are animate, and are called fishes of the sea and birds of the heavens.

The Sixth state is, when from faith and thence from love he speaks true things and does good things, the things he then brings forth are called the living soul and creature. And because he then begins to act from love as well as from faith he becomes a spiritual man which is called an image of God. His spiritual life is delighted and sustained by the things that are of the knowledges of faith and of the works of charity, which are called his food; and his natural life is delighted and sustained by the things that are of the body and the senses;

from which there is a combat until love reigns and he becomes a celestial man.

They who are regenerated do not all arrive at this state, but some, and the greatest part at this day, only to the first; some only to the second; some to the third; the fourth, and the fifth; few to the sixth, and scarcely any to the seventh.

The Seventh state signifies a condition of complete regeneration."

From the above outline our readers can gather at least a faint idea of how completely Swedenborg does away with all simply external interpretations of the Pentateuch, and when he proceeds to deal with the Book of Revelations he finds no difficulty in explaining the many elaborate hieroglyphics with which the mysterious Apocalypse abounds.

It is indeed to his "Apocalypse Unveiled" that we must turn for anything like an adequate view of his special doctrine concerning the Church of the New Jerusalem, which he regards as a new dispensation of truth, in the advantages of which the world is now measurably sharing, though the full glory of the new age has not yet burst upon us. This most wonderful of all his writings was never completed or published by the author, although carefully prepared for the printer as far as the middle of the nineteenth chapter. The general plan of the work closely resembles that of the "Arcana Cœlestia"; the full text of each chapter is given, then elaborate expositions of single verses follow; some of which are treated at great length, others briefly.

According to Swedenborg a new age of the world began in 1757, and it was after that year that he undertook to minutely explain the Apocalypse, which he declares (particularly in its closing chapters) symbolically describes the ideal condition of humanity yet to be realized.

John the Revelator is said to represent those who are in the good of life from faith in the Lord who remain steadfast through the desolation of the church, and who are the first to become aware of their Lord's coming, which being "in clouds," and in the midst of "seven golden candlesticks," represents a manifestation of light in the midst of obscurity in the letter of the Word. The seven churches are the members of the Christian Church in seven distinct conditions. What was seen through the door in heaven (Chap. 4) was the ordering of all things in preparation for judgment. Those who sit on different-colored horses mean those who variously understand the significance of the Word. Souls under the altar are those who have lived a good life reverencing the Lord, and though oppressed by rulers of the external church, have been preserved by divine care. The rolling away of heaven as a scroll represents the dissolution of that fictitious heaven which pretended Christians form for themselves as soon as their inner condition is disclosed by the light of the Lord's coming. The mystical 144,000 are they of the true church of every kind who are sanctified within. The "woes" follow the exploration of the states of those who rely on faith without charity. The woman clothed with the sun (Chap. 12) signifies the new church that is to come; the man child whom she brings forth is the strong doctrine of that church

which is opposed frantically by the dragon which
represents the false doctrine of faith alone. The
ruling of the nations with a rod of iron by the man
child represents the power of the new doctrine
which will be illustrated both from the letter of the
Word and by rational argument from the facts of
nature. War in heaven results in the overthrow
of those fictitious states which outwardly appear as
heavens until their inner lack of true affection is
discerned. The golden vials full of divine anger
signify the holy good and truth of heaven flowing
in and making evil secreted in the church manifest,
that it may be vanquished. Babylon described as a
"harlot," reveals the state of those who misuse their
position in the church for ends of self-aggrandise-
ment. The "Beast" is the letter of the Word in the
hands of those who pervert it to base ends. The
coming church, confirmed in genuine truth, is described as the bride of the Lamb, clad in fine linen;
the doctrine of this church is described as a Holy
City descending from God out of heaven into which
there shall not enter anything false or defiling. The
foregoing are but a few out of multitudinous
explanations of striking metaphors with which
this marvellous book abounds, but though few
they suffice to afford some clear insight into Swedenborg's general line of interpretation. In addition
to all this remarkable expository comment Swedenborg has given us an immense number of personal
experiences of a superphysical character not only in
his "Diary" but scattered through almost all his
works. To any unprejudiced reader many of these
narrations may serve the double purpose of ac-

quainting us not only with Swedenborg's spiritual experiences but also with his own mental bias, which was particularly strong in certain definite directions. Being educated as a Lutheran he seems to have inherited a certain affection for some forms of Protestant Christianity and a very decided dislike for Roman Catholicism, and this, as Emerson has pointed out, together with many similar incidents, serves to foster the opinion, entertained very widely, that however true a seer he may have been his revelations were all more or less colored by the mental medium through which they flowed; they are therefore no more to be regarded as infallible than those of other seers.   But this rational position is so distasteful to extreme Swedenborgians that they appear resentful when this great man, whom they so very highly extol, is placed upon something like the same level with other great philosophers who have also enjoyed spiritual revelations.   The remark of the apostle Paul, "We have this treasure in earthen vessels," is universally applicable to all human experience, and it is just at this point that simple Theism proves its unconquerable superiority to all sectarian systems, adherents to which invariably claim far too much for some one leader whom they extravagantly exalt, and often far too little for other noble teachers with whose positions they are not in sympathy.   The foolish statement that God makes a perfect revelation through an imperfect medium is a fantastic bubble which bursts as soon as it is pricked, for there is no question of divine but only of human ability at stake; and if we are in this world undergoing gradual training, and it is the divine will that we should unfold by a succession of progressive experiences, we may safely conclude that there is no cut and dried revelation once for all ready to our hand. It is undoubtedly far best for us to be situated exactly as we are, without such a revelation, but with every inducement and ever-increasing opportunity to arrive at more and more knowledge of truth for ourselves by faithfully and continually exercising those very faculties with which we are clearly endowed for the purpose of enabling us to find out truth through the agency of their exercise. Though this common-sense position, as it may well be called, is in entire agreement with all our actual experiences of human education, and is moreover strictly scientific in all its tendencies and implications, it can never satisfy any who demand a complete unveiling of the mysteries of the universe, for they set themselves in an attitude toward revelation which renders it impossible for there to be a gradual unwinding of the scroll of truth to human understanding, seeing that if their position be tenable, all truth must be already in our possession. Needless to argue that no really illumined teacher at any time anywhere ever took so insane a position, which is one, moreover, that no professedly Orthodox or Catholic theologian will attempt to maintain if engaged in controversy with an intellectual opponent.

It is much to be regretted that so few admirers of any great teacher seem willing to place him among the world's enlighteners, simply as one of them, instead of exalting their chosen hero to a

rank enirely beyond that of all the rest.    This
attitude toward Swedenborg, on the part of his
devotees, has led many to turn away entirely from
his revelations because they could not accept them
as infallible, though they doubtless contain much
ennobling philosophy, and can well be studied as
helpful textbooks by all who are seeking to acquaint
themselves with the history of modern seership.
Though, for ourselves, we totally deny everlasting
continuance in hells, which most Swedenborgians
believe is a necessary inference from their leader's
disclosures concerning the spiritual world, we can
entirely agree with Swedenborg's doctrine of dominant affection regulating our condition in the hereafter.    Clairvoyance may be.perfect, to the extent
of clearly revealing post-mortem conditions as they
now exist, without throwing any light whatever on
how radically those conditions may have changed
before another century has rolled away.    We have
not the slightest warrant for supposing that any
soul will choose evil everlastingly, though we can
comprehend the idea that if one did actually desire
to spend eternity in a hell, the privilege would be
accorded him of gratifying his dominant propen-
sity.    But how pitiably absurd is such a vile conjecture in the light of Swedenborg's primary teaching regarding human origin, for he attributes all
life to a sole Divine Being, whose life animates the
entire creation.    Swedenborg accounts for evil by
styling it an inversion of good, but why an inversion
should continue forever can never be explained
reasonably.    There is no diabolical fount of life

whence some portion of the creation has emanated, and if all souls are alike divinely created why should some choose to spend eternity in opposition to their Creator whom Swedenborg beautifully describes as perfect Love and Wisdom? In the hideous and utterly irrational idea of even a greatly modified unending hell we see traces of the pernicious Lutheran doctrine which Swedenborg never completely left behind, though he wonderfully improved and in every way greatly modified it. Running all through Swedenborgian theology is the supposition, to say the least, that some human souls have, during the brief term of a single embodiment on earth, so confirmed themselves in love of evil,—which of course implies hatred of good,—that of their own volition they will remain forever in a state of alienation from all truth and goodness. In this inference we can see nothing but shortsighted failure to discern the true inwardness of human nature. Where those fictitious characters are to be found in real life who have no love of goodness in them we have never been able to discover, though it needs no more than the most ordinary observation to discern widely different degrees of manifest goodness, not only in different individuals, but also in the same individuals at different times and in the midst of varying circumstances. We are often reminded by Swedenborgians that the Lord coerces no one, but leaves every individual free to choose a destiny; but the full acceptance of that proposition does not in the slightest measure sustain the position we are combating, for it can be assented to in its entirety by all who take a reasonable view of human nature and be by them employed to illustrate the certainty that that very freedom of choice upon which Swedenborg insists so strenuously will prove the agent through which the transformation of all hells into heavens will be ultimately accomplished. Were this point only a theological quibble, having no immediate bearing upon our conduct toward our fellow beings here and now, we might well consign it to the category of those mysteries which may be cleared up in a future life, but not in the present; but nothing can be more misleading than to assume that an anthropological doctrine can be void of present influence upon the mutual practical conduct of those who entertain it. The whole question of Prison Reform is affected vitally by the views of human nature which we at this moment entertain, and it is not too much to condemn as shockingly immoral a doctrine of innate and perpetual, therefore presumably irremediable depravity. With the breaking down, in nearly all Christian communities, of the frightful old views of hell which Swedenborg did so much to modify, a wave of humanity is now sweeping over the earth, which promises ere long to completely transfigure all our penal institutions; and so powerfully is the good influence exerted by the "new theology" being already felt that we can hardly take up a periodical, or even a newspaper, without finding some account of good work accomplished through the beneficent influence exerted by the dissemination and application of humane views of human nature. The Southern States of America have long been in the clutch of extreme religious and other phases of conservatism, and it has generally been considered that the North is far more open to accept needed reforms in thought and practise than the South; but it is now happily true that the South is entering upon a new era of prosperity and awakening to embrace the same noble philanthropic spirit which is now making rapid headway in the North and in the West. As recently as March 29, 1910, a representative Southern newspaper, "Virginian Pilot," Norfolk, Virginia, contained the following beautiful account of an address delivered in that city by Judge Benjamin Lindsey, of Denver, Colorado. Our special object in inserting the report in this volume is to show exactly how human nature actually responds in this world to the right sort of treatment, and it is this same human nature with which we have to deal when we are contemplating the future state of our humanity. As we read this noble record of the gracious helpful work of a truly brave and strong, as well as intensely kindly man, let us keep steadily before us the fact that Judge Lindsey is dealing with that element in society which is designated "incorrigible" in many instances by people who can see no latent love of virtue below the mass of débris behind which it is often deeply hid. When theologians as a whole believe that the law which regulates the universe is at least as good and wise as its manifestations in the persons of many living philanthropists, though they may still have much more to learn, they will cease speculating upon the fate of the "finally impenitent."

BOYS' CHAMPION IS ENTHUSIASTICALLY WELCOMED.

Judge Ben. B. Lindsey, of the Juvenile Court of Denver, Colo., one of the most noted workers in the interest of juvenile court work in the United States, and the author of the sensational political story, "The Beast in the Jungle," which has been running in Everybody's Magazine for the past six months, lectured to a large audience at the Academy of Music last night on "Juvenile Court Work." The lecture was given under the auspices of the Co-operative Clubs of Norfolk and Portsmouth and directly under the auspices of the Norfolk section, Council of Jewish Women.

After his lecture, which was received with great warmth, Judge Lindsey was besieged by the representatives of a half dozen clubs and organizations of the city and promised to make his appearance before four of them.

It is no wonder that the "kids" of Denver took Judge Lindsey into their confidence and told him their troubles when no other judge had ever been able to get a word either as evidence or confidence. Judge Lindsey is a man who has a personality which attracts youngsters and inspires confidence. He has an honest, appealing sort of a face with not a hard expression in it, but always a laugh about his eyes when the rest of his countenance seems serious.

He carried his audience away with him last night on many little trips into boys' hearts and boys' lives. He told about things which have happened to about every man who listened to him last night, but most of them had forgotten and were delighted when their memories were refreshed.  He brought out the fact that interest is everything in a child's life and that the child is changing the whole scheme of things.  What is most needed, he said, is a little love in the law and less of that inconsiderate harshness which classes the mischievous boy with the criminal man.  Fewer jails and more schools; more education, more tolerance, more patience and more sympathy, and less browbeating, is Judge Lindsey's prescription for saving boys' futures.  He believes that there is some good in every boy and that the good dominates the bad.

"We are dealing with human hearts and souls and qualities," said Judge Lindsey.  "We ought to deal with a lad as a child is dealt with, and not a criminal.  Give boys what they need—sympathy, assistance, encouragement and co-operation, and see what you get in return.

"Fathers and mothers in the home if they are wise will get the truth from the child taken in delinquency, for if a child gets by with a lie, in many cases, it is lost.  Take them when they are young and mould their character while it is plastic and you make for better men and better citizenship."

Judge Lindsey divided the study of juvenile court work into three classes, each of which, he said, was closely allied with the other.  He cited the physiological, the sociolgoical and the psychology of the boy's nature, each of which must be approached from an entirely different standpoint, but which are very closely linked together.  Because of a total ignorance of these qualities, or perhaps because of an utter disregard for them, Judge Lindsey declared, 100,000 children go to the courts of the country every year, which in a generation makes more than 2,000,000 "kids," as he referred to them, who are up against hard propositions which they don't understand. These conditions are attributable to careless parents, political corruption, and the grinding of the mills of the wealthy, which he declared crushed hundreds of lives which might have become a valuable asset to the nation."

Once let the members of the New Jerusalem Church follow their gifted leader further than the actual words of his writings, now long stereotyped, may be able to carry them and they will see that the greatest honor we can pay to a spiritual pioneer is not to cling slavishly to the letter of the record he has left behind him but to go steadily forward along the line suggested by the obvious trend of his philosophy. If there be any spiritual revelation it must be progressive, and instead of stupidly claiming, as many shortsighted people do, that you must take a revelation in its entirety or else utterly reject it, we claim that all revelations, no matter of what nature, must be fearlessly and dispassionately examined in accordance with the wise injunction, "Prove all things; hold fast that which is good." The scientific spirit needs to prevail in religious as well as in all other circles. Nothing is too sacred for examination; no revelation can be final and none can be complete, because our capacities for acceptance and for comprehension are continually on the increase.

During the Darwin Celebration at Cambridge, England, held in June, 1909, many learned men who expressed the sincerest admiration and esteem for the hero of the occasion did not hesitate to call attention to his limitations while extolling his nobility of character and paying high tribute to the enormous value of his work. If some similar attitude were taken, by his admirers, toward Swedenborg, much good would undoubtedly be accomplished, and we should soon be able to assign to the gifted seer and sage of Scandinavia the place which rightfully belongs to him in his three-fold capacity of Scientist, Philosopher and Theologian. All who wish to estimate Swedenborg fairly, and to profit as much as possible from his immense literary output, should not confine themselves to his theological, but should make a study of his earlier scientific and philosophical writings also, for in these we can trace the gradual growth of his perceptions and watch, with much interest and profit, how he applies the universal law of correspondences to the entire field of nature, which he most industriously examined. Swedenborg's entire work will be far better comprehended, and his mission far more clearly understood, when some review of it in its entirety is undertaken by impartial and unprejudiced examiners. But these are usually difficult to find, because bias does exist, either for or against, to a large extent, even in the minds of men as widely comprehensive as Ralph Waldo Emerson, whose essay on Swedenborg is, to an extent, marred by his evident disrelish for any attempt to map out even a small portion of the unseen universe. Emerson's distinctive bias led him to eulogize Plato, almost extravagantly, while his review of Swedenborg suffered from the same

cause.   Many of Emerson's criticisms of Swedenborg's "heavens" are very just, but there is more
to be said in favor of their naturalness than a man
of Emerson's temperament would be likely to discover.   It is quite true that, when describing domestic life in the spiritual world, Swedenborg's
married angels do appear something like "country
parsons and their wives," though on rather a glorified scale; but it is quite conceivable that Swedenborg was really intromited into just such a state in
the spiritual universe, his clairvoyance enabling him
to see exactly what he described and was in full
sympathy with; and just because his ideals and aspirations concerning the hereafter were not quite
the same as Emerson's, his own selected heaven
would not be the same as that chosen by one whose
tastes and feelings were in many respects unlike his
own.   By carrying out the dominant Swedenborgian
theory of will and choice as ruling factors regulating our condition in the heavens, we can dispose of
many difficulties which appear at first insuperable,
and it must be with Swedenborg himself for guide
that his own philosophy will yet be much more fully
elucidated.   Here we may rest our argument, at
least for the immediate present.   We all make our
own spiritual conditions here and hereafter, and
the same law works uniformly in all worlds and
through all ages.   In accordance with the strictest
implications of this rational and orderly proposition,
we can logically proceed to construct a sound, sane,
and ever-widening philosophy.

# CHAPTER XII.

When rapidly running through some of the contents of Genesis, we dwelt particularly upon those
wonderful Type Men, Abraham, Isaac, Jacob
(transformed into Israel), and then Joseph,—a
character of such rare beauty and comprehensive excellence that words fail utterly to do full justice to
the magnificent ideal thus set before us. Turning
now to Exodus, we find one majestic solitary figure
towering in sublime moral magnificence far above
all the rest, even Moses, the unrivaled prophet who
to this day remains the grandest law-enforcer of
whom we have any distinct record. In Genesis we
are made acquainted with Egypt in the days of its
ancient splendor, when the Pharaohs (Native
Rulers) were just and honorable men and extended
to Joseph, the representative Israelite, not only a
cordial welcome but also assigned him the exalted
station to which his extraordinary capabilities entirely entitled him. Then were the happy days
when Egyptian and Israelite dwelt side by side in
harmony, wisely co-operating for the general good.
In those remote days it appears that Egypt had well-
nigh perfectly solved some of those intricate indus-

trial problems which are greatly vexing the world to-day. The Hebrews were originally a pastoral and agricultural people, while the Egyptians were given to arts and crafts; they were also navigators and chemists of a high degree of proficiency. Racial differences have always existed, and it is perfectly right that we should recognize them still, but difference rightly understood never implies discord; on the contrary, it constitutes the only basis for exquisite harmony. There could be unison but not harmony in song if all voices were of the same pitch and all singers sounded the same note; so is it with the great human chorus composed of the various races of humanity; they are properly distinct, but they never ought to appear discordant.

The Book of Exodus introduces us to a very different state of affairs, when it informs us that "another king arose who knew not Joseph"; a brief, comprehensive sentence containing in germ the entire history of the fatal progress of Egyptian degeneracy, resulting finally in that abject decadence which brought about the complete overthrow of the Pharoic dynasty, tragically described in the graphic account of the destruction of the Egyptian host in the Red Sea, while those who had been cruelly enslaved and maltreated by Egypt's degenerate rulers were making their escape from bondage and taking their first vigorous steps on the road to complete enfranchisement. It is in the midst of a degraded Egypt that the sublime figure of Moses rises into a position of conspicuous leadership. We know quite well that the character of Moses is far from perfect, but perfect characters are never discover-

able among us; we all, even the greatest of us, have
certain very definite moral and mental limitations,
and were we to refuse to accord honor to a great
leader because he exhibited some failings and frail-
ties, we should be compelled to entirely abandon all
that useful, because temperate and sagacious, hero-
worship which, when kept within reasonable limits,
is unquestionably a highly elevating factor in human
development. The beautiful Bible story of Moses
is full of picturesque detail, commencing with the
Ark of Bulrushes in which he is found when an
infant by an Egyptian princess, who takes the
little Hebrew boy into her kindly charge and se-
cures for him all the advantages which the highest
culture of the day could afford. The Hebrew name
*Moshe* means literally drawn up out of the water,
and has no exclusive reference to the mere incident
of a literal rescue from physical drowning at a time
when the curse of anti-Semitism had invaded Egypt,
to such an extent that drastic measures were employed for killing off in infancy multitudes of male
Hebrews. The spiritual significance of the name
*Moshe* denotes one whose consciousness has become
elevated to a higher than the simply intellectual
level; water signifying intellect esoterically. The
life of Moses, which extended to 120 years, is divided into three periods of forty years each. The
First Period is devoted to education; the Second to
civil employment; the Third to seership. We are
told in Exodus that Moses was fully eighty years
of age when he turned aside at Horeb to behold
that great sight, the bush burning with fire which,
however, remained unconsumed. Though very

beautiful poetic allusions have been made to this bush, as though it were a vegetable, by John Green-leaf Whittier, Theodore Parker, and other excellent modern writers, and their references are thoroughly well justified, we know that the original meaning of the bush is human nature itself. Moses was a veritable prince among anthropologists, and because of his intimate and profound acquaintance with human nature essentially, it is truly said that he beheld the Divine Similitude. In the thirteen articles of Jewish faith, compiled in the twelfth century of the present era by Moses Maimonides, we find the following saying: "There hath never risen yet in Israel a prophet like unto Moses; one who hath beheld his similitude." Taking these words in connection with the sublime sentences which precede and follow them, we are fully justified in connecting this statement with the declaration in the first chapter of Genesis that humanity is created in the Divine likeness, therefore those truly great prophets who have revealed Divine Law to humanity with special fulness and clearness, are simply those who have attained to a higher degree of spiritual development than the majority. Reverence for great men may be carried to an extreme, but there is surely no just reason for denying the self-evident fact that once in a while some especially illumined teacher does appear among us, never, properly, as an object of worship, but as a true and faithful guide to some fuller comprehension of the one living and true God whom all the prophets in Israel have most emphatically declared to be the only proper object of human adoration. Let "higher criticism" dispute over historical occurrences as it may, the sublimity of the moral law contained in the Book of Exodus can never suffer in the slightest degree by reason of anyone's alleged ignorance of the time and place of its original enunciation.   The intrinsic value of the Ten Commandments is in no sense affected by any surrounding circumstances in ancient or modern days, and it is surely to the Mosaic type of man that the world is indebted for such clear and wonderful deliverances concerning courses of thought as well as action, necessary not only to the preservation of human society but to its continual elevation to ever higher and higher levels of attainment.   Were the other nine commandments to be treated only as pertaining to outward conduct, the Tenth would always remain so thoroughly related to our most interior life of thought and feeling that its pure spirituality would ever constitute it a beacon light for human guidance, until the blessed time arrives when no commandments will be longer necessary, because a perfect love for goodness and truth will be so fully developed within us that we shall no longer need any external prohibition or exhortation.   Moses may well be regarded as a truly great Adept and Initiate into those universal Mysteries which Theosophists and many others are now endeavoring to unveil and practically apply to existing human necessities.   A people in bondage like Israel in Egypt may well be looked upon as representing a stage in human evolution prior to the awakening of spiritual consciousness.   The Bible seems to tell us that people are very comfortable in servitude until a new love of liberty awakens within them; then they become restless and restive, and in the endeavor to shake off their bonds they always encounter trial from within and persecution from without.  Such has ever been the history alike of individuals and of nations; thus the story of Exodus applies not only to deliverance from physical slavery, but, in a much higher sense, to spiritual emancipation.  Whenever a great crisis is reached in the progress of a nation, some great deliverer arises wonderfully equipped to lead a multitude which could not lead itself; likewise whenever an individual reaches a similar crisis in interior development, some hitherto unknown intuition causes, at one and the same time, discontent with prevailing modes of life and a more or less distinct vision of some higher state attainable.  We observe that Moses is the younger and Aaron the elder brother, but the Divine voice speaks to Moses and through Moses to Aaron, then through Aaron to the multitude.  This statement agrees exactly with the pre-eminence of the younger Jacob over the elder Esau, and gives significance to a famous modern phrase, "That which is latest born is highest born."  Here we can readily trace the complete foundation of the universal truth of involution and evolution, for no matter in what direction we turn for example and illustration, we find it invariably stated, in the most widely divergent treatises, that the lowest forms of existence appear earliest and the highest class come last of all.  We talk very curiously about "olden times" when we mean earlier days; but just as we grow older from year to year, so must time grow older; this year is therefore the

oldest year the earth has known, and as human beings are justly supposed to have been gathering experience through all the years which have passed,
and to be therefore far maturer in judgment at
seventy than at seventeen, so as the earth advances
we have the right to expect that knowledge will
continually increase, therefore the newest generation and the youngest individuals may be in very
truth the oldest.   Moses represents the intuitive man
who sees everything through spiritual perception;
he is therefore purely a prophet, while his elder brother Aaron has only that intellectual understanding
which enables him to deal with those external matters which always pertain to the priestly office.   As
we follow the Book of Exodus from stage to stage,
we find how naturally the author tells us that there
comes a time when Aaron can be made to yield to
the idolatrous wishes of the people while Moses is
absent, but Moses remains relentless in his refusal
to yield to any popular demand which his conviction cannot sanction.   This has always been the
great historical difference between prophet and
priest, and it certainly exists manifestly at the present day.   It is the superb courage, the dauntless
moral bravery of Moses, which singles him out as
a type of very much that is abidingly noblest in
our common human nature, and it is not too much to
claim that every true leader of a multitude must
possess and exhibit, in unusually large degree, those
prophetic qualities which cause their possessor to
brave every possible danger and difficulty for the
purpose of arriving at truth and emancipating, as
far as possible, enslaved humanity.   That very noble

and intensely conscientious political economist, Henry George, whose writings deserve the deepest study, gave many a truly inspiring lecture on Moses, taking that heroic ancient prophet as a type of what a valiant leader in any age and anywhere should be. There must be no temporizing, no pandering to injustice, no seeking to curry favor with unrighteous monopolies for selfish ends, or through timidity, but firm, uncompromising adhesion to one's uttermost convictions of right, no matter at what cost to one's self or whether the very people in whose interest one is specially working recognize the good intentions of the one who seeks to deliver them or not. Without these qualities and qualifications there can be no such prophet as Moses in the modern, any more than there could have been in the ancient world.

The real prophet is so much more than one who simply foretells coming events that, though there may be some element of forecasting in a prophet's ministry, he is before all else a champion of liberty and an exhorter to righteousness.

The curious story of the plagues of Egypt offers food for thought along several distinctive lines, one of which is the nature of magic and the part it played in ancient Egypt and Israel. Nowhere do we find a clearer line of demarcation drawn between white magic and black, than in the trial of strength between Moses and Aaron on one hand and Pharaoh's court magicians on the other. Up to a certain point whatever Moses and Aaron could do, and did, the soothsayers readily duplicated, therefore there could be no victory for either side until the crucial test was made at the time when men and animals

were alike suffering from painful and fatal diseases.   The power to heal by magical means has
been claimed for true prophets and their disciples
in all lands and through all ages, and it has been
quite reasonably maintained that no healing efficacy
can possibly reside in the black magician's art, because he never works with a desire to benefit humanity, but, on the contrary, to unduly exalt himself and enslave others.   We are quite ready to
credit the statement in Exodus that while Moses
and Aaron could and did perform beneficent works
of healing, when the sorcerers attempted to do the
same they only succeeded in enlarging the area of
misery they were thus vainly attempting to reduce.
Reason certainly compels us to decide that in order
to accomplish any really beneficent work in the
world, no matter by what means, we must have the
love of humanity at heart; therefore it has always
been justly claimed that power to heal resides only
among holy prophets, never among those who,
though genuine wonder-workers, producing marvellous phenomena through the performance of magical
rites, are in no way actuated by any sincere desire to confer blessings on their neighbors.

The plagues of Egypt were of a startling nature,
but they were not in themselves edifying, nor could
they throw any light on the divine commission of
Moses.   They were doubtless due, in large measure,
to the exercise of that strange hypnotic power about
which we hear so much at present and which always greatly mystifies those who endeavor to rationally explain the wonders often performed in
India in sight of European travelers by Hindu ma-

gicians.   Turning a staff into a snake and a snake back into a staff may be altogether an illusory phenomenon, the spectators being temporarily affected by the mental power of the magician, and it may also be, as many Theosophists distinctly claim, that these wonder-workers have acquired through rigid self-training a control over Nature-Spirits which can be made to do their bidding.   Causing the waters of the Nile to assume the semblance of blood, and also the mysterious production of quantities of locusts and other pests, would be well within the province of any sort of magician according to universal testimony regarding magic, but there would be nothing in all this to suggest any divine activity.   When we come to the affliction of the beasts, many Jewish commentators have suggested that as certain animals were accounted sacred and unduly venerated in Egypt, the power exerted by Moses and Aaron to subject these creatures to affliction was intended as a convincing rebuke to prevailing idolatry, showing that the bull and other idolised animals were not able to protect themselves against attacks which might be made by men upon them; thereby proving that they were neither divinities nor under the special protection of divinities.   Whatever we may think of that interpretation—and there is something to be said in favor of it—a clear moral issue is at stake only when we reach the point where the great prophets in Israel relieve the suffering alike of men and animals while their opponents can only increase distress.   This is a very old and also a very new lesson, quite as much needed at the present moment as in any time of old, for we are witnessing to-day an almost overwhelming recrudescence of interest in everything avowedly magical, and especially in everything Egyptian, so much so that the weirdest and most fantastic tales have been very recently circulated concerning the dire catastrophes which have befallen impertinent persons who have behaved rudely to a painted mummy case, representing an Egyptian princess, in the British Museum.

We have no right ever to positively deny what we cannot definitely disprove, either on ethical or intellectual grounds; but we have a right to refrain from blindly endorsing almost incredible narratives, and particularly are we justified in discountenancing alarming beliefs concerning the powers of sorcery which, wherever entertained, can have no other effect than to weaken the nervous system and cloud the mind with dim forebodings of disaster. The plagues of Egypt must have had a highly salutary effect in two directions: First, they served to show exactly where a line can and must be drawn between beneficent and maleficent wonder-working; Second, they were instrumental in leading to the dethronement of tyranny and the gradual emancipation of an enslaved multitude.

Turning from an outer to an inner view of these strange records, a mystic commentary thereon will lead us to see in the Egyptians of the Book of Exodus all those, even at the present day, who, because dwelling in the night of ignorance and enslaving superstition themselves, are bent on doing all they can to hold others in captivity.

In the great mass of the Hebrews we may imagine

those who, though by no means as yet fully enlightened, are nevertheless awakening to a sense of their
captivity and becoming filled with what we now
often call divine discontent, are struggling to break
their bonds.   In Moses and Aaron (Moses especially) we behold the picture of those few who are
so thoroughly consecrated to high ideals and so
completely bent, no matter at what hazard to themselves, on carrying forward the glorious work of
liberating the enslaved, that they do all and dare
all to the utmost extent of their ability to accomplish
the noble end to which they feel they have been
called by the divine voice within them.   The two
great and serious problems of moral and industrial
slavery need solution in modern Europe and America
even as they needed solving in ancient Egypt, and
we may well hope that there is to be found a modern
as well as an ancient Horeb and Moses.   The tragic
overthrow of Pharaoh and his host in the Red Sea,
presents in glowing imagery the inevitable disaster
which must finally overtake all governments and
monopolies which fight to maintain themselves at
the expense of every humane consideration.   We
must not gloat over the sufferings of individuals,
who physically perish in the days of some great
revolution which results in the upward progress of
humanity, but we may well triumph in the thought
that cruelty and injustice invariably play a losing
game, for, as Robert Browning beautifully expresses
it, "God's in His heaven; all's right with the world."
This magnificent truth so sublimely uttered and
so constantly reiterated by all the world's greatest
prophets and poets, should prove an anchor of refuge

in every time of trial, no matter how severe our trials may be, by nerving us with that true optimism which can alone sustain us in times of affliction by enabling us to cling with unflinching faith to a doctrine of the universe which places Divinity at its center and destroys all belief in the ultimate triumph of inequity in any portion of it. There are two texts in the Book of Exodus, equally sublime, but adapted to diametically opposite human conditions, which we do well to so lay to heart that we may receive inspiration from them both in times of needed repose and in periods which call for instant and vigorous action. The first of these is, "Stand still and thou shalt see the salvation of God"; the second is, "Speak unto the children of Israel, that they go forward." To understand the import of these two mighty sayings, we must take well into account the circumstances in which they both were uttered. The first came at a time when, if the people had stepped forward, they would have been instantly drowned, and had they gone backward they would have run into the swords of their pursuing enemies. The second applied to taking decisive action at such a period as we often call "the psychological moment." One lesson for us to learn is that sometimes there is nothing for us to do, and then it is that we require to summon all our energy to do nothing. No course to pursue is more difficult and no act is more heroic than to remain quite quiet in a time of panic, when people all around us are frenzied with excitement; and nothing again evinces more thoroughly developed intuition than to make a necessary move at exactly the right moment, and in exactly the way which will prove most permanently effective.

When the people went out of Egypt they carried with them all that was worth conveying away of the religious ideas and ceremonies and also of the social usages of the Egyptians. This is symbolically stated in the statement that they borrowed jewels of gold and silver and "spoiled" the Egyptian. In this single sentence we have a distinct clue to the influence of Egyptian upon Hebrew culture, and we have also a plain intimation that when the old Egyptian civilization came to an end all that was really valuable in it was carried forward to other lands and eventually became incorporated in the institutions of other countries. Figuratively speaking, again applying the story of Exodus to universal human development, we may well decide that nothing worthy of preservation can ever be really lost, though it may often change its outward form, and sometimes remain to a large extent buried (but never dead), to come to active life again when some new age begins to dawn in human history, and some new race is evolving to embody the excellences of the past coupled with new developments unknown in ancient epochs.

# CHAPTER XIII.

Quite a number of different versions have been given of the special lessons intended to be conveyed by the Plagues of Egypt. We have already referred to their magical character, and endeavored to show that they present a very clear distinction between white magic and black—i.e., between Occult Power exercised with beneficent intent in the one case, and for the purpose of working injury in the other. There is yet another reason given for the Plagues than that of showing the distinction between wonders wrought to assist in procuring liberty for the enslaved and similar wonders performed for the purpose of keeping serfs still in bondage, a demonstration of Divine power over the Egyptian Idols which the Ten Plagues specifically attacked. Miraculous or magical power was believed by the Egyptians to be in the possession of their idols, which they always regarded as far more than emblems or symbols; believing as they did that their divinities in some mysterious manner communicated with them through the agency of these images, and also in a very particular manner through the various living creatures which they held particularly sacred. Several writers have not hesitated to affirm that the Plagues were sent almost solely for the purpose of destroying faith in the various Egyptian divinities, a proposition to which we can well assent, provided we are convinced that thirty-five centuries ago the worship of these idols was intimately associated with the perpetuation of cruel slavery and many grossly immoral practices.   There is no suggestion in the book of Exodus that the magicians of Egypt were devoid of power or that their performances were simply conjurors' tricks; but the very word conjuror meant originally one who could conjure or evoke certain unseen influences and compel them to do his bidding.

No objection need necessarily have been taken to any form of Nature worship, provided it had not been abused to the ends of human injury; but directly it had become thus perverted there was surely an excellent reason for protesting vigorously against it, and working wonders with the intent to demolish it.   We must always keep steadily before us the one idea that whatever was done by Moses and Aaron had this sole object in view—the liberation of oppressed people from servitude.   The first wonder destroyed confidence in the power of serpents which were very highly venerated in Egypt and in many other ancient countries, for we are told that Moses and Aaron could perfectly control them and cause them to appear and disappear at will. When man can show conclusively that these reptiles are completely subject to his sway, they can no longer be regarded as proper objects for human adoration, for it is self-evidently absurd to bow be-

fore inferior creatures which are subject to our will
and cannot protect themselves against any assault
we may make upon their alleged superiority.   To
pollute the waters of the Nile, the sacred river of
the Egyptians, was to prove that their river deities
were unable to protect the stream against the as-
saults made upon it by those greatest of wonder-
workers, Moses and Aaron, who spoke in the name
of a far more powerful Deity.   We cannot suppose
that any people could be at once led to acknowledge
One Only Supreme Being, but they could quite
easily be induced to admit through the agency of
manifest marvels that the Divinity worshiped by
the Hebrews was an altogether superior being to
their own local divinities; and for the purpose of
the Exodus it was clearly necessary to establish in
the mind of Pharoah and his generals that the divinity worshiped by the Israelites had greater
power than the many gods and goddesses to whom
the Egyptians in general were accustomed to render
homage.   The plague of frogs was directed against
an Egyptian god who was supposed to regard these
unclean creatures as peculiarly sacred, and no sooner
did frogs become a definite nuisance to the Egyptians than they ceased to venerate them, and were
thus rescued from that particular phase of idolatry.
No greater mistake could well be made historically
or otherwise than to suppose that only Hebrews were
liberated at the time of Passover, for the narrative
in Exodus distinctly informs us that a mixed multitude went out of Egypt.   The Egyptians as a nation were not drowned in the Red Sea, but only
Pharoah's pursuing army who had set forth with

the one intention of dragging back into slavery those who were just escaping by way of the Red Sea passage. The various plagues, therefore, were intended to enlighten, not to curse, the Egyptians, though it is said to have come to pass that those who refused to give heed to salutary warnings were overthrown in a time of widespread calamity. The presence of various obnoxious insects in sacred temples as well as in secular houses served to desecrate all those places, and it had long been commonly believed that no insect regarded as unclean could possibly invade an Egyptian sanctuary. That old tradition may well have taken its rise in very ancient times when the priesthood was pure and noble, and did actually possess some real ability to consecrate buildings and sacred vessels as well as to sanctify its own religious vestments, but that time had long passed, and the priesthood of the days of Exodus had become, for the most part, so corrupt that no real sanctity could possibly attach to it or to its ministrations. The subject of the power to consecrate is very finely treated by Annie Besant in "The Changing World," particularly in the section headed "The Sacramental Life," in which she furnishes a large amount of information concerning "Words of Power," to which she attributes the very results in these days which have been claimed for them from time immemorial. So very much, according to this view depends upon the consecrator that no object can be consecrated simply by the celebration of a rite or the employment of a formula; it takes a holy man or woman to perform a holy act; the simple fact of one's being a nominal priest or priestess confers no genuine grace or power. Just as in India a mantra can only be successfully used by a holy person who speaks the right syllables in exactly the right manner, so can we readily discover by observing contemporary mental therapeutic practice that while nothing is easier than to learn a set of formulas and repeat them by rote, the actual efficacy of this mode of treatment depends far more upon the man or woman who makes use of it than upon the formula itself, though it may also be fairly claimed that there is a suggestive value in certain formulated sentences quite apart from the special condition of the individual who employs them. Again and again we are told in Exodus that Moses and Aaron gave credentials of their divine commission by healing the afflicted, a work which Pharoah's magicians utterly failed in accomplishing whenever they undertook it; it was not therefore the production of the Plagues, but their removal, which proved that Moses and Aaron were on the righteous side while their opponents were the servants of unrighteousness. Nothing could well be more odious than to believe that anybody at any time displayed delegated divine authority by producing plagues or causing pestilence, but when we have learned that though that work can be quite successfully performed by black magicians, the power to remove plagues testifies some degree of divine authority the case is entirely different, and by no means irrational or incredible. We are told that the magicians, when they witnessed the power of Moses and Aaron accomplishing wonders far beyond their own power to duplicate, exclaimed, "This is indeed the finger of God," an expression which clearly shows that they were amenable to reasonable conviction and did not hesitate to confess their inferiority when such was clearly demonstrated.   There was in Egypt at that time a singular belief in a divinity who presided over flies, and indeed every creature mentioned in the story of the Plagues was in some way connected with prevailing idolatry.   It was, however, only after the slaying of the first-born sons that Pharoah is said to have become so terrified that he not only let the people go, but urged the captives to depart with utmost haste, lest even greater calamities should fall upon him and his subjects.   This terrible ordeal through which the Egyptians had to pass suggests the outworking of the Law of Karma, which metes out exact justice in the long run to every individual and to every nation.   This slaying of the first-born of the Egyptians may be regarded as the fruitage of the previous slaying of the male children of the Hebrews by command of an earlier Pharoah.   What we do to others we often unknowingly and unwittingly do to ourselves; for all evil thoughts, words and deeds directed against others are like boomerangs: they strike back the individual who throws them out.   Herein lies the open secret of the much-maligned but ever true law of retaliation, expressed in the famous sentence, "An eye for an eye and a tooth for a tooth." This is the law of the universe, and no one can ever evade its operation; but it is a beneficent law, and when rightly interpreted impresses us deeply with a sense of divine equity, but conveys no thought of vengeance, for we need the discipline of suffering ourselves if we have caused others to suffer. There is something actually sublime in that great phrase of Emerson's, "No one can do me an injury but myself," which clearly means that we are never really hurt by any opposition from without, but only by deterioration from within. Knowing that a great many Christians entirely misconceive the law of retaliation and believe that the New Testament condemns it, we hope they will soon come to understand it rightly, and they will when they see that it is at no point in conflict with the Golden Rule which beautifully advises us to do unto others only and exactly what we wish others to do unto us. No great teacher ever instructed his disciples to knock out their neighbors' teeth and pluck out their eyes, but all great teachers have urged upon their students the necessity for just and kindly conduct in all the relationships of life; consequently, if Christians obey the Golden Rule they will not find the Jewish law working against them in any particular, even though it be carried out in its minutest detail. We do not mean to say that all Jewish legislation, any more than all Christian legislation, has been either just or merciful, but we are not now endeavoring to deal with the particular acts of certain individuals, but only with the broad outlines of a code of morals set forth in the Pentateuch. In the literal enforcement of equitable law we must always be compelled to make the utmost compensation or restitution in our power for all injuries we have inflicted on others; but this certainly does not mean that others are to perform upon us the same ferocious acts that we have performed on our neighbors, for no good end would probably be served by that kind of savage retaliation. There can be no real justification for inflicting any penalty on anyone except with some benevolent end in view; but as different people are reached by different methods, adapted to their varying stages of moral and mental development, seemingly harsh measures are often kind in reality, while very lenient ones are frequently ineffective. We must, however, be very careful, if ever we feel disposed to take the law into our own hands, for we are wisely told in the Bible that retribution belongs to God, and all matters will be adjusted equitably through the outworking of an unchanging universal law with which we must simply endeavor to place ourselves in harmony. We should do all in our power to discourage any form of gloating over the discomfiture of our personal antagonists, and if we celebrate the Passover in any helpful manner, we must rejoice only in a commemoration of human liberation from slavery and think of the means provided to accomplish this noble end merely as those best suited to a bygone age in a distant country. The lesson of the Passover itself is universal and perpetually enduring, even in the case of curious ceremonial details, such as the eating of bitter herbs and unleavened bread, which have a far deeper significance when viewed esoterically than any mere remembrance of a hurried flight from Egypt on a certain eventful night between three and four thousand years ago.

Even the curious traditional songs sung in Jewish homes on Pesach Eve are replete with deep interior meaning, though such curious specimens as

"One Only Kid" may well be classed with fables and folk-songs in general. Children always love songs, fables, parables and all kinds of object lessons, and they grasp what there are intended to teach far more readily than they learn by the less attractive methods employed by teachers who exclude symbols from their curriculum. "One Only Kid" is a fair specimen of ancient combinations of allegory and anecdote. The main object of the song is to demonstrate the instability of all mortal things and the sole permanence of Deity and of God's unchanging law. The child sings at time of Passover celebration of his father's buying a kid, which was eaten by a cat (originally some large member of the feline family was indicated). Now the cat was a very sacred animal in ancient Egypt; so sacred was it held that cats mummied thousands of years ago are yet in a good state of preservation in the British Museum. But after the cat had slain the kid, a dog came and bit the cat. Now the dog was held sacred in Babylonia and Assyria, to which power Egypt was rendered tributary after the Israelitish exodus. History is therefore taught in the quaint old melody as well as religion. The dog in turn is beaten with a stick, which is emblematical of Persia, where it was a type of the strictest possible administration of justice, as we learn from the Zend-Avesta. Then a fire burns the stick, and this is said to represent the conquest of Persia by Alexander of Macedonia, who rushed forth like a devouring flame, and in less than seven years completely overthrew Persian supremacy. The fire now is quenched by water, which typifies the Roman power which swept like a flood over the major portion of the then known world.   Eventually an ox appears, and drinks up the water which had quenched the fire, and this is looked upon as an emblem of Moslem rule.   But the ox meets its fate at the hands of a butcher, who is said to signify the Crusaders who as relentlessly attacked the Mohammedans as they had attacked those whom they had previously conquered.   But there comes a time when the butcher must fall before the sword of the Angel of Death, who will ultimately remove all strife from the earth and usher in the glorious age of universal peace foretold by all the greatest of the prophets of all climes and ages.   The Holy One (Blessed be He) slays the Angel of Death who has removed the butcher who slew the ox which drank the water that quenched the fire that burnt the stick which beat the dog that bit the cat that ate the kid.   Finally the prophets assure us all wars will cease and this planet will reach the zenith of its perfection and become the abode of only holy and happy multitudes. Such is the predicted end of the world, for by end is meant object in view.   To what end are you working? is a familiar inquiry.   Wisely indeed does John Uri Lloyd, in his wonderful romance, "Etidorhpa" (Aphrodite spelled backward), represent a radiant maiden appearing to a venerable man who had undergone the weirdest imaginable experiences, and saying to him, "I am the end of the world," a highly significant sentence, meaning that the object of all terrestrial experience is to bring forth perfected humanity, which must be the only sane and satisfactory solution of our planet's tragic history.

The Pillar of Fire which went before the children
of Israel during their forty years' march through the
wilderness between Egypt and Palestine, has been
accounted for literally by some modern students on
the basis of discoveries in the vicinity of Mount
Sinai in Arabia, pointing to the volcanic character
of the district.   A simply materialistic version of
the fire by night and cloud by day is that the crater
of the volcano furnished exactly such phenomena.
Be this as it may, and the suggestion is quite credible,
the esoteric meaning of the narrative is in no way
impaired by any physical discoveries.   Natural facts
have all a spiritual origin, and they are always made
use of illustratively in all the sacred literature of
the entire world.   The inner meaning of all spiritual allegories must have reference to continuous
human experiences, therefore let us be ready to endorse whatever material science may reveal concerning outward phenomena, and at the same time
search diligently for those deeper truths of human
experience which relate us with the usually unseen,
but by no means permanently unknowable spiritual
universe.

We should have to write volumes, not chapters,
did we attempt, even in outline, to review and
comment upon the many thrilling incidents we have
left untouched in this brief mention of the Book
of Exodus.   Among the most powerfully suggestive
are the stories of Quails and Manna and the fash-
ioning and destroying of the Golden Calf.   The
story of food supplies is an intensely profitable topic
on which to meditate, for the heaven-sent manna
suggests an explanation of the nature of evil so

lucid and comprehensive that he who runs may
clearly read. Provision for human necessities comes
sweet and wholesome from heaven to earth, typify-
ing all human faculties and all natural and proper
means for sustaining our exterior existence; but if
we do not make a right use of faculties and opportunities, and moreover if we do not use these at the
proper time as well as in the right way, they become perverted, unwholesome and offensive. If
we are gluttonous and over-eat of the good food
provided, we are made seriously ill by "quail," when
we could be healthily sustained by "manna." All
things are good in their right place and time; per-
version, excess and misappropriation are the sole
causes of the many miseries we bemoan. In the ab-
sense of Moses (who denotes intuition and spiritual
guidance in general), and when only Aaron (who
signifies unillumined intellect) is leading us, we are
sorely apt to revert instead of to advance, and to require a material idol, like an image of the Egyptian Apis, to adore instead of trusting in the true
spiritual Divinity. The nations to be exterminated
before we can enter our Land of Promise figuratively denote all dispositions and practices which
are called in the New Testament "fleshly lusts which
war against the soul." We must all accomplish our
own individual as well as our collective exodus,
which is naught else, in its last analysis, than complete freedom attained from all kinds of servitude,
through strict adhesion to the voice of the Divine
within, obedience to which can alone secure complete
emancipation from every phase of thraldom which
yet embarrasses the human race.

# CHAPTER XIV.

There is a great fascination attaching to the name
of Gautama, the Buddha, almost all over the world
to-day: partly on account of the wide reading of
Sir Edwin Arnold's extremely beautiful poem, "The
Light of Asia," and partly by reason of the extremely widespreading interest in a general study of
Comparative Religion. To some minds Buddhism
appeals as a system of philanthropic philosophy, not
properly religious, because it appears that there are
no definitely theological elements in the system as
originally taught and promulgated, but as definitions of religion are many and varied, and as several
hundred millions of our fellow human beings accept
it as their religion, and declare that they take refuge
in Buddha as confidently as the devoutest Christians
take refuge in Christ, Buddhism may fairly rank,
not only as a religion, but as one of the great religions of the world. James Freeman Clarke, in
his splendid treatise, "Ten Great Religions," has
styled Buddhism the Protestantism of the East,
though from its present ceremonial aspects it far
more closely resembles Catholicism. It differs radically from Brahminism in its repudiation of caste

215

and by its insistence upon a philanthropic life, regardless of ritual observances. Though recently readmitted into India, for many centuries Buddhists were forced to live outside the land which gave their religion birth, and it was in Ceylon and in Thibet that the two great divisions of the Buddhist faith found their representative respective homes. Northern Buddhism is distinctly Theistic, consequently it cannot be pessimistic, for Theism and Pessimism are diametrically opposed; but Southern Buddhism has been accounted atheistic and also pessimistic. We incline to another view of Buddhistic teaching in its entirety from that taken by those who make these claims concerning even a section of it. The character of the traditional Buddha, Prince Gautama, is extremely beautiful, though it is by no means perfect in all regards. About 600 B. C. this prince was born in India, at a time when mighty teachers were about to stir the world in many districts. Old legends state that the birth of the child who was to become a Buddha was heralded by many wondrous signs, such as are traditionally associated with the advent of all great spiritual leaders. One testimony is that certain eminent astrologers declared that the infant prince would either become a singularly powerful earthly monarch or else renounce the world and become the Buddha he became, the choice being in his own will. His father earnestly desired that he should take the regal earthly pathway and did his utmost to further that ambitious end, but from very early years the boy showed indifference to worldly honors, and began to evince extreme solicitude for the downtrodden

and afflicted wherever he beheld them.   All in vain
did the king make efforts to keep all sight of human
distress beyond the sight of his youthful son; the
boy could not be effectually shielded from the vision
of prevailing misery, and it is related in many an
Indian tale that if his father's orders were strictly
observed, so that no pitiable spectacle of misery
could reach the lad's outward gaze, the Devas would
present to him pictures of distress, the contemplation
of which, though only saddening him at first, soon
aroused within him an unconquerable determination
to break away from royal restraints and plunge into
the vortex of suffering humanity to discover the
cause for such harrowing phenomena.   At the early
age of sixteen the young prince was married to a
charming princess, to whom he was devotedly attached, and his life in general was one spent in
the midst of all procurable mental and physical de-
lights.

But nothing could silence the distress which increased within him whenever he mentally contrasted
his own luxurious lot with the wretched portion of
multitudes of others who apparently deserved as
well at the hands of the universe as he.   Unrest increased within him to such an extent that he could
enjoy nothing while he felt that others were suffering whom possibly he might relieve.   It was with
that sentiment his incipient Buddhahood began to
dawn, and it was that same emotion which led him
to renounce every delight in life and to go forth
on the serious quest for knowledge regarding the
source of human misery which no splendor and no
personal affection could induce him to ignore.

It was in the very earliest stages of his career that this ardent lover of afflicted humanity inclined toward pessimism, and it is never an occasion for surprise when the young and tender-hearted give way to feelings akin to despair on their first introduction to sorrow and death, which are always heartrending spectacles until we have learned to regard them with philosophic calm and as not ultimately irreconcilable with Divine beneficence. Grief and death as ends in themselves never can be thus reconciled, but as factors in evolution they come to be seen as transmutable into very decided blessings; and as Gautama proceeded along his upward spiritual journey he not only apprehended that glorious truth, he taught it with joyful enthusiasm to all disciples who would accept it.

In his early hermit days he followed the rigidly ascetic path which gave him discipline but could not bring him joy. No satisfaction could he win from the teachings of the ascetics with whom he consorted; he could only learn the lesson pointed out by the author of Ecclesiastes, that from the standpoint, first of the sensualist and then of the intellectualist, whose eyes have not yet been opened to discern spiritual realities, "all is vanity and vexation of spirit." Teachers of conventional religion could recommend fastings and all manner of austerities. and these the growing Buddha tried, but they could not yield him peace, nor could they answer the mighty question, the true reply to which he was determined in some manner to obtain. It is recorded that he lived a domestic life for thirteen years, for his age is given as twenty-nine when he took the decisive step and broke away from family ties to enter upon a mission to the suffering of the world. Much might be said *pro* and *con* as to the value of the example hereby set, and it would need considerable caution to handle this episode judiciously and helpfully. Certainly this was no case of desertion or of leaving a family unprovided for, because a palace remained the home for wife and child, while the husband and father was out on his pilgrim mission. Oftentimes we hear men eulogized for going to the battlefield, and it is by no means uncommon for patriotic wives, regardless of the greatest personal suffering, to rejoice in the valor of their husbands; surely then, if warfare can supply sufficient reason for leaving home and kindred, the consciousness of a mighty spiritual mission may be urged with even greater earnestness. There is always something intensely noble in the spirit which prompts to voluntary self-sacrifice for good of others, though there is something mean and contemptible in that hysterical thought about one's personal salvation which has prompted many to seek refuge from the world in convents and monasteries, lest they should suffer individual contamination by associating with unrighteousness. Whenever there is an apparent conflict between a lesser and a larger work, it is always heroic to choose the larger, especially when that choice involves relinquishment of domestic joys and other legitimate pleasures which are standing in the way of the fulfilment of a larger ministry. Gautama soon began to teach that every man must work out his own salvation; there is no place for any vicarious atonement in his system. But how is salvation to be worked out? That is the vital question. The Buddha's doctrine of the Way of Enlightenment differed widely from the inculcations of the Brahmin priests, for as he discovered truth by delving into the inmost recesses of his own being, so did he counsel his disciples to do the same. Concerning the Ultimate Reality he never dogmatized, but he declared when one reached the state of Buddhahood he perceived it without speculation. Between Nirvana and Para-Nirvana, enlightened Buddhists make a great distinction, Nirvana being a condition of rest and peace, while Para-Nirvana signifies a state of realization of Divine Unity beyond the power of language to describe. The general philosophy of Buddhism is summed up in the teaching concerning the four Great Truths, which are: Concerning Suffering; Concerning the Source of Suffering; Concerning Cessation of Suffering; Concerning the Way that Leads to Release from Suffering. Suffering is due to attachment to the illusions of the mortal plane; therefore deliverance from pain can only be accomplished by the transference of our affections from the transitory to the permanent. Instruction on this theme carries us far along a most important pathway, but is a road we need to tread very cautiously, lest we mistake callousness for spirituality. Against this danger Mrs. Besant has warned her readers very clearly, and it would be well for all who show a tendency to confound indifference to human affection with hopeful signs of spiritual development to read very thoughtfully the excellent counsels and warnings given by this representative Theosophist, whose

appreciation of the excellences of Oriental philosophy is unsurpassed in any direction. There can
be no real emancipation from suffering until we
can no longer derive benefit from its continuance.
The only sane and sensible view to take of suffering is that it is a corrective and educational experience, entirely good and indeed altogether necessary,
so long as we can only learn certain needed lessons
through its agency, then not only superfluous, but
actually impossible when we have outgrown conditions in the midst of which it can serve a useful
purpose. This is the teaching of the entire book of
Job, a magnificent poem, dramatically portraying the
uses of affliction and calculated to inspire the studious reader with a sense of profound gratitude for
the ministry of those painful experiences which
lead up to a blissful knowledge of truth otherwise
unattainable. To call Buddhism pessimistic is almost as absurd as to call Judaism pessimistic, because individual Jews may appear to be pessimists;
yet the parrot cry is raised continually that Buddhists are all pessimists, and seek a substitute for
bliss in the oblivion of annihilation. The Buddhist Church has indeed become so largely formal-
istic that ritual observances, to which its alleged
founder attached no importance whatever, have been
allowed to obscure the pure ethical teachings of the
greatly unfolded soul on whose doctrine the institution professes to be founded, and it is always possible for doubt and pessimism to grow and thrive
where only ceremonoy and tradition are insisted on.
The doctrine of Karma, to which Buddhists all
adhere, is an optimistic view of ultimate attainment

when rightly comprehended. The source of suffering is in the illusory belief, with which we are all to some degree tinctured, that the outward shapes of things are the only realities, therefore we cling frantically to those transitory vehicles of the spirit, and suffer bitterly when they are disintegrated. If it be asked why humanity falls into this illusion, an answer is readily forthcoming—viz., that as we need our outward bodies temporarily, and we should not be likely to preserve them if we did not value them, the over-estimate we place upon them is simply an exaggeration of their importance. It is not by steeling ourselves against affection and becoming anchorites that we can tread Buddha's eight-fold path to blessedness, but by learning to see things in due relative proportion and find this abiding entity, though the mortal sheath may disappear. Suffering ceases when we have outgrown all desire for separated existence, but we have no right to infer from this that there is no individual immortality; rather can we behold a glorious vision of life immortal when all entities composing our humanity are so perfectly united in mutual love that they constitute an indivisible unity. "Kill out the sense of separateness," exhorts Mabel Collins, in "Light on the Path," which is a paradoxical presentation of Buddhistic doctrine. Separateness does not mean individual distinctness, but mutual antagonism, and just so long as the slightest vestige of antagonistic feeling remains in any consciousness, the possessor thereof has not yet attained the bliss of the condition called Nirvana, which we are assured the Buddha reached before he quitted his mortal em-

bodiment. The Sublime Eight-fold Path consists
of Right Views; Right Aspirations; Right Speech;
Right Conduct; Right Living; Right Effort; Right
Mindfulness; Right Recollectedness. William Wal-
ter Atkinson, editor of "New Thought: A Jour-
nal of Practical Idealism," published in Chicago,
has styled Buddhism "Negative Idealism," in contradistinction from "Positive Idealism," for which
he particularly stands; but though he thus designates
the system (we think too sweepingly), he very wisely
adds: "The two phases of Idealism are but two sides
of the shield of Truth"; a most admirable remark.
Our only regret is that the maker of it should have
previously called Buddhism pessimistic. It is, of
course, impossible to speak authoritatively for the
Buddhist Church in any section of the world, unless
one is an accredited official thereof, but it is not
with later developments, in many cases loaded with
undesirable accretions, that we need feel concerned
if we wish to discover what was the original Buddhistic doctrine. An impartial outsider desiring to
learn the tenets of primitive Christianity would very
naturally turn to the New Testament for information, rather than to any one of the numerous sects
and parties in Christendom which differ so widely
one from the other. It has been reported that the
Japanese, who were some time ago contemplating
the adoption of a new State Religion to supplant
their (at that time) unsatisfactory Shintoism, undertook to seriously consider Christianity. Christian missionaries had long been active in Japan, and
much benevolent and educational work had been
carried on in connection with the best of the mis-

sions.   Propositions were therefore made that Christianity be carefully examined with a view to testing its adaptability to the religious needs of Japan, when straightway appeared about thirty distinct varieties of Christianity, each one put forward by its advocates as the nearest to the original Gospel of Jesus. What effect could so bewildering an array of rival Christianities have on the examiners but to cause them to decide that their own Shintoism was far less confusing, and though it might not be ideal, it was at any rate better adapted to Japan than such a bewildering array of competing denominations. Now if there are so many varieties of Christianity after nineteen centuries since its primitive inception. it is not surprising that in the course of about twenty-five centuries different phases of Buddhism have appeared, each sect or party claiming to give the truest and completest version of Gautama's original enunciations; but on that account we have no right to discard what we can clearly see is "wheat," because we refuse to endorse the "tare" which has sprung up in the same field with it.   Institutionalized Buddhism is not the Buddha's simple doctrine unalloyed with foreign elements, but all the established systems do contain very much that is worthy of a great world-enlightener, together with much that is conspicuously unworthy.   In the Christian world we can trace the form of the Roman Catholic Hierarchy to the Roman Empire, and in Presbyterianism we can see the plan of the Roman Republic.   No great spiritual teacher ever surrounded himself with the pomp and circumstance of a regal court, and in the case of the Buddha all accounts declare that though he was born into it he voluntarily renounced it.   It is quite possible to carry out ceremonies in the name of one who cared nothing about them, provided he did not expressly forbid them, but to claim that he established them is sheer imposture which may delude the ignorant but can never deceive the educated.   It is always the "letter" which killeth while the "spirit" giveth life, and yet it seems impossible to clothe any spirit without some letter. Organized Buddhism has erred exactly where all other systems have erred—viz., in over-emphasizing non-essentials, until with the lapse of ages the garments have come to be so highly prized that the original wearer has been quite obscured by such massive drapery and such heavy veils.   Buddhism to-day is emerging from its long captivity and will soon present a smiling face to the world, no longer shrouded with the veils of cumbersome unnecessary ritual observances, and no longer exploited by ignorant and oppressive priests.

Nowhere in modern literature have we such a complete and beautiful setting forth of the essence of Buddhism as in Sir Edwin Arnold's poem, "The Light of Asia," which, though composed by a patriotic Englishman, received unqualified endorsement at the hands of the High Priest of Buddhism in Ceylon. Dr. J. M. Peebles and other distinguished American travelers have met with cordial welcome in that lovely island where, at Colombo, there has long been established a Buddhist School for Girls, under the kindly auspices of the Theosophical Society, where English women teach Cingalese maidens much that is highly useful and quite in harmony with the ancient Buddhistic faith.

It may seem strange to some that British women should engage in such a work, but it is one of great utility and calculated to accomplish a widely beneficent end. India and Ceylon are parts of the British Empire, therefore it is the plain duty of enlightened British people to do their utmost to bring about good-fellowship between the native populations and the British. Instead of endeavoring to take from them their ancestral faith and bid them scorn it as a "heathen abomination," it is the clear duty of those whose "souls are lighted with wisdom from on high" to so walk in the light of that wisdom as to hasten the dawning of that glorious new morning when in the sunlight of a larger knowledge of truth the several nations of the earth shall see their way to righteous federation. There can be a fraternity of religious systems, each one purified from the excresent accretions which have long concealed much, though never the whole of its indwelling excellences. Buddhism makes a brave showing when restored to its original simplicity, and the heroic figure of Guatama stands forth as one who loved all forms of life and found an expression of Divinity in everything. "Cosmic Consciousness" is a favorite phrase with many people to-day, and it is to the life and teachings of the Buddha that we may well turn for a beautiful historical example of it. With the iron rules of Caste a lover of the entire human race can have no sympthy, especially when such rules are applied to serve the ends of oppression and result in ignoring individual worth,

while slavishly bowing before inherited position.   It
was the special glory of Gautama that he taught
his country people the essential truths contained in
their beautiful historic Vedas, which are full of
exquisite spiritual teaching, fundamentally at variance with the religious tyranny established in India
against which the Buddha's most vigorous protest
was made.   We may sum up the essential teachings
of the purest forms of Buddhism in two splendid
words — Philanthropy and Purity — the same two
majestic substantives which Canon Hensley Henson
of Westminster employed in a noble sermon which
he preached on Trinity Sunday, 1907, in St. Margaret's, Westminster, when he summarised the essentials of universal religion in exposition of the
famous text from the Epistle of James, "Pure religion and undefiled before God and the Father is
this: To visit the fatherless and widows in their
affliction, and to keep himself unspotted from the
world."   Not a hint here of any belief in any dogma
as necessary to salvation.   But this we are told is a
Christian saying.   Let it be so; it is also in strict
accord with original Buddhism, and may well form
a link between sincere and spiritually-minded people
adhering to either cult or creed.

# CHAPTER XV.

MAGIC IN EUROPE IN THE MIDDLE AGES—ITS CON-
NECTION WITH MYSTERIOUS HEALING AND
MARVELLOUS DELIVERANCES.

Though Judaism is, on the whole, a distinctively Theistic and Ethical Religion, comparatively little given to either Mysticism or Magic, there have been many notable instances of thoroughly respectable and noble-minded Jews, among whom are to be found some distinguished Rabbis, who have practised magical arts and taught them to a few carefully selected disciples. There are numberless passages in the Old Testament which contain ferocious denunciations of Babylonian sorcery and witchcraft, as we have endeavored to show in other sections of this volume; but the aim of these denunciations was to entirely discountenance all dabbling in vicious psychic practises which had for their object the working of some sort of injury. Laws against witchcraft, which are not yet entirely erased from modern statute books, were originally intended to inflict severe penalties upon all who sought by magical means to endanger the safety of individuals, or to work harm upon a community by attempting to blight the harvest, poison the wells, or in some other manner work grievous injury upon a community. Obviously such laws were not directed against any who sought to practise a White Art, which had for its sole objects healing the sick and in other ways conferring blessings upon humanity; but as neither priests nor legislators always knew just where to draw the line between White and Black Magic, and moreover as charges of witchcraft, brought often against unpopular but entirely innocent persons, served to divert attention from the real culprits when offences had actually been committed, legislation against witchcraft very often defeated, rather than served, the ends of justice. It also encouraged many degrading superstitions which retarded the progress of sanitary science, while it engendered and fostered that very state of dread of some malign influence at work against us, which is one of the most deterrent influences which can possibly be set in motion when a patient is nervously unstrung and needs confidence in Divine, not diabolical, agency, to help him to recovery.

The great beauty of Judaism, as a religious system, is that it requires no belief in devils on the part of its adherents, but rather discountenances than encourages such belief; at the same time Jews, as a community, have seldom been entirely free from some dread of evil spirits, though the fundamental teachings of Judaism are quite at variance with any doctrine of evil spirits such as orthodox Christianity still foists upon the world and which, in a modified form, many Spiritualists and Occultists still engender.

One of the most curious and interesting literary examples of Jewish belief in Magic is to be found in a treatise entitled "The Book of the Sacred Magic of Abra-Melin the Mage, as delivered by Abraham the Jew unto His Son Lamech." A translation from the original Hebrew into French, contained in the Bibliothèque de l'Arsenal, Paris, has been rendered into English by S. L. MacGregor-Mathers, whose works on Rosicrucianism and other mysterious and unusual themes are of great interest to those who desire to step aside from the beaten paths of literature and stray into weird and fascinating byways. The English translator of this curious MS., which goes back, in the original, to 1458, declares that Bulwer Lytton and Eliphas Lèvi were acquainted with this MS., which contains much material from which such a story as Lytton's "Zanoni" might easily have been embellished. The treatise is divided into three books, the first of which deals principally with the travels of the author, which were quite extensive and brought him into close association with many highly placed and well-distinguished personages. The second book is filled with matter pertaining to Ceremonial Magic, which, like all treatises of this sort, arouses much more curiosity than it satisfies. It is excellent reading for any who want to know exactly what the best type of Mediæval Magicians really believed, and how they set to work to accomplish their mysterious performances, and it has the great advantage of containing a large amount of excellent moral counsel, to the effect that all who engage in such occult undertakings must do so with a full sense of the grave responsibilities they are assuming, and always with righteous ends in view. The third book describes enchantments of various kinds, some of which enter upon the field of necromancy, and prove that it was actually believed that within the space of seven years after death it was possible to induce the departed spirit to temporarily reanimate the discarded physical frame, if that had been preserved through the interim. It is quite clear that the noblest among magicians declared that such a feat should never be attempted except in cases of extreme gravity, and only where it was highly important to gain information directly from the departed spirit; but happily for the world of to-day, those most absorbed in Spiritualism are seeking only to get in touch with their departed friends by employing methods which have no connection with the arts of necromancy.

Evil spirits are said to be rightly obedient to the will of the trained magician, who puts them to work as servitors, but if he loses self-control or permits himself to misuse magic for base ends, he then becomes subject to the dark forces, who cause him much suffering as well as inconvenience. There can hardly be any doubt that much good has often been accomplished in connection with the better kinds of magic, particularly in the wide domain of therapeutic practise, where we know the influence of ideas and suggestions over physical conditions is inestimably great.

It is recorded that this magical Abraham healed a multitude of disorders of many varieties, including leprosy. There is nothing incredible or irrational in this statement, for there is no reason why any disease should be looked upon as essentially

incurable.   On this whole subject of seemingly miraculous healing the popular mind needs a great
deal of setting straight, and we see many signs of
promise that popular fallacies are soon to be dis-
pelled by the appearance on the scene of practical
activity of a large number of well-equipped mental
practitioners, who will give rational accounts of
their ministry and thereby deliver the topic of Suggestive practise from the many phantasies which
still surround it.   Ceremonies carry great weight
with many people, who seem as yet quite unable to
grasp the simpler and directer teachings of Psycho-
Therapy.   From five to six centuries ago the masses
were far less acquainted with the rudiments of rational psychology than they are to-day, and had it
not been for the incantations of wonder-workers on
their behalf, many a sufferer would have remained
incurable, incurability being an entirely relative
term.   A case may be quite incurable in one set of
circumstances and readily cured when the patient
is transferred to different surroundings.   Change
of mental attitude is the prime essential in nearly
every malady, and there are indeed no cases of any
sort where faith and hope and courage are not extremely valuable helpers.   Is is said that as many
as 8,413 persons were healed through the agency
of the magician whose work we are now considering, and it is highly important to note exactly the
position taken by the healer concerning the nature
of his ministry.   Abraham was born in 1362; his
age was therefore forty-eight in 1410, when he
calls himself ninety-six, in consequence of a curious
reckoning which makes a magical year only six

months in length. Abraham teaches that the best years of a man's life for the practise of ceremonial magic are from twenty-five to fifty, probably because he had discovered that, on an average, the mental and physical faculties are simultaneously most active during that period, though there are many undisputed instances of great mental and physical vigor appearing in combination much before the age of twenty-five and very long after fifty. The following quotation is very explicit in showing how magicians have claimed to be able to secure for their clients the efficient services of unseen servitors, and though we may incline to attach far more importance to the patient's own mental attitude than to magical rites *per se,* we cannot deny that there may be serving spirits ready to obey the will of a magical director, much as nurses stand ever ready to obey the instructions of doctors under whom they are working and in whose skill and wisdom they have confidence.

"Up till now I have healed of persons of all conditions, bewitched unto death, no less than 8,413, and belonging to all religions, without making an exception in any case. I gave unto mine Emperor Sigismond, a very clement prince, a Familiar Spirit of the Second Hierarchy, even as he commanded me, and he availed himself of its services with prudence. He wished also to possess the secret of the whole operation, but as I was warned by the Lord that it was not His will, he contented himself with what was permitted, not as Emperor, but as a private person; and I even by means of my art facilitated his marriage with his wife; and

I caused him to overcome the great difficulties which opposed his marriage. I delivered also the Count Frederick by the means of 2,000 artificial cavalry (the which I by mine art caused to appear according unto the tenor of the twenty-ninth chapter of the Third Book here following), free out of the hands of the Duke Leopold of Saxonia, the which Count Frederick without me would have lost both his own life and his estate as well (which latter would not have descended unto his heirs).

"Unto the Bishop of our City also, I showed the betrayal of his government at Orembergh, one year before the same occurred; and I say no more concerning this because he is an Eccesiastic, passing over in silence all that I have further done to render him service.

"The Count of Varvich was delivered by me from prison in England the night before he was to have been beheaded.

"I aided the flight of the Duke and of his Pope John, from the Council of Constance, who would otherwise have fallen into the hands of the enraged Emperor M; and the latter having asked me to predict unto him which one of the two Popes, John XXIII and Martin V, should gain in the end, my prophecy was verified; that fortune befalling which I had predicted unto him at Ratisbon. At the time when I was lodged at the house of the Duke of Bavaria, for matters of the greatest importance, the door of my room was forced, and I had the value of 83,000 Hungarian pieces stolen from me in jewels and money. As soon as I returned, the thief (although he was a Bishop) was forced to

himself bring it back to me in person and to return with his own hands to me the money, jewels.
and account books, and to give me the principal
reasons which had forced him to commit the theft,
rather than any other person."

A great many more instances of various kinds,
equally wonderful, are given, but the few we have
quoted are typical and serve to show what were
the stupendous claims made for his art by Abraham,
who always used it conscientiously.

Works of this kind abound in literary and historic interest, and they are also freely interspersed
with salutary moral counsels, but we doubt whether
there are many among us who can put the magical
formulas to any practical account; and is there any
good reason why we should actually attempt to do
so?   Professedly Occult literature is largely given
over to uncanny narratives, some of them calculated
to induce a creepy dread, especially at Christmas-
tide, when ghost stories are especially popular, but
this feature, at least in our opinion, needs to be repressed rather than exaggerated, and of one thing
we may be quite convinced—viz., that if there be
such malign or uncanny psychic influences in our
immediate vicinage as many people continue to believe, our surest protection against them is to cultivate such heroic faith in the omnipotence of goodness that we shall cherish no lurking dread of evil.
The talismanic value of diff·rent psalms is insisted
upon by many mediaeval writers, and there is doubtless considerable reason for attributing to them extraordinary efficacy, because they breathe a spirit

of perfect trust in Deity and discountenance all fear of evil influences, both seen and unseen.

In a very curious and scarcely reliable production, called fantastically "The Sixth and Seventh Books of Moses," we find the entire Psalter endowed with magical potencies. Each one of the 150 psalms is said to be a talisman against some kind of sickness or danger. Whether the entire Book of Psalms can be usefully employed in such a manner is open to controversy, but we can readily see how a recitation of such psalms as the 23d and 91st in particular, may prove of great assistance in times of severe mental distress and difficulty. The peculiar tenacity with which people cling to the Psalter lends color to the claim that it possesses some magical qualities, but in its accepted English version, at any rate, it needs a large amount of revising and a vast deal of wise interpreting to make it suitable for such undiscriminating use as the Church of England, in its daily services, makes of it. Swedenborgians and Mystics get over all moral difficulties, when they encounter imprecatory clauses, by declaring that as to their interior meaning they refer, not to personal enemies but to impersonal lusts "which war against the soul." When we wisely pray for the destruction of our enemies we are really seeking the annihilation of our own vicious tendencies, the encouragement of which may certainly render us susceptible to unholy influx, no matter from what source it may proceed. Were this view always taken and explained to choir boys before they sing in cathedrals and parish churches, there would be no valid reason for protesting against the unceasing use of the entire Psalter; but how often is this matter explained? and when it is not, the pernicious influence of supplicating the Almighty to destroy one's personal foes, if one be supposed to have such, is terrible in its effects upon the ethics of the rising generation. The wide incompatibility between Mediæval magic and the best kinds of modern mental therapeutic systems, is that the former is loaded down with belief in enemies against whom we must work by the employment of magical spells, while the latter endorses the sublime saying of Emerson, "No one can do me an injury but myself."

Christian Scientists, while verbally repudiating any endorsement of magical theories and practises, are strangely inconsistent in clinging to their pet bug-a-boo "malicious animal magnetism."   Were they as a denomination once for all to give up that old devil with a new title, they could soon make for themselves a noble place among the advanced philosophers of our day; but just so long as that recrudescence of a most objectionable part of the superstitious belief of old-time magicians clings to their movement, they will engender the very dread of evil which their famous text-book "Science and Health with Key to the Scriptures," by the founder of the cult, Mary Baker G. Eddy, renders utterly illogical in the celebrated phrase "All is good; there is no evil."   Whatever that sentence may exactly mean,—and many different interpretations have been placed upon it,—it cannot logically be accepted in connection with any dread of evil.   All the good accomplished by old-school magicians, and all the good done by modern mental therapeutists is accomplished by strengthening the will and calming the mind of sufferers, to whom evil appears a great and terrible, usually an invincible, reality. Abraham's story of conjuring up artificial soldiers seems all of a piece with some scenes in Marie Corelli's "Sorrows of Satan," particularly the magical appearance and disappearance of phantom servitors at the "Willowsmere" festival which was organized by "Lucio Rimanez." We are treading on very treacherous ground if we venture to speak dogmatically concerning the possible connection between our ordinary external life and mysterious unseen influences, and we have no right whatever to wilfully close our eyes in the face of any well-supported evidence. It is however very necessary to insist that great danger to health and reason attend upon dabbling in ceremonial magic to gratify morbid curiosity, and far greater are the penalties we shall have to pay if we allow ourselves to be actuated by any malicious motive. No matter in what department of Psychical Research we may be seeking for knowledge we must never fail to remember the wise words of Alfred Tennyson, who sometimes felt an intense desire to rend the veil and gaze upon what lies behind it. To all everywhere who are thinking of embarking upon the dimly-lighted ocean of magical evocation, or even attempting to get into conscious communion with their departed (or at least unseen) loved ones, we commend the following quatrain from "In Memoriam."

"How pure in heart and sound at head,
With what divine affections bold
Should be the man whose thoughts would hold
An hour's communion with the dead.

They haunt the silence of the breast,
Imagination calm and fair,
The memory like a cloudless air,
The conscience as a sea at rest.

In vain shalt thou or any call
The spirits from their golden day,
Unless, like them, thou too canst say
My spirit is at peace with all.

But when the heart is full of din
And doubt beside the portal waits,
They can but listen at the gates
And hear the household jar within."

We notice in these exquisite lines how the thoughtful poet has assigned doubt to the same low place to which all magicians persistently consign it.   Doubt, they declare, renders all attempts invalid, chiefly on account of the weakening effect doubt has on the doubter.   And here let us learn a much-needed lesson ere we attempt to succeed in any form of mental practise.   Thoughts are transmissible; mental states are communicated from practitioner to patient and from teacher to pupil. How, then, can we reasonably expect to prove successful in a work we undertake half-heartedly?

The particular methods employed, in a majority of instances, are not nearly so important as the mental state of the one who employs them. Henry Wood and other able modern writers have reviewed the medical practice of the Middle Ages most instructively, and while we cannot approve of all the strange medicaments and weird practices advocated, to study a Mediæval pharmacopœia is to gain much insight into the enormous influence that mental states have always exerted over physical conditions. When we treat the subject of Healing in Bible Times impartially, we shall be able to trace exactly the same influences at work many centuries earlier in Asia Minor which reappeared and held the centre of the stage in Europe during periods nearer to the present day.

As the same law works universally, time and place may be accounted well nigh negligible factors whenever we are considering problems, the solution of which is only to be found by studying deeply our human constitution.

# CHAPTER XVI.

## ANCIENT MAGIC AND MODERN THERAPEUTICS— PARACELSUS AND VON HELMONT.

Ennemoser's "History of Magic, translated from the original German into excellent English by William Howitt (to whose other works we have referred), contains an enormous amount of intensely interesting information concerning all mysterious arts and practices, many of which serve to throw a vast deal of light upon matters usually regarded as too obscure or fanciful to merit much serious notice, but which are certainly engaging the profound attention of many of the most brilliant intellects of the present day. Theosophists and Occultists in general have no difficulty in ascribing mysterious phenomena to the action of various orders of Nature Spirits (sometimes designated sprites), who can be rendered submissive to the commanding will of a qualified magician, and if the existence of these fascinating creatures be conceded, an explanation of magical phenomena is by no means difficult. Animals are rightly subservient to humanity, and they gladly obey and serve those who treat them decently; indeed, they are often so greatly devoted to humanity that they continue to evince affection even when the treatment they receive is cruel and barbarous.

On the unseen side of Nature, magicians claim there are races of sub-human entities who sustain a similar relation to humanity to that sustained by animals on the common objective plane, and while it is less easy to gain ascendancy over these races than over physical animals of domesticated types, it is no more difficult for the trained magician to make them his servitors than for an animal trainer to subdue the ferocity of the natives of the jungle, who, by combined firmness and kindness, can always in time be rendered docile, provided the trainer does not allow himself ever to lose self-control. It is not, however, by any means exclusively with "Nature Spirits" that magicians deal, for a very large portion of their most effective work is due to mesmeric or hypnotic influence, also to the projection of thought-forms, which appear as definite on the mental plane as do ordinary material objects on the physical.

We will now proceed to consider a few of the methods employed by the ancient Hebrew Prophets when engaged in their benevolent work of healing the seriously afflicted, and in some cases raising to life again the seemingly dead. Concerning the actual raising of the dead, we know nothing. Bible narratives only inform us that certain people declared that others had actually died when they were so far beyond the reach of ordinary methods that they certainly would have died very shortly had they not been restored by the power of God working through the prophets. We hear a great deal in these days about Divine Healing, and we often wonder whether it can be ever justifiable to apply so

great an adjective to any form of healing in particular, seeing that we have no right whatever to
limit our idea of Divine activity to those particular
modes of practice which we personally employ, or
of which we specially approve.  An honorable physician who conscientiously administers medicine has
quite as much right to affirm that he believes it to
be God's will that outward remedies should be administered, as any Christian Scientist has to say
that a certain school of mental practice is of divine
appointment.  It is just at this point that Christian Scientists make themselves ridiculous by claiming everything for those particular methods which
they as a denomination endorse and adopt, while
they discountenance all beside.

It is quite true that the Jewish religion, as well
as the Christian, can reasonably appeal to the Scriptures in support of the plea that even if every wonder of healing now claimed by Christian Scientists
is all that it is said to be, there are no miracles
performed in this century any greater than those performed long ago in ancient Israel, and at a later
period by Christian apostles.  Elijah and Elisha are
two of the greatest prophets mentioned in the Old
Testament as functioning especially in the rôle of
healers.  Both of these mighty men are said to have
raised to life again a widow's son who was pronounced dead, and both of them, according to the
record, employed what we might call in these days
a combination of mental, spiritual, and magnetic
methods.  Prophetic doctrine and practice do much
to confirm the idea that God works through all
natural instrumentalities, but as man possesses far

more of the Divine Spirit than does any sub-human creature, human ability far transcends any curative virtue which we may find in vegetable or mineral. The most extreme cases of suffering, together with the severest and farthest advanced stages of fatal disease, naturally require a mode of treatment far more powerful and effective than ordinary simpler cases; therefore it was always believed that only the greatest among the prophets were able to heal leprosy or to raise to life those who appeared dead, though they might have been only in a dying condition.   There is one case which suggests more food for thought, perhaps, than any other in connection with Elisha's ministry, viz., the case of Naaman the Syrian Captain, who was directed by a Hebrew maiden who waited on his wife to the great prophet in Israel, who is said to have received him at first very curtly and to have positively refused to perform any magical acts, no matter how much treasure Naaman was ready to heap upon him.

This story brings out in prominent relief the opposition to ceremonial magic entertained by the Jewish Prophets at a time when it was almost universally believed that sicknesses were caused by evil spirits and that these could be driven out by enchantments.   Wherever such a belief is entertained, man is usually made to appear a puppet in the hands of unseen forces, frequently malignant, which can be driven away by some subtle processes performable only by trained exorcists.   This theory of suffering, and its remedy, has the very great moral disadvantage of implying that our own mode of life has little (if anything) to do with our general health; a doctrine which is utterly opposed to all the salutary teaching of the Pentateuch, which devotes a large amount of space to minute directions concerning methods of living which, if duly observed, prevent diseases even more effectually than they provide remedies for those which may have already appeared in a community. From the standpoint of sanitation alone, the Mosaic law is highly admirable, and this has been so completely proved many times in Europe during Christian centuries, that one of the charges brought against the Jews in times of general pestilence was that they practiced unholy magical arts which enabled them to withstand the ravages of plagues which decimated surrounding Gentile populations. The real cause of this surprising immunity was a strict observance of the sanitary laws laid down in the Torah. We are now witnessing a very wholesome revival of popular interest in sanitation; few (if any) physicians to-day refusing to admit that if we live clean and wholesome lives we need not suffer as communities from Zymotic and Tuberculous diseases.

The fresh air cure for consumption, taken in connection with general cleanliness and a simple nutritious diet, works hand in hand with all intelligent mental healing. Whatever elevates the mind fortifies the body; whatever depresses the mind, weakens the body; and in like manner whatever injures the body reacts prejudicially on the mind. The absurd and blasphemous idea that God sends sickness (except in the very restrictive sense that we bring it upon ourselves when we act in opposition to some law of nature, which is necessarily an outward ex-

pression of Divine order), receives no sanction at
the hands of the Bible, though many ministers of
religion have told God in their prayers that He
has been pleased to send sickness upon members of
their congregations, whereas, if they had taken the
prophetic attitude, they would have prayed that those
who were afflicted might come into a fuller knowledge of Divine law and learn to harmonize their
lives with its requirements.   When Elisha told
Naaman to wash seven times in Jordan, so that he
would recover from leprosy, he greatly insulted his
haughty visitor, who became very angry, and indig-
nantly refused to pay attention to so impertinent a
direction; but after Naaman had returned home,
and found his disease making still further progress,
he gradually changed his mental attitude, and, returning to Elisha, expressed willingness to comply
with his directions.   Bathing seven times in Jordan
signifies reforming his own life, not simply or chiefly
taking a number of baths in a sacred stream.

The vital point in the narrative is where the
prophet tells his patient that he must do something
for himself, and not expect the doctor to do everything for him.   This is a very bold position to take
when one is dealing with Army officers or any other
people of distinction, who are accustomed to give
orders and receive homage rather than obey the
directions of others.   Probably no one short of a
prophet would have sufficient bravery to speak his
mind quite plainly to a very wealthy patient occupying a singularly high position in society.   There are
no incurable diseases, *per se*, but there are many disorders which are seemingly incurable because we

are not in possession of the necessary means for
their vanquishment.  The law regulating the isola-
tion of lepers may be regarded as a useful and humane one, considering the fact that where no remedy
is at hand it is not kindness to the sufferers, but
injustice to the populace, to permit persons with
infectious diseases to mingle freely with people in
general who may be susceptible to contagion.  Pre-
cautionary measures are, of course, inferior to prophetic power to heal, but we do not attain unto
higher powers or greater knowledge by foolishly
disregarding useful sanitary regulations.  There are
probably some people to-day who can quite safely
mingle with lepers, and there are certainly a few
who know of a cure for leprosy; and it is not too
much to hope that in the near future knowledge
of how to heal disorders long regarded incurable
will have become common mental property.  When
this happy state of things has come permanently
to exist, we may rest assured that the teaching
given by true doctors, who are far removed from
pharmacists, will be of such a character that the
most disagreeable diseases of which people are now
most afraid will soon entirely cease, and their very
names be blotted from our dictionaries.

Though in a very large majority of instances we
may fairly attribute so-called magical cures of disease to faith and imagination in the patient—imagination being a therapeutic agent of immense power
and value—it by no means necessarily follows that
there is no value whatever in magical ceremonials
which are conducted with earnest confidence by dis-
ciplined magicians, and there is yet another aspect

of the subject which must not be overlooked, viz., the actual efficacy, on the psychical as well as on the physical plane, of certain medicaments employed in occult medical arts.   Dr. Franz Hartmann, in a very instructive treatise on this question, has shown how different orders of practitioners in the Middle Ages had recourse to knowledge of the potencies of many plants and herbs not included in the common pharmacopœia.

The general doctrine of Occultists of all schools being to the effect that there are various planes of Nature, unseen as well as seen, and that we can learn how to render the unseen as well as the seen serviceable to us—a plant or herb in the eyes of an Occultist is an existence on some other plane in addition to the physical—therefore it can be reasonably claimed that occult medication is applicable to the psychical as well as to the physical side of human necessity.   Some of the grosser means employed in Europe a few centuries ago may appear disgusting, as well as stupid, from the standpoint of fastidious sentiment, but we cannot boast of a medical system to-day entirely free from extremely disagreeable practises.   If we take exception to some of these, we are instantly told by their advocates that a doctor's work is to strive to the utmost to deliver his patient from the clutch of disease; therefore, we cannot be fastidious where life and death may be involved; and this position is fundamentally so sound that it is well-nigh indisputable.   We can, however, raise our protest against lymphs, serums, etc., which we know to be foul and pernicious, and especially against such as can only be obtained at the expense of great cruelty, which is never tolerated, whether practised on man or beast, by any Occultist of the beneficent type.   It is highly noteworthy that the most vigorous protests against vivisection proceed from students of Occultism who have plunged somewhat deeply into the abyss of mystery which has for ages enshrouded all magical ceremonial.

Dr. Anna Kingsford and Edward Maitland, who gave us "The Perfect Way," were among the most vehement denouncers of all experiments on living animals; and the Theosophical Society, as a body, is at present definitely active in the interests of the suppression of vivisection, not only out of regard for the sufferings of animals, but also in the interests of humanity, whose cause can never be truly served by outraging humane sentiments which, in addition to cultivating much that is sweet and beautiful in our dispositions, also serve the purpose of safeguarding us on unseen planes of Nature.   It may prove interesting and instructive to briefly outline a few of the prominent methods in vogue among magicians, so far as they have been publicly recorded, that we may compare them with some of the therapeutic measures accounted valid to-day. In comparatively recent times no name stands out more conspicuously in the annals of magical healing than that of Theophrastus Paracelsus, who founded a very remarkable school in which Magnetism was extolled as the mighty agent through which healing is to be accomplished.   We are so thoroughly used to the term "magnetic healing," and it is often so vague as well as comprehensive. that it seldom conveys any very clear idea of claims made or methods employed beyond the commonly accepted idea that magnetizers put their hands on their patients and claim that some efficacious emanation is transferred from one body to another.   Paracelsus, being a man of profound learning and deep insight into the hidden realms of Nature, would naturally give us views on magnetic healing very different from those expressed by comparatively illiterate people who often accomplish much good without any scientific understanding of how they do it. Paracelsus taught a doctrine, with certain modifications of his own, which had been handed on from age to age from the remotest period of which we have any records, and it was to his combined knowledge and skill that he owed his marvellous abilities as wonder-worker as well as teacher.

We can all teach theoretically what we have intellectually grasped, but to make practical demonstrations of our knowledge requires much more than mental information; thus it has always been proven that a peculiar mode of life must be followed by those who would successfully officiate as demonstrators of healing by magnetic means, for in magnetic treatment the individuality and personality of the operator must be involved to a much greater extent than in a conventional practise of medicine where the written prescription is regarded as a factor of prime importance.   But though the administration of compounded medicine constitutes a large part of accepted medical practice, it is well known, and freely admitted throughout the medical profession, that the personality of the doctor weighs very

heavily in the scale of his failure or success, and as
a personality which some people may think charming
is distasteful to others, and magnetic emanations
which quiet some sufferers disturb others, uniform
success in all cases judged similar from symptoms,
rarely if ever falls to the lot of any practitioner.
Occultists teach that we have peculiarities of inner
as well as of outer organizations which need to be
ministered to in a specific manner, and because the
broad term magnetism is often employed to cover
the psychic effluence of a mental as well as physical
practitioner, such a saying as I like, or I do not like,
that person's magnetism, is heard frequently in
circles where the scientific aspects of the question are
totally unknown.   The system of Paracelsus has
sometimes been denominated "mineral," because he
taught that the mineral as well as the vegetable and
animal kingdoms contains a subtle elixir of life
which can be scientifically distilled when one is suf-
ficienly acquainted with magical formulas.

Had Paracelsus lived at such a time as the present,
he would probably have had much less recourse to
a terminology which has been called "mystical jargon," as this hieroglyphic means of communication
between teachers and pupils, and between fellow initiates, was not intended only to preserve secrets from
the "profane," but was very largely employed as a
necessary precaution in times when every one sus-
pected of practising magic was in serious danger.
With a key to interpretation of mysterious symbols,
one can readily uncover a good deal of the teaching of Paracelsus, but his entire body of doctrine
is written in a double cipher, so that it has inten-

tionally two distinct but closely related meanings,
one pertaining to the literal practise of the healing
art, the other to the demonstration of arcane teaching concerning the work of transmutation, which
has, in its turn again, two distinct significations.
There can be no doubt that Paracelsus was naturally quite highly gifted, and that he also used his
talents with a very special view to rescuing the practise of medicine from the abject degeneracy into
which it had fallen in his day, when the disciples
of Galen spent most of their time in foolish controversy and dispute, and accomplished very little in
the way of healing.

The claim of Paracelsus was that he went direct
to Nature, repudiating all the teachings of the
schools which in his day were very nearly worth-
less.  He had studied Metallurgy, and had become
a mining expert; he travelled widely, and gathered
information wherever he went, all of which he
turned to excellent account.  His biographers say
of him that he learned of all kinds of people, and
was never too proud to accept knowledge from even
the very humblest.  When he had already acquired
great fame as a healer of wounds, as well as possessor of an immense amount of miscellaneous information, he became a lecturer in the University
of Basle, to which the most celebrated men were
attracted from all over Europe.  He manifested in
his teachings great veneration for Hippocrates, who
had pursued the very method by which he himself
sought truth.  He declared that apothecaries were
opposed to him because he would not endorse their
charlatanry; his own recipes were very simple, never

consisting of from forty to sixty ingredients, as did
those of the Galenic doctors.  In an essay on the
power of the magnet, he says: "The magnet has
long lain before all eyes, and no one has ever
thought whether it was of any further use or possessed any other property than that of attracting
iron.  Sordid doctors complain that I will not follow the ancients, but in what should I follow them?
All that they have said of the magnet amounts to
nothing.  Place what I have said of it in the balance,
and judge.  Had I blindly followed others, and not
myself made experiments, I should know no more
than what every peasant sees, that a magnet attracts
iron.  A wise man must inquire for himself, and it is
thus I have discovered that the magnet, besides this
obvious power of attracting iron, possesses another
and concealed power.

"In sickness, you must lay the magnet in the
center from which the sickness proceeds.  The magnet has two poles, one attracting, one repelling.  It
is not a matter of indifference to which of these
poles a man applies.  In falling sickness and every
kind of epilepsy, where the attack affects particularly
the head, it is proper to lay four magnets on the
lower part of the body with the attracting pole
turned upward, and only one on the head with the
reflecting pole downward, and then you bring other
means to their aid."  Paracelsus considered that
more valuable information was condensed in these
few paragraphs than was spread over all the ver-
bose statements of the ordinary physicians of his
time.

Paracelsus was also an astrologer, and laid great

stress on Siderial magnetism, which he regarded as both spiritual and physical. In this he agreed substantially with the renowned Chaldeans of old, who attributed the influence of the planets to their spiritual energy far more than to their physical movements. He has much to say concerning "Magnes Microcosmi," the little world which he regards as the universe in minimum. Man, he teaches, contains the four great elements, fire, air, water and earth, and must be nourished by them, not only palpably through the stomach, but also imperceptibly through the magnetic force resident in all nature, from which every individual draws specific nourishment. He has also much to say concerning our reciprocal relations with the Sun and the various planets, maintaining that they receive from us even as we receive from them. His celebrated "Magisterium Magnetis" is a tincture extracted from the magnet which he declares is a specific capable of drawing out every variety of diseases from the human body. He even went so far as to claim that this mysterious tincture communicated its properties to all objects near it, and that it did not only attract iron, but also other bodies of various kinds.

Paracelsus compares the human body to wood, and the life within it to fire. He calls magic the philosophy of Alchemy. He declares that a certain attractive power is born with all men, and through this power we become capable of continually attracting into our bodies the properties of the elements. In close harmony with this idea, he explains the cause and method of infection, which he rightly considers to apply to the contagion of health

as well as disease, a claim which lies at the root of
all modern as well as ancient magnetic treatment.
This remarkable man declared that though he
founded his doctrine on his own experience, he discovered it to be in very close accord with the teachings of the Bible, which he had studied so fully that
he knew almost the entire Book by rote.   It certainly does seem remarkable that people who profess
to credit as genuine the wonderful accounts of magnetic healing, which are scattered all over the Bible,
should take exception to the laying on of hands
and other simple magnetic methods as means of
cure, though it may be argued that the mineral magnet is not mentioned in the Scriptures in connection
with the work of healing accomplished by either
Jewish prophets or Christian apostles.   The spirit
of the elements, claims Paracelsus, rules the lower
propensities of man, but as there is in reality only
one life, a common essence pervades all forms of
existence.   All created things he denominates letters
and books, describing human origin and descent.
The human body is, according to his system, a perfect microcosm which man himself must learn to
completely control, for while the body comes from
the earth, the spirit comes from a higher world.   Concerning divination, he has much to say, especially
with regard to the Astral body, which he clearly
distinguishes from the elementary body which rests
during sleep, while the Astral continues active.   In
this Mediæval teaching we find the word "astral
directly derived from the stars, from which it is
said to emanate, and among which it is capable of
travelling.   Animals as well as men possess Astral

bodies, and are therefore capable of experiencing presentiments. Paracelsus wrote a curious book on "Fools," whom he declares all contain some measure of wisdom, which occasionally breaks forth like sunshine through a fog. This comparison agrees well with many present-day statements concerning the human aura, which is really an atmosphere or photosphere surrounding every individual, bright and luminous in the case of highly developed natures, dark and murky in cases where little progress above animality has been made. We find in the teachings of Paracelsus a firm belief expressed in the efficacy of enchantments, but while he believes in the power of curses as well as of blessings, he makes it clear to students that it is only the weak, the foolish and the vicious who can be seriously affected by any sort of malediction, while blessings can be fully received by the most highly cultured and spiritually advanced members of the human race. With regard to the highest kind of magic, he says that to practice it requires a powerful imagination, in addition to firm faith; no ceremonies are really necessary, and they are usually nothing but humbug. "The human spirit is so great a thing that no man can express it; as God is eternal and unchangeable, so also is the mind of man. If we rightly understood this mind, nothing would be impossible to us. Imagination is invigorated and perfected through faith; every doubt seriously hinders a magical operation, for it is faith that establishes the will. Because men do not perfectly imagine and believe, their arts are uncertain while they might be perfectly certain."

Another very wonderful man—one of the worthiest and ablest of the successors of Paracelsus —was Baptista Von Helmont, who, on account of his vast knowledge, acute judgment, and amazing penetration, created a new epoch in medicine. In the history of magnetism he takes the very first rank, since he brought into this dark field a clearer light than anyone before or since has done. Deleuze, in his famous work on "Animal Magnetism," speaks of Helmont in terms of unstinted praise, and gives a great deal of interesting information concerning his life and methods. He was the first to give the name of gas to aerial fluids. In Ennemoser's "History of Magic," we are told that this good and great man had often to defend his doctrine and practice against the stupid charge that its origin was diabolical, and to the satisfaction of the learned and intelligent of his day, his logical rebuttals proved quite convincing, though the ignorant and fanatical still clung to that senseless and debasing delusion.

Concerning Magnetism he says that it is of a heavenly nature and unrestrained by the boundaries of space. Whoever, therefore, avails himself of magnetic means, undertakes a God-pleasing business. Regarding the power of suggestion, he has left many worthy sayings on record, proving that our modern methods were well known and largely practised by Alchemistical Philosophers, who in some notable instances seem to have attributed all efficacy to suggestion, though incantations and other ceremonies were often used; in this they forestalled the conclusions of many learned psychologists of to-day. The power of evil is very much restricted in the doctrine of Helmont, who by no means denies it in toto, but distinctly shows how evil (i. e., disorderly) influences can be operative only on the surface of existence, while whatever is good (i. e., orderly) possesses practically unlimited power, because it is working with (not against) the great purpose of the universe. The use of herbs entered largely into Helmont's practise, and to many vegetable products he assigns magical properties; as, for instance, when he says that if you hold a certain extraordinary herb crushed in your hand, and at the same time hold the hand of another person, he or she will retain a great liking for you for at least several days. A singular story is told by this acutely observant man of a sensitive woman, who invariably suffered an attack of gout if she occupied a seat on which a brother of hers used to sit regularly five years previously; this man had suffered acutely from the distressing malady. Persons of blunt and irresponsive temperament may readily laugh at such tales, because they have no experiences of their own calculated to confirm them, but highly sensitive natures know that such facts do occur, and it is quite in accord with the best and wisest sanitary regulations of our day to admit the reality of such phenomena sufficiently to induce us to cremate all articles which have been long associated with chronic invalidism as well as with avowedly infectious maladies.

Helmont, in common with all magicians, does not only acknowledge the power of men over animals, he also teaches the influence exerted by animals over all ordinary men, and he tells many a weird tale of animal fascination, and cites some of his own experiences in support of his contention. Fascination is a very powerful weapon with which animals are equipped, and without it in the struggle for existence many would have been swept away which now exist and multiply. Psychometry is now confirming many of Helmont's narratives, and as it certainly seems that the average sensitiveness of civilized humanity is palpably increasing, we may soon need to know quite a great deal of mystical philosophy to enable us to enjoy good results of this increasing sensibility, instead of being embarrassed and debilitated thereby. A very beautiful summary of Helmont's truly sublime philosophy we present in the following quotation: "When God created the human soul, He imparted to her essential and original knowledge. The soul is the mirror of the universe, and stands in relationship to all living things. She is illuminated by an inward light; but the tempest of passions, the multitude of sensual impressions, the dissipations, darken this light, whose glory only diffuses itself when it burns alone, and all is peace and harmony within us. When we know ourselves to be separated from all outward influences, and desire only to be guided by this universal light, then only do we find in ourselves pure and certain knowledge. In this state of concentration, the soul analyses all objects on which her attention rests. She can unite herself with them, penetrate through their substance, penetrating even to God Himself, and feeling Him in the most important truths." Another great statement of this wonderful man reads thus: "The physician chosen of God is accompanied by many signs and wonders for the schools. He will give the honor to God, as he employs his gifts to assuaging the sufferings of his neighbor. Compassion will be his guide. His heart will possess truth and his intellect science. Love will be his sister; and the truth of the Lord will illumine his path. He will invoke the grace of God, and he will not be overcome by the desire of gain. For the Lord is rich and bountiful, and pays hundredfold in heaped measure. He will make his labor fruitful, and he will clothe his hands with blessings. He will fill his mouth with comfort, and His word will be a trumpet before which diseases will fly. His footsteps will bring prosperity, and sickness will flee before his face, as snow melts in a summer morn. Health will follow him. These are the testimonies of the Lord to those healers whom He has chosen— this is the blessedness of those who pursue the way of kindness; and the Holy Spirit will, moreover, enlighten them as the Comforter."

# CHAPTER XVII.

## JEANNE D'ARC, THE MAID OF ORLEANS.

Among the most remarkable seeresses known to modern Europe, the name of the famous Maid of Orleans stands eminently conspicuous, particularly when we take into account the period in which she lived and the people among whom she moved. Five hundred years or less ago, woman's position in Europe was widely different from what it is now; thus it was far more remarkable that a simple peasant girl could successfully head the French army during the fifteenth century than that such a phenomenon might occur to-day. From whatever standpoint we approach Jeanne's history, we cannot well call it other than miraculous, and as a psychological study it far outdistances in general importance all considerations pertaining to the immediate cause which she espoused or the particular victories she accomplished.

Domrémy, her birthplace, was a romantic village on the border between France and Prussia, and many were the legends which clustered thickly around it regarding apparitions of saints and angels which gathered about the spot. A particularly romantic story concerned a famous tree in the village, which had the reputation of being a trysting-place between spirits and mortals, and it was under its shade that the simple maiden first heard mysterious voices and became imbued with the conviction that she had a mighty mission to fulfil under celestial direction.   S. Margaret and S. Catherine, patron saints of Domrémy, are said to have appeared to her when she was a mere child, and gradually unfolded to her the overwhelming tidings that she must place herself at the head of the French army and secure the coronation of the Dauphin after she had routed the English troops, which were then largely occupying her native country.

We often hear it said in these days that women cannot carry arms, and therefore have properly no right of suffrage; but this assertion was completely refuted nearly five hundred years ago, when an innocent maiden accomplished, as a general, what no man among her countrymen seemed able to achieve.  The story of the Maid of Orleans settles the sex question at its very outset by demonstrating that individual ability is the only passport to certain victory, and we can never tell when genius will appear clothed in male or in female habiliments. Sometimes a youth, at other times a maiden, will be raised up to accomplish daring deeds that none but the greatest of heroes can undertake successfully, and we never know whether such genius is likely to rise from the ranks of nobility or peasantry; but when it does appear, it carries all before it like some mighty cyclone against which all opposition must inevitably prove fruitless.  It is unquestionably not the ordinary normal vocation of a woman to become a soldier, and warfare itself may become defunct much sooner than most of us suppose; but when the times required an intrepid military commander to save a land from foreign dominance, it came to pass that the unseen powers which govern mortal destinies did at least on one highly memorable occasion raise up an untutored maiden to wave the banner and carry the sword successfully on the field of martial conquest.  The many difficulties which Jeanne had to encounter were so formidable and well-nigh insuperable that they might easily have daunted the courage of even a seasoned warrior; but the innocent child, with unshakable confidence in her Heaven-directed mission, brushed all these obstacles aside with the power of that unflinching faith which does indeed, figuratively speaking, remove mountains.  Though her mother, a very spiritually-minded woman, readily listened to the maiden's thrilling accounts of angelic interviews, her father, even though he may not have entirely discredited them, was so shocked at the idea of his daughter heading an army that he made no secret of his sentiment that he would rather see her drowned than embark on so utterly improper an undertaking.  But an uncle favored her enterprise, and under his guardianship she set forth on the arduous and perilous career which she was fully convinced could end in no other way than gloriously; for not only did she believe that two saints were promptting her; she felt that the mighty archangel Michael was her chief inspirer, and with this conviction to buoy her spirits, her courage never faltered even in the face of the most determined opposition which she encountered from ecclesiastical dignitaries as well as from the secular authority.  The story of her movement from place to place, until she finally reached the Dauphin, and eventually secured his coronation at Rheims, reads like a fairy tale, a work of fiction almost too highly colored to take rank with serious novels. But we are dealing with actual history, not with sensational romance, and here indeed is demonstrated the truthfulness of the long-celebrated adage: "Truth is stranger than fiction."

The clairvoyance of the Maid of Orleans was triumphantly demonstrated on the occasion of her first encounter with the man whom her bravery was to elevate to the throne, for though he had completely disguised himself, and placed a substitute in his accustomed place, this ruse proved entirely ineffectual. The Dauphin, who was a very impressionable man, became greatly interested in Jeanne's mission, and soon became willing to render her the aid she needed to equip an army. One of the most remarkable incidents in the Maid's career was her extraordinary discipline, which manifested itself immediately in the improved conduct of the soldiers and in the amazing courage with which she inspired all under her command. Being herself of a highly religious nature, and deeming it of the utmost importance that religious rites should be faithfully observed, she readily induced the army to pay renewed attention to their long-neglected devotions, and she soon succeeded in inspiring a demoralized body of men with real reverence for all the virtues she so highly exemplified in her own heroic person. There is a marvellous contagion in perfect trust and quenchless bravery, and from whatever viewpoint

we may regard the story of visions and voices from
the unseen world, we must be ignorant indeed of
the first principles of psychology if we fail to perceive how mighty an effect on others one's own
indomitable courage can exert.   Whether the commander be Alexander, Cæsar, Napoleon, Wellington,
Washington, or the Maid of Orleans, no army has
ever proved continuously successful except when
headed by some intrepid general whose own conviction was unflinching that victory must surely wait
upon obedience to his (or her) command.   It seems
incredible that Joan of Arc could have accomplished
even the simple leadership of a battalion had she
not been able to impress those under her with something of her own confidence in Heavenly guidance,
for an immature maiden at the head of a regiment
of soldiers is a spectacle so grotesque, when viewed
from any ordinary standpoint, as to suggest a farce
rather than a serious battle.   Doubtless the charm
of her personality had something to do with her
successes, but we must keep steadily in mind that
here was no voluptuous woman appealing to the admiration of beauty-loving men, but a saintly virgin
whose especial charm consisted in her supreme devotion to spiritual ideals, her confidence in celestial
prompters and her unflinching determination to serve
her country at all hazard, guided as she believed by
the very finger of the Almighty.   It seems from all
histories that a certain magical charm was exerted
by her banner, the very sight of which nerved her
troops to daring, as they had accepted the suggestion that that symbol was a token of Heaven's approval of their march.   A very noteworthy incident

in this astounding record is the well-attested fact
that when the Maid followed implicitly directions
given by the spirit-voices, she was invariably victorious, but when she had accomplished, to the full,
the special work to which those voices led her, she
subsequently permitted herself to be led into battle
when they were silent, victory no longer crowned her
leadership, but she sustained serious physical injuries at the hands of the opposing troops, and soon
entered upon that sad episode in her formerly triumphant career which finally reached the tragic end
of martyrdom.  Among the many histories of this
truly wonderful girl, perhaps the most fascinating
of all is the volume of "Personal Recollections,"
translated from the French by that always delightful writer Samuel Clemens, familiarly known as
Mark Twain, who says: "The details of the life of
Joan of Arc form a biography which is unique
among the world's biographies in one respect.  It is
the only story of a human life which comes to us
under oath, the only one which comes to us from
the witness-stand.  The official records of the Great
Trial of 1531, and of the process of Rehabilitation
of a quarter of a century later, are still preserved
in the National Archives of France, and they
furnish with remarkable fulness the facts of her
life.  The history of no other life of that remote
time is known with either the certainty or the comprehensiveness that attaches to hers.  The Sieur
Louis De Conte is faithful to her official history in
his personal recollections, and thus far his trust-
worthiness is unimpeachable; but his mass of added
particulars must depend for credit upon his word

alone." The story, as told by this well-recognized authority, is divided into three books, written with a peculiarly vivid charm which makes the reader feel that he is himself living amid the extraordinary scenes so graphically depicted, and the original French seemingly has lost nothing by translation into Mark Twain's wonderfully beautiful English. To review this narrative with any degree of fulness would be to practically re-write it; but the following extracts from the story of Joan's trial and martyrdom may tend, in some slight degree, to familiarize our readers with what actually occurred at the time when a recognized saint of the Roman Catholic Church of to-day earned her right to beatification. "At nine o'clock the Maid of Orleans, deliverer of France, went forth in the grace of her innocence and her youth to lay down her life for the country she loved with such devotion and for the king who had abandoned her. She sat in the cart that is used only for felons. In one respect she was treated worse than a felon, for whereas she was on her way to be sentenced by the Civilon, she already bore her judgment inscribed in advance upon a mitre-shaped cap which she wore.

"In the car with her sat the Friar Martin Ladvenu and Maitre Jean Massieu. She looked girlishly fair and sweet and saintly in her long white robe, and when a gush of sunlight flooded her as she emerged from the gloom of the prison and was yet for a moment still framed in the arch of the sombre gate, the massed multitudes of poor folk murmured, 'A vision! a vision!' and sank to their knees praying, and many of the women weeping;

and the moving invocation for the dying rose again, and was taken up and borne along, a majestic wave of sound which accompanied the doomed, solacing and blessing her, all the sorrowful way to the place of death. 'Christ, have pity! Saint Margaret, have pity! Pray for her, all ye saints, archangels, and blessed martyrs; pray for her! Saints and angels, intercede for her! From thy wrath, good Lord, deliver her! O Lord God, save her! Have mercy on her, we beseech Thee, good Lord!'

"It is just and true, what one of the histories has said: 'The poor and the helpless had nothing but their prayers to give Joan of Arc; but these we may believe were not unavailing. There are few more pathetic events recorded in history than this weeping, helpless, praying crowd, holding their lighted candles and kneeling on the pavement beneath the prison walls of the old fortress.

"And it was so all the way. Thousands upon thousands massed upon their knees, and stretching far down the distance, thick sown with the faint yellow candle-flames, like a field starred with golden flowers.

"But there were some who did not kneel; these were the English soldiers. They stood elbow to elbow, on each side of Joan's road, and walled it in, all the way; and behind these living walls knelt the multitudes.

"By-and-bye a frantic man in priest's garb came wailing and lamenting, and tore through the crowd and the barrier of soldiers, and flung himself on his knees by Joan's cart, and put up his hands in supplication, crying out!

" 'O, forgive; forgive!'

"It was Loyseleur!

"And Joan forgave him; forgave him out of a
heart that knew nothing but forgiveness, nothing
but compassion, nothing but pity for all that suffer,
let their offence be what it might.   And she had no
word of reproach for this poor wretch who had
wrought day and night with deceits and treacheries
and hypocrisies to betray her to her death.

"The soldiers would have killed him, but the Earl
of Warwick saved his life.   What became of him
is not known.   He hid himself from the world somewhere, to endure his remorse as he might.

"In the square of the Old Market stood the two
platforms and the stake which had stood before
in the churchyard of St. Ouen.   The platforms were
occupied as before, the one by Joan and her judges,
the other by great dignitaries, the principal being
Cauchon and the English Cardinal, Winchester.   The
square was packed with people, the windows and
roofs of the blocks of buildings surrounding it
were black with them.

"When the preparation had been finished, all noise
and movement gradually ceased, and a waiting still-
ness followed which was solemn and impressive.

"And now, by order of Cauchon, an ecclesiastic
named Nicholas Midi preached a sermon, wherein
he explained that when a branch of a vine—which is
the Church—becomes diseased and corrupt, it must
be cut away or it will corrupt and destroy the whole
vine.   He made it appear that Joan, through her
wickedness, was a menace and a peril to the
Church's purity and holiness, and her death there-

fore necessary.  When he was come to the end of
his discourse, he turned toward her and paused
a moment, then he said: 'Joan, the Church can no
longer protect you.  Go in peace!'

"Joan had been placed wholly apart and conspicuous, to signify the Church's abandonment of her,
and she sat there in her loneliness, waiting in patience and resignation for the end.  Cauchon addressed her now.  He had been advised to read the
form of her abjuration to her, and had brought
it with him; but he changed his mind, fearing that
she would proclaim the truth—that she never know-
ingly abjured—and so bring shame upon him and
perpetual infamy.  He contented himself with ad-
monishing her to keep in mind her wickednesses, and
repent of them, and think of her salvation.  Then
he solemnly pronounced her excommunicate, and
cut off from the body of the Church.  With a final
word he delivered her over to the secular arm for
judgment and sentence.

"Joan, weeping, knelt and began to pray.  For
whom?  Herself?  Oh, no—for the King of France.
Her voice rose sweet and clear, and penetrated all
hearts with its passionate pathos.  She never thought
of his treacheries to her, she never thought of his
desertions of her, she never remembered that it was
because he was an ingrate that she was here to die
a miserable death; she remembered only that he was
her King, that she was his loyal and loving subject,
and that his enemies had undermined his cause with
evil reports and false charges, and he not by to defend himself.  And so, in the very presence of
death, she forgot her own troubles to implore all in

her hearing to be just to him; to believe that he was good and noble and sincere, and not in any way to blame for any acts of hers, neither advising them or urging them, but being wholly clear and free of all responsibility for them.  Then, closing, she begged in humble and touching words that all here present would pray for her and would pardon her, both her enemies and such as might look friendly upon her and feel pity for her in their hearts.

"There was hardly one heart there that was not touched—even the English, even the judges, showed it, and there was many a lip that trembled and many an eye that was blurred with tears; yes, even the English Cardinal's—that man with a political heart of stone but a human heart of flesh.

"The secular judge who should have delivered judgment and pronounced sentence was himself so disturbed that he forgot his duty, and Joan went to her death unsentenced—thus completing with an illegality what had begun illegally, and had so continued to the end.  He only said—to the guards:

" 'Take her'; and to the executioner, 'Do your duty.'

"Joan asked for a cross.  None was able to furnish one.  But an English soldier broke a stick in two, and crossed the pieces and tied them together, and this cross he gave her, moved to it by the good heart that was in him; and she kissed it and put it to her bosom.  Then Isambard de la Pierre went to the church near by and brought her a consecrated one; and this one also she kissed, and pressed it to her bosom with rapture, and then kissed it again and again, covering it with tears and pouring out her gratitude to God and the saints.

"And so, weeping, and with her cross to her lips, she climbed up the cruel steps to the face of the stake, with the friar Isambard at her side. Then she was helped up to the top of the pile of wood that was built around the lower third of the stake, and stood upon it with her back against the stake, and the world gazing up at her breathless. The executioner ascended to her side and wound the chains about her slender body, and so fastened her to the stake. Then he descended to finish his dreadful office, and there she remained alone—she that had had so many friends in the days when she was free, and had been so loved and so dear.

"All these things I saw, albeit dimly and blurred with tears; but I could bear no more. I continued in my place, but what I shall deliver to you now I got by others' eyes and others' mouths. Tragic sounds there were that pierced my ears and wounded my heart as I sat there, but it is as I tell you: the latest image recorded by my eyes in that desolating hour was Joan of Arc with the grace of her comely youth still unmarred; and that image, untouched by time or decay, has remained with me all my days. Now I will go on.

"If any thought that now, in that solemn hour, when all transgressors repent and confess, she would revoke her revocation and say her great deeds had been evil deeds, and Satan and his fiends their source, they erred. No such thought was in her blameless mind. She was not thinking of herself and her troubles, but of others, and of woes that might befall them.   And so, turning her grieving eyes about her, where rose the towers and spires of that fair city, she said:

"'Oh, Rouen, Rouen!   Must I die here, and must you be my tomb?   Ah, Rouen, Rouen!   I have great fear that you will suffer for my death.'

"A whiff of smoke swept upward past her face, and for one moment terror seized her and she cried out, 'Water!   Give me holy water!'   But the next moment her fears were gone, and they came no more to torture her.

"She heard the flames crackling below her, and immediately distress for a fellow creature who was in danger took possession of her.   It was the friar Isambard.   She had given him her cross and begged him to raise it toward her face and let her eyes rest in hope and consolation upon it, till she had entered into the peace of God.   She made him go out from the danger of the fire.   Then she was satisfied, and said:

"'Now keep it always in my sight until the end.'

"Not even yet could Cauchon, that man without shame, endure to let her die in peace, but went toward her, all black with crimes and sins as he was, and cried out:

"'I am come, Joan, to exhort you for the last time to repent and seek the pardon of God.'

"'I die through you,' she said, and these were the last words she spoke to any upon earth.

"Then the pitchy smoke, shot through with red flashes of flame, rolled up in a thick volume and hid her from sight; and from the heart of this darkness her voice rose strong and eloquent in prayer, and when by moments the wind shredded somewhat of the smoke aside, there were veiled glimpses of an upturned face and moving lips. At last a merciful swift tide of flame burst upward, and none saw that face any more, nor that form, and the voice was still.

"Yes, she was gone from us; Joan of Arc! What little words they are, to tell of a rich world made empty and poor!

"Joan's brother Jacques died in Domrémy during the Great Trial at Rouen. This was according to the prophecy which Joan made that day in the pastures, the time that she said the rest of us would go to the great wars.

"When her poor old father heard of the martyrdom, it broke his heart, and he died.

"The mother was granted a pension by the City of Orleans, and upon this she lived out her days, which were many. Twenty-four years after her illustrious child's death, she travelled all the way to Paris in the winter time, and was present at the opening of the discussion in the Cathedral of Notre Dame, which was the first step in the Rehabilitation. Paris was crowded with people, from all over France, who came to get sight of the venerable dame, and it was a touching spectacle when she moved through those reverent, wet-eyed multitudes on her way to the grand honors awaiting her at the Cathedral. With her were Jean and Pierre, no longer the light-hearted youths who marched with us from Vaucouleurs, but war-worn veterans with hair beginning to show frost.

"After the martyrdom, Noel and I went back to

Domrémy, but presently, when the Constable Riche-
mont superseded La Tremouille as the King's Chief
Adviser, and began the completion of Joan's great
work, we put on our harness and returned to the
field and fought for the King all through the wars
and skirmishes, until France was freed of the English.   It was what Joan would have desired of us;
and, dead or alive, her desire was law for us.   All
the survivors of the personal staff were faithful to
her memory and fought for the King to the end.
Mainly we were well scattered, but when Paris
fell we happened to be together.   It was a great day
and a joyous; but it was a sad one at the same time,
because Joan was not there to march into the cap-
tured capital with us

"Noel and I remained always together, and I was
by his side when death claimed him.   It was in the
last great battle of the war.   In that battle fell also
Joan's sturdy old enemy, Talbot.   He was eighty-
five years old, and had spent his whole life in battle.
A fine old lion he was, with his flowing white mane
and his tameless spirit; yes, and his indestructible
energy as well; for he fought as knightly and vigorous a fight that day as the best man there.

"La Hire survived the martyrdom thirteen years;
and always fighting, of course, for that was all he
enjoyed in life.   I did not see him in all that time,
for we were far apart, but one was always hearing
of him.

"The Bastard of Orleans and D'Alençon and
D'Aulon lived to see France free, and to testify
with Jean and Pierre d'Arc and Pasquerel and me
at the Rehabilitation.   But they are all at rest now,

these many years.   I alone am left of those who fought at the side of Joan of Arc in the great wars. She said I should live until these wars were for-gotten—a prophecy which failed.   If I should live a thousand years, it would still fail.   For whatso-ever had touch with Joan of Arc, that thing is im-mortal.

"Members of Joan's family married, and they have left descendants.   Their descendants are of the nobility, but their family name and blood bring them honors which no other nobles receive or may hope for.   You have seen how everybody along the way uncovered when those children came yesterday to pay their duty to me.   It was not because they are noble; it is because they are grandchildren of the brothers of Joan of Arc.

"Now as to the Rehabilitation.   Joan crowned the King at Rheims.   For reward, he allowed her to be hunted to her death without making one effort to save her.   During the next twenty-three years he remained indifferent to her memory, indifferent to the fact that her good name was under a damning blot put there by the priests because of the deeds which she had done in saving him and his sceptre, indifferent to the fact that France was ashamed.   In-different all that time.   Then he suddenly changed, and was anxious to have justice for poor Joan, himself.   Why?   Had he become grateful at last? Had remorse attacked his hard heart?   No; he had a better reason—a better one for his sort of man. This better reason was that, now that the English had been finally expelled from the country, they were beginning to call attention to the fact that this King had gotten his crown by the hands of a person proven by the priests to have been in league with Satan, and burnt for it by them as a sorceress —therefore, of what value or authority was such a kingship as that? Of no value at all; no nation could afford to allow such a King to remain on the throne.

"It was high time to stir now, and the King did it. That is how Charles VII. came to be smitten with anxiety to have justice done the memory of his benefactress.

"He appealed to the Pope, and the Pope appointed a great commission of churchmen to examine into the facts of Joan's life and award judgment. The Commission sat at Paris, at Domrémy, at Rouen, at Orleans, and at several other places, and continued its work during several months. It examined the record of Joan's trial, it examined the Bastard of Orleans and the Duke D'Alençon, and D'Aulon, and Pasquerel, and Courcelles, and Isambard de la Pierre, and Manchon, and me, and many others whose names I have made familiar to you; also they examined more than a hundred witnesses whose names are less familiar to you—friends of Joan in Domrémy, Vaucouleurs, Orleans, and other places, and a number of judges and other people who had assisted at the Rouen trials, the abjuration, and the martyrdom. And out of this exhaustive examination Joan's character and history came spotless and perfect, and this verdict was placed upon record, to remain forever.

"I was present upon most of these occasions, and saw again many faces which I have not seen for a

quarter of a century; among them some well-beloved
faces—those of our generals and that of Catherine
Boucher (married, alas!), and also among them certain other faces that filled me with bitterness—those
of Beaupere and Courcelles and a number of their
fellow-fiends.  I saw Haumette and Little Mengette
—edging along toward fifty, now, and mothers of
many children.  I saw Noel's father, and the parents
of the Paladin and the Sunflower.

"It was beautiful to hear the Duke D'Alençon
praise Joan's splendid capacities as a general. and
to hear the Bastard endorse these praises with his
eloquent tongue, and then go on and tell how sweet
and good Joan was, and how full of pluck and fire
and impetuosity and mischief and mirthfulness, and
tenderness and compassion, and everything that was
pure and fine and noble and lovely.  He made her
live again before me, and wrung my heart.

"I have finished my story of Joan of Arc, that
wonderful child, that sublime personality, that spirit
which in one regard has had no peer and will have
none—this: its purity from all alloy of self-seeking,
self-interest, personal ambition.  In it no trace of
these motives can be found, search as you may, and
this cannot be said of any other person whose name
appears in profane history.

"With Joan of Arc, love of country was more
than a sentiment—it was a passion.  She was the
genius of Patriotism—she was patriotism embodied,
concreted, made flesh, and palpable to the touch
and visible to the eye.

"Love, Mercy, Charity, Fortitude, War, Peace,
Poetry, Music—these may be symbolised as any shall

prefer; by figures of either sex and of any age; but a slender girl in her first young bloom, with the martyr's crown upon her head, and in her hand the sword that severed her country's bonds—shall not this, and no other, stand for PATRIOTISM through all ages, until time shall end?"

Such, in brief, is a fair record of one of the most marvellous cases of inspired bravery and true martyrdom the world has ever known. There may still remain psychological mysteries connected with the Maid's career which neither physical nor psychical research has yet been able fully to fathom, but that is no reason why we should withhold our consent to such abundant testimony as has clearly been afforded to the super-physical element in the career of this mysterious girl whose name, nearly five centuries after her departure from the physical body, is gaining continually added fame and lustre. Europe as well as Asia, the Christian centuries as well as older times, have all borne witness to the reality of spiritual interposition in the affairs of humanity on earth, thereby entirely putting to flight the erroneous assumption that this world stands alone in space, or that its inhabitants while incarnate are isolated from companionship with intelligent entities on other than physical planes of manifestation. Whenever a work needs to be done, fitting instruments are raised up to accomplish it, and these in the present, as well as in the past, appear often at first entirely unsuited to the mighty tasks they have been selected to fulfil. Time vindicates all things. Justice reigns, and must forever triumph.

# CHAPTER XVIII.

## ANDREW JACKSON DAVIS, A NINETEENTH CENTURY SEER—A GLIMPSE AT HIS PHILOSOPHY.

Among the truly wonderful pioneers of the great new wave of thought which during the past century largely revolutionized the entire thinking world, the name of Andrew Jackson Davis, author of "Nature's Divine Revelations," "The Great Harmonia," and many other wonderful literary productions, deserves to hold a singularly high and honored place. We hear so much of the influence of heredity and of environment, that we are generally much astonished when we find a highly gifted writer displaying amazing knowledge on almost every subject, if concerning his ancestry and early history we know nothing in any way remarkable.

The mother of Andrew Jackson Davis seems to have been a good, honest, ordinary woman, displaying no remarkable traits or characteristics, and as to the boy's early history we can only discover that he attended common country schools and was in early youth apprenticed to a shoemaker. Without some spiritual theory to account for genius, we can only remain utterly bewildered in presence of the great library of outwardly unassuming but intellectually imposing volumes which have recently been re-

issued by the Austin Publishing Company, Rochester, N. Y., and which carry us back to the 'forties
and 'fities of the nineteenth century.   Quite apart
from the phenomenal character of their authorship,
the works themselves are a stupendous revelation,
embracing as they do profound and learned treatises
on all the natural sciences, besides undertaking to
give us wonderful enlightenment concerning the
(ordinarily) unseen universe.

In the case of Emanuel Swedenborg, we can trace
the gradual evolution of a mighty intellect.   Swedenborg was born into a distinguished family of scholars, and he gradually ascended by well-defined successive steps from treatises on natural science and
philosophy to dissertations concerning the spiritual
universe.   But while Swedenborg was over fifty
years of age when he undertook to unveil the wonders of life in spiritual spheres, the Seer of Poughkeepsie was under twenty, and quite illiterate in
the collegiate sense, when he began unfolding with
marvellous insight and wealth of diction the wonders of those innumerable super-physical states and
conditions concerning which the majority of even
the best-informed among scholars professed to know
next to nothing.   Were the works of Davis wild
romances or accounts of rhapsodic visions lacking
alike in logical coherence and continuity, we might
quickly dismiss them as psychic vagaries, and pay
no serious attention to their inculcations; but in
Davis's writings we are brought face to face with
a fund of scientific and historical information which
renders the books marvels of erudition even if we
pay no heed to the accounts of unseen spheres which

we are told the youth clearly beheld when in a superior condition.   It was in 1846 and 1847 that the
first of these great works was brought to public
notice, therefore just before the year when the
"Rochester Knockings" are said to have inaugurated
the advent of Modern Spiritualism.   Davis was
therefore a forerunner of all those modern prophets
who startled America with their disclosures concerning life beyond death, and all of whom in the
early days of the Spiritualistic movement seemed to
take a somewhat different view of their relation to
the world of spirits than that claimed for himself
by Davis.   We all know that the common idea of
mediumship is of a state or condition in which the
medium is under the control or direction of some
outside influence, and usually it is claimed that such
influence works *through* the medium, whereas in the
"superior condition" of Davis, which in this respect
largely resembled that of Swedenborg, he claimed
to see and hear for himself what was going on in
other worlds, or on other planes of existence, by
virtue of the enlargement of his own perception enabling him to see much further into the universe
than is possible with only ordinary faculties.   We
read in his Autobiography, called "The Magic
Staff," that at first he was magnetized or mesmer-
ized, and while in the magnetic or mesmeric state
exhibited singular lucidity.   But the men who thus
operated with him were entirely incapable of trans-
mitting through his agency the wondrous information which soon began to pour in torrents through
his lips, though their manipulations do seem to have
opened a door into the trance condition, which soon

gave place to a higher state of independent clairvoyance. How far magnetism or mesmerism can
prove a genuine aid to psychic development is a
very open and much-disputed question, but the bulk
of testimony in this direction, which we may reasonably deem reliable, is that it does often prepare the
way for higher developments which follow, principally by removing that extreme self-consciousness,
which, when coupled with inordinate attention to the
external side of things, is doubtless the chief barrier in the way of mental and spiritual lucidity.
Though it is quite clear to every logical thinker
that no one can impart knowledge which he does
not possess, it is by no means unreasonable to assume that certain obstacles may be removed, which
are usually in the way of receiving information
psychically, through the agency of the mesmerist.
In the middle of the last century mesmeric opera-
tions were greatly in vogue among many learned
doctors, prominent among whom stood the famous
Dr. Gregory of Edinburgh, whose long-famous
work, "Animal Magnetism or Mesmerism and Its
Phenomena," contains a great many thoroughly well
authenticated accounts of remarkable clairvoyance
induced by mesmeric treatment. But most of this
clairvoyance was very much of a piece with the
thought-transference, telepathy, and mental telegraphy, about which we are now hearing and reading constantly. Contrast the meagre results of many
recent endeavors to communicate with the unseen
world on the part of such distinguished scientific
celebrities as, for example, Sir Oliver Lodge, with
the magnificent inspired output of the Seer of

Poughkeepsie, and we are only the more bewildered with the dazzling splendor of a revelation which has been almost entirely overlooked by the scientific world, even while a distinguished portion of it has been engaging itself with an attempted solution of the very problems which this revelation seems so very largely to have solved.  But we must not forget that however satisfactory as well as wonderful this revelation may appear, it does not seem to supply that distinctly evidential individual testimony to personal immortality which our modern seekers are striving to obtain, unless we admit the many instances of recorded clairvoyance with which his writings abound as supplying such evidence.  We can quite readily imagine the attitude taken by our modern Psychical Research Committees regarding conclusive evidence, and should we press such alleged evidence upon them, they would naturally inquire where is your proof that such visions are other than results of a fertile and highly vivid imagination? To this inquiry we can indeed offer no reply which might prove universally conclusive.  Still, it may reasonably be argued that the information given is so extensive, profound, and rational that the very large probability is that it emanated from the source whence its recipient declared that it did proceed. But in these days "cross-correspondence," and other new phases of telepathic intercourse, hold the center of the stage in certain scientific circles, and these phenomena are indeed intensely interesting and deserve the fullest attention at the hands of earnest students everywhere.  But on that account we are by no means justified in narrowing the field of our vision and confining our researches within the very limited domain in which many investigators seem desirous of pursuing their inquiries.   Having glanced over the contents of a valuable recent book by Sir Oliver Lodge—which has been widely reviewed in periodicals of all descriptions and has furnished texts for many lectures and essays—we find the most characteristic evidences of both mundane and supra-mundane telepathy to consist in dialogue of an extremely commonplace nature, a fact which Professor Hyslop and many other earnest investigators regard as confirmatory of the fact that individuality is expressed much more fully by means of an exhibition of minor peculiarities than through the agency of profound utterances which, however valuable from a philosophical standpoint, convey no convincing impression of having emanated from a particular individual intelligence.   One of the special characteristics of the avowed inspiration of A. J. Davis is that he received it from a "sphere" of intelligence rather than from any special individual, and for that very reason it may lack a peculiar personal character, such as characterizes friendly messages between companion souls, while it gains immensely in profundity of sentiment and grandiloquence of speech.   The work of Davis was evidently far more to set people thinking concerning mighty problems relating to universal life than to give them private information relative to their personal affairs; yet, because the smaller can always be included within the greater the diligent student of the Harmonial Philosophy can find almost every question fully answered which pertains to the personal side of life here and hereafter. The "magic staff," which Davis said he was recommended, by his spiritual prompters, always to rely upon in every time of doubt and difficulty, was couched in these words: "Behold, here is thy magic staff: UNDER ALL CIRCUMSTANCES KEEP AN EVEN MIND. Take it; try it; walk with it; talk with it; lean on it; believe on it forever." We are told that these words came to him in radiant light, but a doubt seized him, and he asked: Is that longest sentence my magic staff. "Under all circumstances keep an even mind," is that the mystic cane which I thought I had lost or forgotten? In a twinkling the sheet of whiteness vanished, and in its place beamed forth YES. This satisfied him, and from that day forward he declares that he always leaned on that reliable staff, which never deserted him throughout his long, eventful life, which only closed when he was past eighty-three years of age. This revelation came to him in 1844, some time previous to the more wonderful experiences which quickly and thickly followed, till at length we find no less than twenty-seven wonderful volumes growing under his hand, in consequence of his always following the guidance of that marvelous inspiration which exalted him to the rank of a truly marvelous prophet and philosopher. Personal details are always interesting when they concern remarkable personages, for they serve to throw some light upon the temperament as well as character of those who are destined to perform unusual work in the world. Davis says of himself, when reviewing his boyhood years: "I had a love of truth; a reverence for knowledge; a somewhat cheerful disposition; a deficient imagination; unbelief or ignorance concerning the existence of ghosts, etc.; dread of death, and a still greater dread of encountering what might exist beyond the grave; a tendency to spontaneous somnambulism; an ear for what I then called imaginary voices; a memory defective as to dates; a mind nearly barren of ordinary education; a heart very sympathetic in cases of trial and suffering; and lastly I was disposed to meditation and the freedom of solitude." Speaking of his physical condition, he says that his body was imperfectly developed; breast narrow; spine short and weak; stomach very sensitive; muscular fabric unsound and inefficient; nervous system highly impressible, and he ends this uninviting description of his personal appearance and condition by declaring that he was not calculated to inspire strangers with much interest in his existence. These statements are of great scientific interest in so far as they furnish overwhelming proof that the development of the psychic faculty in a delicate lad, when wisely carried forward, far from leading to physical disability or mental deterioration, served to build up a robust mind and body, which not only endured considerable physical and mental exertion through a protracted lifetime, but also served the benign and noble purpose of conveying a vast amount of health-giving information to multitudes. That there are dangers connected with sensitiveness of every kind, no reasonable student will deny, but these are often greatly exaggerated, and in no instances is this rendered so painfully apparent as among people who foolishly discountenance and berate all exercise of supraphysical faculty. Among the many works of Davis his "Lyceum Manual" is singularly fascinating and affords a beautiful and comprehensive basis for the healthy instruction and exercise of children and young people in liberal Sunday Schools.   Though the Lyceum Movement has somewhat waned in America, it has taken deep root, and is now greatly flourishing all over Great Britain and in many of the British Colonies.   The system of teaching and exercising is so beautiful and natural that it unfolds the whole nature of the youth or maiden who follows it out in its entirety, and instead of forcing upon children doubtful theological dogmas, which no one attempts to fully comprehend, young people in a Lyceum are gently led on through a contemplation of the beauties of external nature to penetrate into the mysteries of the yet more glorious spiritual universe.   In the Fifth Volume of the "Great Harmonia" we are confronted with almost a complete epitome of the teachings of the world's greatest seers and sages, from very ancient to quite modern times, and through all these narratives we can trace far more than ordinary insight into the underlying principles which these master minds have clothed in systems of thought and embodied in schools of philosophy, the influence of which is at this day even greater than when these mighty doctrines were originally promulgated.   We here append a few citations:

From "The Great Harmonia," Volume II, entitled "The Teacher," we extract the following (page 250): "I consider motion the first manifestation of mind—an indication of the Great Mind which resides back of, and in, Nature; and a prophetical indication of the existence of a corresponding mind as an ultimate or perfection of Nature.

"I consider Life the first development of Motion, and the second indication of intelligence.

"I consider Sensation the first development of Life, and the third indication of future or ultimate Intelligence.

"I consider Intelligence the highest development of Motion, Life, and Sensation, and a perfect manifestation of the internal living and unchangeable organization, and when I employ the terms Soul, Spirit, and Mind, I mean the internal and immortal individual. When Motion, Life, Sensation, and Intelligence are conjoined and organized, I term that organization a unity of elements and attributes; and these elements and attributes arrange according to their natural order, under the comprehensive terms of Love and Wisdom—terms which are perfectly expressive of the natural characteristics and legitimate manifestations of those internal principles. Therefore, when I use the nouns substantive—Soul, Spirit, Mind, and Individual—the thought which suggests their employment is resting invariably upon the inward *Homo*, upon the individual Oneness, which is constructed upon those principles which elevate that oneness above the plane of change and disorganization. Hence the question is answered affirmatively —the terms are unqualifiedly synonymous."

The question referred to was: Are Soul, Spirit, and Mind synonymous? — one which is so frequently asked to-day that we selected the answer to it out of an immense variety of replies to all sorts of questions put to A. J. Davis, thinking it might

serve almost better than any other to elucidate the
philosophy of the Poughkeepsie Seer in his own
words.

We will not attempt any commentary upon the
words quoted, because we desire to acquaint our
readers with what a truly remarkable seer has uttered, rather than to put any gloss of our own upon
his words by argument or comparison.   Concerning the final destiny of the individual immortal
human entity, Davis says, in reply to a query thereon
(page 254): "The Spirit will have no '*final home*';
because to an immortal being rest would be intolerable—it would be next to annihilation." . . . "But
the spirit will progress eternally!  It will always be
in harmony with surrounding circumstances, and
thus will always reside in heaven.  The same differences will exist in future spheres of life as exist
in this world,—I mean those differences which are
established by the real intrinsic perfection of the constitution, education, and harmony of the individual.
But the spirit will walk in those shining paths which
angels tread, in opening communications between the
celestial inhabitants of celestial spheres and those
high-born spirits of our earth."  Only one more quotation will we offer from the vast mass of material
at our disposal, as the object of this essay is to whet
our readers' appetites for the massive volumes from
which these brief excerpts are extracted.  This last
morsel is from "What and Where is God?" (page
270): "Surrounded by an inconceivable number of
forms and organizations,—each one of them occupying a specific and progressive position in Nature,—
the human mind can but perceive that the cause of

them must be, Himself, an infinite Cause; that to produce organizations he must be, Himself, first, Intelligent; and that to produce an infinite machine, he must be, Himself, not only organized and intelligent, but he must have had some glorious end or result to accomplish, according to which his Universal Machinery was constructed.  Surely, this is plain reasoning.  God, therefore, philosophically considered, is an infinite Cause; Nature is an infinite Effect; and the object, for the accomplishment of which the whole was thus constituted, is the infinite Use or End.  God is the Great Positive Mind;—all else is Negative." Atheism indeed receives no support from Davis, as it receives none from any of the world's spiritual enlighteners; but neither does any narrow theology receive endorsement — an all-embracing God is the only real Deity.

# CHAPTER XIX.

BIBLE SYMBOLISM—AARON'S BREASTPLATE AND OTHER TYPICAL ORNAMENTS AND EMBLEMS— THE MORAL INFLUENCE OF BEAUTY AND THE SIGNIFICANCE OF COLOR.

Among the most attractive symbols of antiquity none can be more beautiful and expressive than precious stones, and these have always figured very largely in religious ritual as well as in secular adornment. Nowhere in the Bible can we find a more impressive instance of the use of glittering gems than in the breastplate of the Jewish high priest, Aaron, whose adornments are minutely described in the twenty-eighth chapter of Exodus, verses 15-21, as follows: "Thou shalt make the breastplate of judgment with cunning work, after the work of the ephod thou shalt make it; of gold and of blue, and of purple, and of scarlet, and of fine twined linen shalt thou make it. Four-square it shall be, being doubled; a span shall be the length thereof, and a span shall be the breadth thereof. And thou shalt set in it settings of stones, even four rows of stones; the first row shall be a sardis (ruby), a topaz, and a carbuncle; this shall be the first row. And the second row shall be an emerald, a sapphire, and a diamond. And the third row a ligure (cyanus), an agate, and an amethyst. And the fourth row shall be a beryl, and an onyx, and a jasper. They shall be set in gold in their inclosings.   And the stones shall be with the names of the Children of Israel, twelve, according to their names, like the engravings of a signet, every one with his name shall they be according to the Twelve Tribes." This magnificent breastplate, called Urim and Thummim, was regarded in ancient sacerdotal days as a special instrument for obtaining information from Heaven, a fact which throws much light upon the sacred magic of the Israelites of old.   A very interesting and elaborate dissertation concerning this breastplate is contained in "The Science of Correspondences Elucidated," by Edward Madely and B. F. Barrett, in which the authors claim that we have a key to its interior significance by dividing its four sections thus:   First row downward, predominating color, Red, Celestial Love of Good.   Second row, Reddish Blue, Celestial Love of Truth.   Third row, Whitish Blue, Spiritual love of Good.   Fourth row, Bluish White, Spiritual Love of Truth.   The distinction here made so definitely between Truth and Good is in strict agreement with all of Swedenborg's discriminations, with which these authors are in complete accord, and we shall all do well to ponder thoughtfully exactly wherein the difference really lies. Truth is of the enlightened understanding and addresses itself to intellect, to reason in particular, while Good has to do directly with our affections, which, though intimately associated with our understanding, are nevertheless distinct from it.   As very great interest is now being widely taken in some supposed connection between the twelve Signs of the Zodiac, the twelve Tribes of Israel, and certain precious stones, our readers may be interested to know that an ancient tradition assigns a ruby to Reuben; an emerald to Judah; a cyanus (lapis-lazuli) to Gad; a turquoise (beryl) to Zebulon; a topaz to Simeon; a sapphire to Dan; an agate to Asher; an onyx to Joseph; a carbuncle to Levi; a diamond to Naphthali; an amethyst to Issachar; a jasper to Benjamin. Turning to Numbers, Chapter II, we find the following classification of the twelve Tribes, with their standard bearers: Judah heads the three tribes to the East; Reuben to the South; Ephraim to the West; Dan to the North; the Camp of the Levites and the Tabernacle of the Congregation being in the midst. The same order is indicated in the order of march described in the same book (Chapter X) when the Ark of the Covenant is carried in front of the army. The different arrangements at various times, and in altering circumstances, readily suggests varying significations denoting the changing states of human experience. Red stones always occupy the place of highest esteem, because red is the first of the primaries and is universal in its correspondence, it being the color of the completed octave. As Adam only means a red man, and red is the lowest of the seven prismatic hues according to rate of vibration, it is not only a title applied to the sensuous man, not yet awakened to spiritual consciousness, but is equally applied to those who are regenerated, whom we designate "second Adam," like the upper A which commences a new scale in music. "Stones of Fire" are often mentioned in the Bible in connection with great judgments and mighty deliverances, which are frequently referred to as

preceded by "hailstones and coals of fire."   In the
extremely fascinating imagery of the marvelous
book of Ezekiel we find allusions to precious gems
which throw a large amount of light upon their
mystical as well as magical significance.   By the
use of these two terms in the above connection we
mean by magical all that pertains to the working
of outward wonders by the employment of prescribed and tested ceremonial rites; by mystical we
mean interior results obtained in a spiritual manner
without any recourse to ritual of any description.
The mystical method is very much higher and more
abidingly reliable than the magical, though both are
mentioned with approbation in the Bible, each being
adapted to a particular stage of human conscious
susceptibility to Divine and Celestial influxes.   In
the twenty-eighth chapter of Ezekiel we are told that
the King of Tyre has been in Eden, the Garden of
God, where every precious stone was his covering
until he fell into iniquity and was consequently
expelled and dethroned.   When, in the days of his
moral uprightness, this monarch was figuratively on
God's holy mountain it is said that he walked to
and fro amid "stones of fire," at which time he was
designated "a covering cherub."   This clearly shows
that in ancient times such expressions were used to
denote high offices held by holy people who were
worthy of such exalted station, and not permitted to
retain it in any case after they had disqualified themselves by the practice of unrighteousness.   Many
people to-day are asking whether any value attaches
to the actual wearing of gems, or whether we must
attribute all alleged and seeming efficacy to the force

of auto-suggestion.    A reasonable reply to such
enquiries must be at least threefold.    First, we must
remember that jewels are imprisoned sunlight and
they have truly a force of their own, to which
highly sensitive people are peculiarly susceptible ; this
is a demonstrable scientific proposition which can
be tested and proved experimentally by Materialists
as readily as by Occultists.    Second, associations
with gems are extremely permanent, and these are
psychical as well as physical, as psychometry abundantly reveals ; a gem is extremely retentive of any
influence it has absorbed, and many precious stones
—opals and pearls especially—are very susceptible
to the condition of the persons who wear them.
Third, individual taste has much to do with the
effect which a stone will have on its wearer, but
tastes, preferences and antipathies are revealers of
character and temperament, and unless there is some
very forcible extraneous cause for our likes and
dislikes as applied to gems and colors we invariably
are attracted instinctively to those stones and colors
whose vibrations agree with us and help us, while
we are similarly repelled by such as either over-
stimulate or depress us, in consequence of their rate
of vibration being either too high or too low to meet
our necessities.    The High Priest in ancient Israel
wore a breastplate composed of twelve precious
stones because he must represent all the twelve tribes
equally, and a man capable of filling so highly representative a position worthily must be beyond the
ordinary run of attractions and repulsions.    A thoroughly balanced man or woman admires all beautiful
objects in nature and in art, and feels at home with

all of them, at the same time understanding their
respective uses and significances and employing them
accordingly.   Among gems the diamond is the most
universally admired and worn; this is largely on
account of its bright all-including whiteness, out of
which every brilliant hue can sparkle in the sunshine,
and also in artificial radiance.   Almost every one
feels at home with the diamond, just as we are all
at home with white, while different limited colors
affect us differently in our varying moods and seem
highly appropriate in such situations as demand
them, but quite out of place in other circumstances,
though in themselves they are always beautiful.
There is not the slightest reason why we should not
avail ourselves of the beauty of nature, and surely
nothing can be more unnatural and ridiculous than
to dispense with all adornment when nature is so
lavishly profuse with decoration, and it requires no
more time or effort, in the long run at any rate, to
make life outwardly as well as inwardly beautiful,
than it does to peg along in a manner calculated to
lower instead of raise the tone of our vitality, and
thereby lessen instead of increase our working capacity.   Though we all know that foolish extravagance
in dress and adornment, together with all other
forms of ostentatious display, are not productive of
desirable results in human society, we ought not
ever to be unmindful of the fact that sordid ugliness and crime are often very intimate associates.
John Ruskin never hesitated to preach his gospel of
beauty as a moral elevator, and it certainly does
appear that, on an average, there is far less crime
where beauty is cultivated than where ugliness reigns

supreme.   Drunkenness is often largely due to a state of mental dulness bordering on despair.   Men and women work in dingy workshops and live in dingy dwellings unworthy of the name of homes, and with what result?   They almost invariably exhibit signs of moral, mental and physical deterioration, and are very rarely as cheerful in disposition or as optimistic in sentiment as those who surround themselves with more attractive objects.   We may well feel compassion and express sympathy for all who are apparently compelled to live in gloomy places, but there can be no valid excuse for deliberately planting ourselves in such surroundings, except for the benevolent purpose of ministering to those who are incarcerated therein.   When we have the choice of circumstances in our own hands it would be well indeed did we invariably elect to surround ourselves with beauty, and it was originally intended that the people at large should be instructed in this lesson by beholding the extreme beauty of the sacred places in which they performed acts of worship.   Those who seemingly require no special temple and no officiating priests can certainly lift their souls in aspiration amid the glories of undisfigured natural surroundings, and as the highest compliment which can be paid to any artist is to assure him that his work is a perfect facsimile of nature, we can have no greater beauty even in structures of the rarest magnificence than we behold in those charming districts of the world where natural scenery is allowed to remain untampered with.   The Garden Cities now springing up in England are exerting a highly beneficial effect upon the civilization of the country, because they are helping people to get further away from that hideous artificiality which has for a long time past exerted an undermining influence upon health and morals.  Rapid transit is beginning to prove an immense benefit to multitudes by making it quite easy for men of family to transact business in the centre of a great city and bring up children in the very heart of a lovely country.  Dress as well as circumstances and diet receives a great deal of attention in the Mosaic Law, and not only the attire of those who are set apart to perform peculiar religious functions, but the ordinary costume of the masses, receives some definite notice.  It is an undeniable fact that Jews to-day, as a community, are very fond of jewelry, and it has been said that the very word jewel pertains to Judaism.  Be that as it may, the Old Testament lays great stress on personal adornment, in addition to cleanliness, in many imposing instances, and in so doing it does not show itself barbaric, as some foolish people suppose, probably because all unsophisticated peoples are, like children, fond of bright colors and general display; but in this matter, as in very many others, it evinces singularly deep insight into what is conducive to general well-being.

Colors apart from jewels (which, however, embody them in the most perfect manner and to the fullest possible degree) have a value and exert an influence far beyond what is ordinarily supposed. Dr. Edwin Babbitt, in his famous treatise, "The Principles of Light and Color," has given out an immense amount of information of extreme value, which has not received anything like the degree of attention its great merit richly deserves, though we are happy to say that the large illustrated volume, rather too ponderous for general reading, has found its way into a very large number of libraries in many lands, and we have good evidence that it has beneficently influenced the practice of many progressive doctors, and also helped many sufferers on the road to recovery by explaining to them a rational, and not difficult, mode of home treatment. In any country retreat or seaside resort it ought to be easy to open up a Solarium and apply the Light and Color treatment, provided a director can be found for each institution who really understands the science of the system, and is provided with an adequate mechanical equipment; and even without a full supply of chromo-lenses and thermolumes, a great deal of useful work can be done by simply fitting up a few rooms with the necessary colored window glass. The house ought to be so situated that it commands more than an average amount of sunlight, and the various rooms—in the Northern Hemisphere with Southern, and in the Southern Hemisphere with Northern exposures—should be equipped with colored windows, always kept scrupulously clean, so that the special rays of light needed in different conditions can be enjoyed to the full by those undergoing treatment. But though it is to sunshine primarily that we must look for the color vibrations necessary, we have in electric light so valuable an adjunct that at seasons of the year and in localities where the sunshine is often very limited we can arrange electric light fixtures so that we obtain almost the same results by night as by day, and in cloudy as in brilliant weather. A thoroughly equipped Solarium, furnished in every detail in accordance with the prescription of certain highly trained and widely experienced Occultists, would be nothing less than a magnificent Temple of the Sun, in which patients to-day might receive treatment identical with that which made many an ancient temple famous. Multitudes of sufferers all over the world are readily amenable to Solaric and Electric t.eatment simply and beautifully administered, and in these days when new methods are eagerly sought after and painstakingly examined, the time is indeed opportune for a revival of this best, simplest, humanest method of healing through direct co-operation with Nature in one of her most glorious and attractive forms the world has ever witnessed. With the rapidly increasing sensitiveness of the present generation crude methods and gross remedies are passing out of vogue; there is, constantly, a loud and imperative call for measures which will prove effective and convincing and in no way injure or terrify nervous invalids. In Solaric treatment, accompanied by wise and beneficent Suggestion, we find exactly what our age requires, viz., a Psycho-Physical method which embraces a reasonable appeal to the mind and also satisfies a widespread demand for something which can be readily comprehended by persons who have not grown to a state where they can be fully satisfied with methods exclusively metaphysical. Nature everywhere employs Form, Sound, and Color; we are, therefore, thoroughly in accord with Nature if we avail ourselves of these three great aids to harmony, which were all acknowledged and employed by the greatest healers of antiquity, whose marvelous achievements stand out to-day on the pages of world-wide history, not only challenging our attention and exciting our wonder, but bidding us drink from the same overflowing natural fountain from which they drank so wisely and so copiously, that we too may demonstrate in our age, as they did in theirs, the boundlessness of the supply furnished to us by the glorious central luminary which is the agent of all our life and the active sustainer of all growth and beauty.

The seven prismatic hues may be regarded as four landings and three stairways, symbolically speaking. Red is the first floor, Yellow the second, Blue the third, Violet the fourth. Orange is the first staircase, Green the second, Indigo the third. Red always excites the physical system and can be most advantageously employed to antidote all sluggish and costive conditions. Orange is less physically stimulating than Red, and as it inclines toward Yellow, which stimulates intellectual activity, it is extremely useful in those numerous instances where a mild tonic and purgative is required for mind and body at once. Yellow is, *par excellence*, an excitant of the intellect and it exercises a cooling, refreshing, and mildly stimulating effect upon those whose work requires constant and diligent attention to intellectual pursuits. Green is the home color of our planet, and standing in the middle of the scale is a corrective of nostalgia and a most harmonizing and tranquilizing color to employ in all places where many people exhibiting diverse characteristics are required to congregate. Blue is the decidedly ethical harmonizer and is to be specially recommended in all cases where passions are too easily excited and where material objects exert too great a sway.   This color is a soporific, a true conqueror of insomnia and nervous headaches; fevers yield to its tranquilizing influence, as its action is to cool the blood, lower the pulse, and generally soothe senses while tending to free the mind from anxiety and worry, leaving it free to engage in the profitable contemplation of ideal conditions.   Purple (or Indigo) excites toward spiritual contemplation and always suggests intellectual, coupled with moral, dignity.   Violet is the spiritual color, *par excellence*, and it is found extremely effective in aiding well-conducted psychic experiments.   To fit up a private solarium is not very expensive, as only eight rooms are necessary, though we can easily add profitably to their number.   One room must have clear white glass, as white is the common unifier, and the other seven chambers must have respectively one each of the seven prismatics. A ninth room for the introduction of Rose Pink would be a great advantage, as this lovely color, though not one of the mystic seven, is of immense value in counteracting despondency and all pessimistic tendencies.   Pink is the color of hope, and quite often light streaming through pink windows or electric light globes will drive away all tendency to gloom and to despair, and so invigorate a melancholy sufferer as to go far to prevent insanity and suicide.   We trust that these few hints on Color Treatment will serve to awaken increased interest in this momentous theme, which needs to be pursued indefinitely.

# CHAPTER XX.

LIFE AND MATTER—THE LATEST VIEWS ON EVOLU-
TION—POSITION OF SIR OLIVER LODGE.

Among modern thinkers of high repute in the
English-speaking sections of the scientific world
scarcely any name stands out more prominently at
present than that of Sir Oliver Lodge, the distinguished president of Birmingham University in England. Standing, as this conspicuous educator does,
in the very front rank of modern teachers,—who
while strictly scientific have also a deep regard for
the noblest elements in religion,—this truly learned
man presents us with far more moderate views of
the general doctrine of evolution than we need ever
expect to find in the writings of materialistic evolu-
tionists like Haeckel on the one hand and conservative theologians on the other. The present attitude taken to Charles Darwin, as evidenced during
the celebration at Cambridge in 1909, shows that the
foolish idolatry which was at one time lavished on
that great biologist's writings by his fervid admirers, equally with the absurd denunciation of his
views poured forth by his vituperative opponents,
has practically died away, and given place to a much
fairer and milder estimate of the great scientist and
his remarkable discoveries. There was a time when

the theory of evolution was regarded with horror by the Church of England, and hailed with delight by professing atheists, who thought they found in it complete confirmation of their denial of Deity. But all such views have now been relegated to the limbo of forgetfulness, at least in scientific circles; though they still survive among the unthinking and the illiterate.   Darwin himself was never dogmatic, and he repeatedly warned the public against accepting as final theories which he put forth tentatively. He was, however, very positive in his declaration of ascertained facts, and he always contended that the only reasonable method of dealing with facts was to allow them to speak for themselves, regardless of any theories which might stand in the way of their impartial investigation.   Prof. Alfred Russel Wallace, who was quite independently a co-discoverer with Darwin of many important facts bearing directly on the theory of evolution is a confirmed Spiritualist, while Darwin was a confessed agnostic. This circumstance is quite sufficient to show that the theory of evolution, even when accepted in its entirety as it is by Wallace, does not by any means preclude a studious observer of natural phenomena from keeping a perfectly open mind with reference to evidences concerning other planes of existence than the physical; natural facts of a material character neither serving to confirm or deny the reality of a spiritual universe.   Sir Oliver Lodge is far less agnostic than Darwin and less spiritualistic than Wallace, his position being that of an earnest student of psychic phenomena whose general attitude to all things super-physical remains to an extent indefinite, *i. e.,* from the standpoint of those who consider nothing definite unless it be incontestably dogmatic. We may safely say that a truly scientific attitude of mind, being always open to evidence and constantly engaged in experimentation, must of necessity consider a great many questions as remaining always open; for if we are continually learning more and more of Nature's processes, we are compelled often to take and hold hypothetical positions on our way to ultimately certain conclusions; and even certainties are not finally final, for there is always something yet to be discovered which may throw fresh light upon questions we may now consider definitely settled. Though this position is very unsatisfactory to minds which long to rest in completed certainties, to the truly inquiring intellect this constant search for added knowledge constitutes life's chief delight, and it is certainly quite consistent with the ennobling thought that this world is a school in which we are being gradually educated to prepare us for higher seminaries when we have graduated from this particular college in the universe.

There are certain sublime statements expressed in noble poetry, such as Whittier's splendid couplet: "Step by step since time began We see the steady gain of man," which harmonize exactly with all reasonable views of evolution now entertained and promulgated by the world's leading intellects who are devoting themselves to ever-enlarging research into the mysteries of Nature. Such a title for a book as "Life and Matter," at once challenges attention, because it distinctly separates the idea of Life from the thought of Matter, thereby carrying us back to the earliest and most satisfying view of the unchanging relationship between the two.   Life is the acting power; Matter is the substance acted upon, and it is through Matter of some grade or other that life is made manifest.   Such in brief is the consensus of modern scientific as well as theosophical teachings.   Matter can be of many grades, or planes, therefore we are not left to restrict the use of the word to the gross matter of the physical aspects of our globe.   Once let this proposition be fully established and all difficulty vanishes when we are endeavoring to consider substantial worlds beyond as well as within the limit of our ordinary physical senses. Psychical Research, in which Sir Oliver Lodge has long taken very prominent part, has thoroughly convinced him, as it has also convinced many other prominent scientists, that telepathy, mental telegraphy, clairvoyance, and much else commonly regarded as mystical may be after all quite as natural and orderly as those more generally accepted uses of mental faculty with which the public at large has already become much more familiar.   We are constantly making fresh discoveries concerning our inner selves which are adding considerably to our self-knowledge.   We have looked upon ourselves for so long as confined within very narrow fields of action that we are naturally surprised, and to some extent bewildered, when we come to find out that no such limits need necessarily confine us.   Every fresh scientific discovery and mechanical invention compels us to set to work to readjust our views of human capacity, and by the time we have become thoroughly accustomed to the achievements of the

present day, we have admitted very much that our
not very remote ancestors would have considered
either incredible or supernatural.   The scientific
world does not attempt to draw any definite line
between natural and supernatural, because it humbly
confesses that it has by no means reached a perfect
knowledge of the natural; and until one has done
this, and knows that he has done it, it is self-
evidently absurd for him to talk about what lies
beyond nature.   The wise expression, "different
planes of nature," used frequently by Annie Besant
in her highly instructive book, "The Changing
World," suffices to convey the idea that our present
mental evolution is opening up before us some considerable knowledge of other grades of matter than
those acknowledged by old school materialists, who
in the face of all evidence in support of psychic experiences simply waived the whole question aside as
one pertaining to a mixture of humbug and halluci-
nation.   Sir Oliver Lodge speaks of "would-be
materialists," and of Haeckel's "conjectural philosophy," and he goes very far to prove that much has
been accepted in Germany and elsewhere as demonstrated science which actually rests on no firm scientific foundation.   In a chapter entitled "Monism"
he says: "Between science and philosophy there need
be no permanent barrier, nor need it be regarded as
otherwise than permissible for a man of science occasionally to look over into the philosophic region and
survey the territory on that side also, so far as his
means permit.   And if philosophers object to this
procedure it must be because they have found by
experience that men of science who have once trans-

cended or transgressed the boundary are apt to lose all sense of reasonable constraint and to disport themselves as if they had at length escaped into a region free from scientific trammels—a region where confident assertions might be freely made, where speculative hypothesis might rank as theory and where verification was both unnecessary and impossible."

Sir Oliver Lodge, after the above opening paragraphs, goes on to review Haeckel's views quite radically, and soon proceeds to prove the inconsistencies of that eminent German advocate of Scientific Monism, who now complains that many of his former colleagues have deserted him, and he in his advancing age is left as an almost solitary witness for a position which was extremely popular in the earlier days of the controversy pertaining to evolution. "The Riddle of the Universe," considered by many readers to be Haeckel's masterpiece, contains a vast amount of valuable as well as interesting matter, and on the question of the rights of animals this veteran takes ground almost identical with that occupied by the great bulk of professed Theosophists. It is only where he is negational that his views come sharply into collision with those of nature students, who, while fully appreciating the values and beauties of the external aspects of the universe, are at the same time keenly alive to the yet sublimer wonders and more expansive glories of regions undiscoverable by simply physical investigations. Life, according to Sir Oliver Lodge, is "a guiding and directing principle," and he very pertinently asks us to consider "whether guidance and intelligent direction are really possible, or whether everything proceeds according to some blind necessity from which will and purpose are altogether excluded." It is when discussing the difficult and intricate question of human free-agency that this ripe thinker contributes, in our judgment, a particularly valuable contribution to modern thought. On that vexed problem he says: "Life is something outside the scheme of mechanics—outside the categories of matter and energy; though it can nevertheless control or direct material forces—timing them and determining their place of application—subject always to the laws of energy and all other mechanical laws; supplementing or accompanying these laws, therefore, but contradicting or traversing them no whit."

From the foregoing we can readily trace an attitude of mind very similar to that of nearly all Theoosophists, whose particular contribution to philosophy is the stress laid by them on the incessant orderly activity of intelligent entities on other planes of Nature than the physical; it being asserted uncompromisingly that just as we on earth have limited and ever-increasing ability to direct exterior nature, but never except through the agency of unvarying law, so on the other side of the veil of sense, where clairvoyance may sometimes penetrate, intelligent entities more powerful, because wiser than we, are manipulating events precisely as we manipulate them, so far as necessary conformity with law is concerned, but in consequence of far greater acquaintanceship with law, manifesting ability to produce results very far transcending all we can yet accomplish.

# CHAPTER XXI.

## THE LAW OF SEVEN AND THE LAW OF UNITY.

In a curious old book of Arcane Teachings we find the sevenfold idea carried out with great wealth of detail, particularly as regards the Seven Cosmic Laws which regulate the Universe, at all events so far as humanity on earth has yet discovered them. These Seven Laws are enumerated in the following definite order:

1. Law of Orderly Trend, under the operation of which order is universally made manifest from the groupings of atoms in the formation of the minutest organism to the arrangement of planetary bodies in the constitution of gigantic Solar Systems.

2. Law of Analogy, through the operation of which we can trace a perfect agreement, or exact correspondence, between all forms of manifestation in whatsoever direction we may investigate. What is true of Matter is likewise true of Energy and Mind. The great Hermetic axiom, "As above, so below," is revealed through the changeless operation of this everywhere-to-be-discovered law. An ancient Arcane axiom, "Ex Uno disce Omnes" (By the discovery of one, learn thou of all) applies throughout esoteric or occult teaching to all those diverse but intimately inter-related plans of Nature

concerning which so much is written in the popular Theosophical literature of to-day.

3. Law of Sequence, in which is included all activities grouped under the general heading "Cause and Effect." This is the Karmic Law, the basis of Lex Talionis, or Law of Retaliation, which certainly does manifest itself throughout the Universe, despite the frantic endeavors of humanity to evade its operation. Nothing can occur by chance, there must be an efficient precedent for every consequent; nothing stands alone, therefore no act can be rightly looked upon as isolated.

4. Law of Rhythm, through the incessant working of which depends the variety manifested in the Cosmos. Everything is perpetually vibrating. To understand how to regulate vibration is to possess the Key to relatively unlimited power.

5. Law of Balance, by means of which is found the true explanation of equilibrium, or compensations. To understand the working of this Law is to know the secret of Power and Poise.

6. Law of Cyclicity, which causes all things to move in Circles. Teachers of Arcane Science tell us that the wise and strong convert circles into spirals. and therefore instead of moving continually round and round, they rise in spirals, thus accomplishing those wonderful achievements which mark off Adepts or Initiates from the multitude of their contemporaries.

7. Law of Opposites, which is universally expressed in male and female, thesis and antithesis. In the knowledge of this law is to be found the great magical secret of regeneration which is essen-

tially identical with transmutation and transubstantiation. The practical object and boundless result of understanding and applying these Seven Laws (or to speak still more accurately, seven manifestations of One Law) is to enable those who have attained this Knowledge to accomplish *Magnum Opus* through the joint activity of the will and intellect of the operator. Herein lies the Key to an actual demonstration of those transcendent abilities which are so largely claimed by many modern teachers who, though their theories are sound and excellent, do not as a rule succeed in making any very startling demonstrations of unusual power over environment.

The four following aphorisms are worthy of the deepest consideration:

1. The One Law *is*.
2. There is naught higher or elder than the One Law.
3. The One Law is Absolute, beyond Time, Space and Change, transcending the Three Principles and Seven Laws.
4. The One Law is the Efficient Reason of All-Things.

To consider these four aphorisms deeply and in detail would necessitate very profound study and the expenditure of much time and mental energy, but any student who will devote time and solitude to such deep and profitable meditation will surely be amply repaid both as regards mental illumination and increased ability to govern circumstances. The doctrine of Determinism taught in Arcane Philosophy is quite at variance with Fatalism, Pessimism and all other abnormal and corrupted systems which have owed their origin to garbled and distorted views concerning the operation of the changeless order of the Universe. No special event is divinely predetermined, foreordained, or predestined, but there is a sequence of causes and effects which no human power can vary. It is our reliance upon this very steadfastness of Nature which renders scientific progress possible, for without reasonable certainty that we shall reap according to our sowing there could be no rational engagement in any branch of enterprise.

Among the strikingly unique expressions employed by teachers of Arcane Philosophy, we find not the familiar *Ex Nihilo nihil fit* (out of nothing is made nothing) but *Ex Nihilo Omnis fit* (out of No-Thing all things are formed). This No-Thing of the Alchemists signifies original Cosmic Substance, unparticled, undifferentiated, from which all expressed objects proceed and into which they will at some time and in some way return. Such archaic teachings as these, coming from the wise instructors of our race in times of old, harmonize at every point with all those marvelous and fascinating scientific revelations which characterize the vigorous enterprise of the present (twentieth) century. What, we may well ask, is meant by Matter when modern scientists declare that, to the best of their knowledge, it is but a combination of *ions* or *electrons?* What, again, we may enquire has become of the stupid old materialism which was more difficult to grasp than even the wildest theological fantasies, if mind and life are traceable in all discovered substances from protoplasm to the human frame? Substance,

Motion, Consciousness, are the three Principles we encounter everywhere.  We are living not in a dead but in a living, not in an unconscious but in a conscious universe in which death is only change of expression and birth but assumption of some new garment.

As we are properly far more intensely interested in our human development and in the exercise of dominion over our environment than in any abstruse or abstract dissertations concerning the constitution of the Universe, we only follow the path of wisdom when our studies of the profound Mystery of Universal Law lead us to apply the truths we intellectually grasp to the constant betterment of our actual conditions.

For many centuries in India mighty philosophic concepts have been tacitly admitted by multitudes who have altogether failed to make practical application of the philosophy contained in Upanishats, Bhagavat-Gita, and other holy treatises venerated, often superstitiously, but seldom made use of in the only way which leads to the elevation of a nation. Western "hustle" together with Eastern *laissez faire* make an excellent combination, but one without the other is so unbalanced that it must inevitably lead to stolid resignation to a supposed inevitable or else to frantic hysterical endeavors to force results without regard to the orderly working of evolutionary development.

# CHAPTER XXII

## SPIRITUALISM AND THE DEEPENING OF SPIRITUAL LIFE.

This great topic immediaely invites two important questions: First, what are we to understand by Spiritualism? Second, what is meant by the deepening of our spiritual life?

In reply to the first inquiry it seems safe to say that the irreducible minimum of agreement among Spiritualists is the simple declaration that we are here and now spiritual entities, and being such survive the change commonly called death. Though this direct and widely inclusive statement is common to all who call themselves Spiritualists, it by no means covers the entire ground of spiritual philosophy. It is, indeed, little more than an introduction to it, for Spiritualism is so immensely wide in its ever-extending ramifications that there is scarcely a topic engaging human attention which does not come legitimately within the embrace of its implications.

There can be but three systems of philosophy appealing to thinkers: Spiritualism, Materialism, and Agnosticism. Materialism is practically dead in scientific circles; the ground is, therefore, virtually left to Spiritualists and Agnostics, who are now pretty evenly dividing intellectual territory.   Of these two philosophical systems, one (Spiritualism) is decidedly affirmative, the other (Agnosticism) avowedly indefinite; and because of the incontrovertible fact that all human knowledge is only relative, there must always remain some place for a confession of ignorance on some questions, together with a most positive enunciation of knowledge concerning other matters.   No intelligent man or woman can be exclusively either gnostic or agnostic, but there are many thoughtful persons whose intellectual position is one of wise caution, who do not hesitate to avow their positive conviction that the fundamental propositions of Spiritualism are fully demonstrable.

By reason of the exceeding wideness of the ground which must be traversed, many eminent men of science, including Sir William Crookes, are indisposed to speak as fervently on the side of pronounced Spiritualism as the no less famous Dr. Alfred Russel Wallace, a circumstance which may be jointly attributed to varying degrees of first-hand evidence and to difference in natural mental predilection in the case of these equally distinguished scientists.   We should always keep before us, in every discussion, the important fact that phenomena appealing strongly in the most favorable manner to one type of mind may prove actually distasteful to another type; this alone suffices to account for those diametrically opposed statements which we constantly encounter over illustrious signatures.   To some people the thought of physical manifestations, ranging from "raps" to "materializations," is far from accep-

table.   They have no hope or desire that such phenomena may genuinely occur, while to many others,
equally intelligent, these manifestations carry definite convictions and are sources of considerable comfort and joy.   Unless we can approach so great a
subject as Spiritualism without prejudice or predilection of any sort, we are apt to be unwittingly
unjust at some point in our investigations.   Only
the thoroughly fair-minded, be they statesmen, scientists, clergymen or conjurors, are really competent
to so investigate as to reach conclusions which will
prove of genuine importance.   Probably for this
very reason much controversy is still raging, practically all over the world, concerning the use and value
of Spiritualism, granted that its basic claims be reasonably established.

Our present theme necessitates an excursion into
moral fields, into distinctively ethical as well as intellectual pasture-ground, for to "deepen spiritual life"
must certainly mean vastly more than to convince
the intellect of the survival of the human individual
beyond physical dissolution.   The first momentous
question to be raised concerning any philosophy that
we are invited to investigate is, What does it teach
concerning human nature?   As we are all human
beings, that is the chief fundamental question of
importance.   As a candidate for general acceptance
among philanthropists, Spiritualism has always this
to commend it, that it elevates the idea of human life
far beyond the level of materialistic negation, and
it also disowns those mistaken views of religion
which teach the depravity rather than the nobility
of the root-nature common to us all.   As "psychical

research" continues, it is constantly bringing to light
more and more evidence of the amazing greatness of
the life we are living now and here, and so great
has been the recent addition to the sum of our
knowledge of psychology that the "subjective mind,"
or "sub-self," is responsible for many psychic marvels which before the days of Thomson Jay Hudson and his successors were compactly attributed
to the action of our "departed" friends.   Such a
statement, though possessed of some superficial plau-
sibility, is by no means either radical or rational
when sifted to its foundations or carried forward to
its ultimates, for instead of added knowledge concerning our own nature in the present world destroying the thought of spiritual communion, every addi-
tional discovery in the realm of telepathic and kindred action only goes to prove how spiritual intercourse is actually effected between living entities as
at present situated.   We are discovering and applying certain hitherto unknown possibilities resident
within us.   We find we are able to send and receive
mental telegrams, cablegrams, and aerograms, seemingly without respect to physical distance, but always
in accord with some mysterious law which we as yet
but very imperfectly comprehend; all of which goes
far to prove that we are functioning as spiritual
beings at the present time, and that our external bodies are far less of us than we have generally been
disposed to believe.

All this ever-extending knowledge of our interior
being is rapidly sweeping away those old-time objections to Spiritualism which were based on extremely
limited and almost entirely materialistic views of

human nature.　But this widening view of our common nature does not only afford us a larger idea of our capabilities, scientifically speaking; it gives us boundless reason for insisting with ever-increasing, confident earnestness upon the goodness of our nature, for this wonderful "sub-consciousness," about which so much is being written and said, is by no means diabolical but rather celestial in its inherent tendencies, when these are rescued from the clutch of excrescent attachments, which often veil, though they cannot destroy, the essential entity or ego.　"Subjective," "sub-conscious" and "subliminal" are, as we all know, three words greatly in evidence in contemporary literature, and though they are certainly inadequate to account for all that many of their most frequent users seek to explain by means of them, they can well serve a definite, even though it be a distinctly limited, purpose.　The prefix "sub" is so often used in two opposite ways that it is not always clear in what sense it is employed by a particular author unless we are familiar with his distinctive employment of the term.

F. W. H. Myers, in his very valuable treatise on "Human Personality, Its Survival of Bodily Death," compares us to trees whose rots are hidden while their trunks and branches are revealed.　If such be a fair analogy, then what lies behind the mortal screen is "subjective" not in the sense of *inferior* but *interior*.　Hudson, in all his writings, consistently used the phrase "subjective mind" in precisely that connection, though he appears to have frequently obscured some of his meanings by persistently employing a single phrase to cover ground

which Mrs. Besant covers by using two definite
titles. Among Theosophists in general, "super-con-
sciousness" is the term employed to convey the idea
of higher planes of Nature, "sub-consciousness" being reserved to describe what is actually, morally and
spiritually speaking, below the level of our present
human elevation. Be this as it may, for we have
no wish to wrangle over phrases, it is clear that the
"Emanuelists" and other useful workers in the
ample field of psycho-therapy appeal with great confidence to what they feel to be some inner plane of
consciousness which often readily responds to benevolent suggestion, and the whole structure of much
mental treatment which is highly useful reposes on
a foundation of faith in the willingness as well as
ability of our inner selves to respond to healthy suggestions. Spiritualists who cling to an old-fashioned
terminology often dispute with students of similar
phenomena who speak another language; it is therefore highly desirable that honest inquirers should
get together and compare notes diligently with a
view to reaching some clear conclusion which may
be mutually comprehensible.

We should all spurn the idea as absurd should
anyone tell us that, because we have certain powers
of our own and do much work individually, therefore we never act in concert with our neighbors;
but such a statement, ridiculous as it must appear,
is not necessarily less logical than the contention
that there is no communion with our friends in
spirit who have "crossed the border" because we
have demonstrated mental telegraphy and telephony
and frequently enjoy inter-communion in psychic

ways while still continuing incarnate. Every fact has a value of its own, and the only rational way of dealing with facts is to compare them one with another with a view to arriving at some lucid synthesis. Spiritualism can reasonably be said to include very much more than a simple establishment of the rudimentary doctrine of survival of bodily death, and this the accumulated history of the past, since 1848, abundantly demonstrates. Spiritualism is the pioneer among all modern cults. The Theosophical Society was founded in 1875, and the Christian Science and many other movements, in their present organized form, are even younger.

If Spiritualists resolve to do the great work which they are well capable of performing to-day, as in years gone by, both in their organised and unorganised capacities, they should especially endeavor to unify the many diverging, but not properly contradictory, schools of thought at present striving for supremacy. There can be no true spiritual life where there is dissension and disunion. Unity, but not uniformity, is ever essential to co-operative activity, and only as co-operators can we live a truly spiritual life. Intellectual differences being clearly unavoidable, we must look for a basis of agreement upon a plane deeper than the intellect, and that plane is the seat of truly philanthropic sentiment. Too often in all our researches into the mysteries of the universe we seem to be actuated solely by a desire to *get,* not *give,* and it is on account of this selfish tendency that we often obtain so very little of permanent value among the floods of messages which reach us through the gateway of mediumship, even

though many communications are received which
from the simply evidential standpoint are truly of
great significance.    There are distinct standpoints
from which to judge all alleged communications,
viz., the scientific and the ethical.    From the scientific viewpoint, as Dr. J. H. Hyslop and other well-
known authors and experimenters frequently declare, the more trivial the message (in some respects) the greater its convincingness, while from
the ethical side a totally different standard of judgment must be considered.    At first we are all naturally curious to know if any psychic phenomena can
be proved indubitably genuine; our interest is cen-
tred entirely in the fact of simple evidence, but after
we have fully established certain rudimentary conclusions, if we are actuated to any appreciable extent by benevolent motives, we desire to do positive
good with our Spiritualism, instead of enjoying
spirit communion simply as a private luxury or an
intellectual entertainment.    Wireless telegraphy had
to be demonstrated before Marconi's famous system
could gain the credence of the commercial world,
but now that it is no longer the startling sensation
it was some years ago, people are wisely endeavoring to make such real use of it that accidents at sea
may be avoided, and in case of danger, relief may
be quickly afforded to all in jeopardy.    We may well
rest satisfied with the thought that on unseen planes
of Nature there exist all sorts and conditions of
entities with whom we can and do commune far
more readily and frequently than we are usually inclined to believe, and it is scarcely going too far to
say that no claim is too extravagant to be within the

scope of possibility where such communion is concerned.

We are accustomed to speak glibly of "supernal"
and "infernal" influences without realizing sufficiently that those entities who are commonly called
"angels" on the one hand and "devils" on the other
are only ordinary human beings, in the one case
*higher* and in the other instance *lower* in development than our immediate selves.   Masters, adepts,
initiates, guardian angels, etc., are only titles given
to human spirits further advanced in power and
knowledge than we are at present.   The fact that
we conceive of them and appear to comprehend their
attributes is excellent proof that we contain all
they express; the only real difference between their
condition and ours consisting in the fact that they
have actually developed many faculties which are
at present dormant in ourselves.   These higher intelligences are commonly called "elder brethren"
by Theosophists, and that is an excellent expression
on account of the clearness with which it suggests
their relation to us and ours to them.   Nothing can
be more self-evident than that we are all substantially well agreed as to what are celestial attributes.
No one takes exception to the words attributed to
the great Master of Christendom: "I am among you
as one that serveth," and "he who would be greatest among you, let him be a minister to all."   The
law of ministration is always strongly emphasized
by spiritually-minded thinkers, and we are actually
getting used to the daring statement made by many
"New Thought" advocates that "God is servant to
man," which is only the other side of a deep, vital

truth expressed familiarly in the time-honored phrase, "We are all servants of God." Great propositions must be turned upside down and inside out before we can intelligently estimate their comprehensiveness. It has often occurred that some single aspect of the advantages of spiritual inter-communion has been studied and valued out of all due proportion to others, and that aspect has often been the one which has appealed to the self-seeking rather than to the neighbor-blessing tendencies of our indubitably complex human character. We wish others to serve us, but we are not as a rule so ready to serve as to be served. We are all ready enough to sing with feeling, "Angels ever bright and fair, take, oh, take me to your care," but we are not, as a rule, quite so ready to pray that we may officiate as angels taking others to our care. It is this aspect which must be brought prominently forward if we are truly in earnest concerning the deepening of our spiritual life, or, in other words, developing real practical spirituality.

We know well enough that there are many good definitions of the great word spirit, but the simplest and most obvious of them all, *breath,* from the Latin *spiritus,* must by no means be ignored. We are often reminded that we have reduced a Latin word of eight letters to an English word of six, and then have forgotten (apparently) the source whence our abbreviated term has been derived. This error is being rapidly corrected by the vast amount of attention now given to breathing exercises of all descriptions, from the simplest to the most complicated, but here again we are con-

fronted with the same old question: Why are we
practising Yoga or anything therewith connected?
The breath of life is the original definition of
spirit, and to breathe rhythmically is essential, alike
to mental and bodily vigor.   Health is now happily
being re-defined as wholeness, therefore religion and
science, long divorced, are now being re-married
with excellent prospects for producing living and
abiding offspring, who will not prove unmindful of
sanitary law as applied to all phases of existence.   A
book of great value, "Religion and Medicine," the
joint product of two distinguished clergymen and a
famous physician of Boston, U. S. A., embodies
many of the latest and most popular teachings of
the Church and the medical profession, when the
two combine to wage a war of extirpation upon all
phases of disease, physical, mental, moral and spiritual, through the benign agency of well-directed
thought, inspired by righteous love, and sustained
by reasonable faith in the essential goodness of our
common human nature.   Rev. Elwood Worcester,
D. D., and Rev. Samuel McComb, D. D., are attached as co-rectors to the now famous Emanuel
Church in Boston, which gave name to the much
discussed Emanuel movement.   Dr. Isidor Coriat is
a physician of distinct eminence.   These three
learned gentlemen have produced between them a
singularly valuable volume, in which ancient and
modern thought and practice are placed side by
side in such a manner as powerfully to suggest the
vital thought of constant Divine immanence and
the permanent certainty of good accomplished, regardless of time and country, if we but place our-

selves in receptive attitude toward beneficent spiritual influx: precisely as, on the physical plane, we
may enjoy fresh air and brilliant sunshine if we
only arrange and open our windows and ventilators
in a scientific manner so as to avail ourselves freely
of the copious natural blessings which are incessantly
at the disposal of rich and poor alike.   It is often
urged by opponents of the "Emanuel" and similar
movements, that the Church of to-day is placing
altogether too much stress upon physical healing and
mundane affairs in general.   A complaint is made,
in ecclesiastical and lay journals alike, that our religion is properly a "spiritual" affair, and therefore
cannot concern itself in any direct way with either
the cure of bodily distempers or making provision
for physical necessities; the good clergymen and
others who are engaging in much excellent, seemingly secular, work, are roundly berated in many
quarters for stepping aside from their proper field
of "spiritual" activities and devoting themselves to
matters of less moment and far lower interest than
the "soul-saving" occupation in which their fanatical critics consider they should be exclusively engaged.   Much the same cry is not infrequently
raised in Spiritualistic societies by people who believe in a kind of narrow Spiritualism, which deals
exclusively with matters pertaining to what is termed
conventionally "the future life" and "the other
world."   Now, our ideal of spirituality, and it
certainly accords completely with Greek philosophy
and primitive Christian doctrine and practice, is
that spirit pervades matter, that the external world
is ensouled by spirit which interpenetrates every

seemingly solid substance, verily occupying the interstices between the electrons into which the atoms of matter are now scientifically broken up. If the newest scientific theory of matter is entitled to serious attention, then we must soon arrive at something like a revival of the ancient alchemical concept of a single primary substance, and we may well remember that the phrase "one element" is found in the poetry of Tennyson as well as in the magical treatises of mystic philosophers and occult scientists to whose long-dishonored discoveries and declarations the learned world of to-day is beginning to render serious attention.

Where is that "spirit world" about which we hear so much; where are those "seven spheres" or where can we locate any "heaven," "paradise," or "purgatory" about which theologians speak so glibly? Omar Khayyam, in his world-famous "Rubaiyat," has answered these questions in a few vivid sentences of fervid verse more fully than they have been dealt with in many a bulky tome of labored philosophy or scholastic theology. A deep student of Sufism (Dr. Norton Hazeldine, now of Los Angeles, Cal.), after having spent many years in Persia and other Eastern lands, has in a singularly beautiful version of the esoteric aspect of the "Rubaiyat," given us the following translation of a portion of the sixty-seventh quatrain:

"Hear ye then this simple, yet most ancient of the truths, how man can gain knowledge of life beyond the tomb. Control thyself, and with thy senses send thy soul into its elements there to wring out

the secret of its Birth and End.   The gentle voice
of the silence whispers soft and low and bids me
write the answer here below: I myself am Heaven,
I myself am Hell. I am the Cause Creative, I am
the Way, the End."

It must always be remembered that the personal
pronoun is used here precisely as Emerson in his
famous saying,

> "I am owner of the sphere,
> Of the seven stars and the solar year,"

has employed it; no private ownership, nothing but
universal participation in public reality is intended
in each instance.

This brings us to our most vital point of all—
the possibility of enjoying an inward life of rest
and peace regardless of how fiercely the tempest
may prevail about us.   Natural analogies are always ready to hand to illustrate this greatest and
sweetest of all important truths—the complete beneficence of all life's varied experiences when, as Sir
Edwin Arnold has phrased it, while treating of
the faith of Islam, they are "viewed from Allah's
throne above."   It seems unthinkable that any reasoning Spiritualist should entertain a pessimistic
or even a semi-pessimistic view of the universe, but
it certainly appears that many people never allow
themselves to carry their own philosophy to its logical final result.   Irrespective of our religious, philosophical, or other ideas and opinions, we are all
compelled to admit that our external life, regard it

as we may, is at least for many of us filled with tragedies. To shut our eyes to manifest phenomena is childish if not absurd, but because we allow that facts occur we are in no way obliged to interpret them pessimistically.

A truly spiritual view of life must ever be one which takes no very great amount of any outward gain or loss when such is contrasted with inward pain and pleasure. In spite of all false utterances to the contrary, the words remain true through all succeeding ages that "a man's life consisteth not in the multitude of the things which he possesseth." It is sometimes irrationally claimed by certain Socialists and others that to fix our thoughts upon a life beyond the present is to encourage the rich in their oppression of the poor, and at the same time to counsel underfed and overworked multitudes to be content with their lot in this world, because everything will be straightened out equitably in some life to come. Needless to say, there is some shallow ground on which such an assertion can be made to stand, but to claim that there is any necessary or logical relation between faith in spiritual realities and encouragement of inequitable social conditions is actually ridiculous. Probably no people in England or elsewhere to-day are exerting themselves more vigorously and tirelessly for the betterment of all social conditions than those whose particular brand of religious conviction is designated New Theology, but the Rev. R. J. Campbell and his associates and sympathizers are in the front rank of those interested in proving the reality of a spiritual life continuous beyond earthly dissolu-

tion.  What is to many a new point of view must
now be taken, and Spiritualists should be among the
first to emphasise the *hereness* and *nowness* of the
spiritual life and its omnipresent activities.  Clairvoyance, clairaudience, clairsentience and all other
extensions of normal faculty simply suggest, in the
most obvious manner, that our universally admitted
five senses, regardless of any greater number which
we may latently possess, are by no means confinable
within any determinable boundaries.  We see, hear,
taste, touch, smell, but how far do these five words
convey ideas to us respectively?  Clear sight, hearing and feeling can only mean more than the average; thus for convenience sake we often repudiate
the old word supernatural and take refuge in *super-
normal.*

But, again, let us inquire what is meant by normal, seeing that we have no fixable standard by
which to determine the limits of normality.  At
least we all agree that our normal is someone's su-
pernormal and may be someone else's subnormal.
In an art gallery, adorned with hundreds of exquisite paintings, we cannot determine for each
other any criterion of judgment except to a very
limited extent, for sight, as well as artistic appre-
ciativeness, differs so widely among us that we can
only speak positively regarding the impression a
certain picture makes on us individually.  On the
walls are noble portraits finely executed, each displaying the features of some distinguished man or
woman who has achieved something noteworthy.
Turning, then, from portraits of individuals, our
gaze rests upon landscapes and seascapes, upon

peaceful valleys and populous marts of trade; again we are invited to contemplate some single flower or a cluster of charming blossoms, and now a bird and then an animal is presented to our view. What is the mission of all this art; why are there painters, and why do we prize and exhibit paintings? Surely we must see in all this display of talent and beauty something far beyond the mere gratification of some æsthetic fancy, or our Art Schools and their students are reduced to the most insignificant caterers to an ephemeral taste for the externally attractive. If, however, as Ruskin taught, art is to be cultivated not for its own but for humanity's sake, we can see in the true artist a conscientious worker in the field of spiritual elevation and reform, for as art is always an avenue through which the populace is ready to be reached, the painter and sculptor must take their places among ministers of a sublime and everlasting gospel, bringing the glad tidings of spiritual reality to a world pressed down to the lowest depths ofttimes by a crushing sense of the unreality of all that it has hugged most affectionately to its bosom. Through a picture or a statue a lesson can be quietly, effectively, and permanently conveyed to multitudes as in no other way. When Mrs. Besant visited Chicago in the autumn of 1907, she greatly impressed the citizens of that vast cosmopolis by calling their attention to the fine work done by many painters whose works were conspicuously exhibited, and at the same time making a strenuous plea for a generally higher range of subjects than those ordinarily selected. Here is a broad suggestion for the popularizing of much that is best in Spiritualism.   Artists who are inspirational and deeply imbued with a keen sense of the possible sublimity of their vocation, have a practically boundless prairie in which to range when determined to consecrate their gifts of conception and expression to the embodying of high ideals on canvas or in bronze or marble.

We none of us dwell sufficiently on the uses of good objects of art in our homes, schools, and public thoroughfares.   The fact that much has been done already, and with excellent results, is only an evidence of how more can yet be accomplished and with still greater righteous consequences if we but embrace our golden opportunities.   Music in one sense is even more effectual than the still arts in arousing emotion and lifting thought above external sordidness; but with all its power and charm, the very nature of music being volatile prevents its occupying the special place which the other arts must occupy.   In a spiritual temple, be it a spacious palace or a humble attic in a modest dwelling house, the fabric should always be able to do a work by itself silently and suggestively, quite without reference to any stated exercises carried on within its walls.   A very good tendency among many Spiritualists to-day is to secure homes for spiritual work, the atmosphere of which can easily be rendered distinctive and uplifting in highly pronounced degree, and to accomplish this excellent end fully we should introduce all possible accessories of a beautiful and useful nature.   But there is always one aspect of spiritual philosophy brighter, wider, and more richly consoling than all the rest, and that is the great

theme of experiences gainable in sleep and trance;
and let us remember that on this point Spiritualists
and Theosophists have a wide and comprehensive
meeting ground.  Only comparatively rarely do we
get definite information of the spirit-world or
"astral plane" while we are awake; this is because
we are so very much engrossed with external interests and business that it is only seldom that we
can bestow serious thought on anything outside our
immediate secular engagements.  But during sleep
our condition is entirely reversed, for no sooner
do we enter the sleeping condition than we turn
our backs upon the outer and our faces toward the
inner world.  During eight hours out of every
twenty-four many people rest completely from all
external cares and responsibilities, and thereby obtain not only complete refreshment but spiritual
equipment for the varied work which daily lies before them.  Just as a well-spent day earns a peaceful night, so does a well-spent night prepare us for
a happy, useful day.  Education while asleep, or in
a state of trance, is one of the most important
and fascinating topics in which Spiritualists can
become vitally interested, and, as a conclusion to our
present essay, we wish to offer a few practical
hints for consciously enlarging the beneficial scope
of our nocturnal inspiration.  After retiring, while
yet awake, it is a very good practice to concentrate
attention thoroughly upon some subject or place
with which, or individual with whom, we would like
to be specially related during slumber or entrance-
ment.  Before going to sleep it is well to resolve
to wake slowly and suggest to yourself, while pass-

ing into the sleeping condition, that you will carry
across the border with you some well-defined remembrance of how and where you have spent your
night.   Very often we gain by that process much
information of great importance, helpful in a large
variety of ways, and most of all do we become
increasingly conscious of the blessed fact that night
by night we can work and dwell among our "departed" loved ones, as day by day we minister and
travel among our still incarnate friends.   With pure
resolve to gather useful knowledge on the psychic
plane and employ it for beneficial ends we can safely
practise an exercise which develops, in an orderly
manner, a faculty of our inner nature and enables
us to answer in a definite affirmative the ever-press-
ing query, "If we appear to die do we yet continue
to live?"

WE ARE HERE AND NOW LIVING IN INFINITY AND
ETERNITY.

When this mighty truth is clearly realized there
is no longer for us any "this" or "other" world.
for we have grown to perceive that boundary lines
of space and time relate only to those exterior
planes of consciousness which it is ever the distinctive province of spiritual discernment immeasurably
to transcend.

# CHAPTER XXIII.

## THE ESOTERIC TEACHINGS OF THE GNOSTICS—THE DIVINE FEMININE.

No more fascinating doctrine than that of Gnos-. ticism can possibly engage our interest, and especially now that the position properly assignable to Woman is one of the burning issues of the times. According to Frances Swiney, who has written a wonderful book treating upon this topic, among true Gnostics, Woman is higher than Man, as *Sophia*, the Divine Feminine, is the central object of Gnostic adoration. In a perfectly synthesized system of thought and practise, we feel well assured that neither sex will be in the ascendancy over the other, but as we have seen so much of ill resulting from masculine despotism and monopoly, Mrs. Swiney's other-extreme doctrine deserves earnest thought and careful consideration, and though at first it may strike the average reader as preposterous, there are a good many sane arguments to be brought forward in support of the main body of it. Gnostics have seen the feminine aspect of Deity rather than the masculine, so they have apotheosized women and relegated men to an inferior rank. Perfect sexual equality everywhere acknowledged is our own forecast for the coming age and the coming race; but we can hardly expect that so thoroughly ideal a condition can be ushered in until many children have been born into mental as well as physical surroundings very far superior in all respects to those which now almost universally obtain, and it can only be through the direct agency of emancipated and consecrated motherhood that a new and higher race can be brought into existence. There is a veritable "mystery of godliness" in the Gnostic philosophy now being brought before the public gaze, but there is also a very important "open teaching" concerning the relation of the sexes which is never properly concealed, as it is of the utmost importance to race improvement that it be publicly disseminated. With the breaking up of old ideas and institutions, now everywhere proceeding, preparatory to the installation of a new order, it is not surprising to find a vast amount of religious, social, and industrial unrest. This is far from being a discouraging symptom or a sign of racial decay; it is, to all who can read the signs of the present day aright, a convincing proof that we are on the immediate verge of a new era, in which we may reasonably expect to behold a condition of humanity far superior to that now extant.

The early Christians were many of them Gnostics, and there are numerous unmistakable traces of pronounced Gnostic teaching in many of the Epistles attributed to St. Paul. This fact makes it very easy for Mystics to remain within the Catholic Church while they hold views entirely at variance with the common outer doctrine promulgated in parish churches and accepted as the all-in-all of

Christianity by the great bulk of priests as well as laity. Dr. Anna Kingsford, author of that very popular treatise, "The Perfect Way, or the Finding of Christ," did not consider her own position in the least degree inconsistent, for she held that there is a "church within a church," which is often referred to in the columns of "The Occult Review" as "The Church of the Holy Grail." St. George Mivart, Father Tyrrell, and many other distinguished scholars of recent date, have stirred up much controversy by their "Modernism," which is not very far removed from Gnosticism in many of its most decided features.

The Gnostic will never be satisfied with literalism, to her, or for him, the inner life or quickening spirit is all that is of real moment. Historical events or episodes sink into insignificance when contrasted with a consideration of the operation of the Divine Spirit within humanity in the living present. Historical discussions are never attractive to the Gnostic or to the Mystic, any further than they may prove useful in showing the perpetual continuity of esoteric doctrine and in illustrating, by famous examples, the place of honor which Gnostic teaching has ever held among the most enlightened and enlightening teachers of the human race. From the Preface to Mrs. Swiney's highly artistic and wonderfully illustrated volume we extract the following: "There have always been minds that have grasped, in some measure, the eternal verities; they have, as it were, caught a transient vision of the whole in all its glory and divinity, and have been surcharged with the Wisdom of the Highest. But the majority of the race have lagged far behind; the general development of the spiritual consciousness in mankind being as gradual as has been the organic evolution.  And thus religious beliefs mark the state of consciousness to which human psychology has attained.  We now smile at the coats of skin and too solid flesh with which primitive man in his grossness clothed the most sublime ideals of his race.  But, even allowing that the transcendent reality was soon submerged under the materialised form through whose medium it was presented to the world, the Divine intuition, like a golden thread of truth, glistens through all the various faiths. Interwoven, in spite of man's incertitude, with the objective manifestations and symbolism was the subjective indivisible entity of everlasting Wisdom. Forms of belief are but the transitory phases of the Soul in its upward path from consciousness to consciousness, from truth to truth, from revelation to revelation, from glory to glory, until it attains the Light of Lights.

"But mankind is loth to recognize the ephemeral character of the distinctive creeds that smother the intrinsic verity under external ceremonial, ritual, dogma, theories, codes, canons, conventions, precedents and definitions, until the outward shell imprisons the living truth in an atrophied contraction. We forget that these evolutionary expositions of faith are but resting-places for the human soul in its sore travail for self-completion, as it emerges from the material depths.  Instead of being rockbound sepulchres, in which we bury our Christs, or marble fanes, crumbling before the onslaught of time, they are only tents that are struck in the dawning, when yet another night of darkness has passed away of the ignorance, fatuity, and misery of humanity.

"We toil during the night, as did the disciples on the Galilean Sea. We behold but the unfathomable blackness of the waters, and the inscrutable vault of the midnight sky. Around us lie obscurity, mystery, and the dreaded Unknown. Yet, when the morn breaks, comes also the sublime revelation. For encircling us are the everlasting hills, and the Christos awaits us on the shore—the shore of a sunlit sea."

Gnosticism and Occultism are very near neighbors and close friends, if they are not identical; therefore we are likely at any time to find these terms used interchangeably. True Occultism is a system which seeks to penetrate below all surfaces and discover what has long been enshrined in seemingly impenetrable mystery. The fixed ceremonies of Ecclesiastic and Masonic bodies can serve a useful purpose by preserving an unbroken tradition. Ceremonies are like letters in words, and words in languages, but letters and words are alike useless and cumbersome unless we employ them wisely for the conveyance of living thought from mind to mind and locality to locality.

According to a Gnostic view of religious tenets, the word tenet is directly associated with tent, a temporary abiding or halting-place, and also a movable dwelling which can be easily folded and carried from place to place, as permanent houses certainly cannot be. There are, however, Gnostic temples as well as tents, but these stand for immovable principles, the same in every clime and age, not for special interpretations placed upon facts at different epochs in human evolution, and by men who though high ecclesiastical dignitaries were often far more carnal than spiritual.

Mead, in his "Fragments of a Faith Forgotten," tells us that during the first century of the present era the Gnostics at Alexandria endeavored to discover a truly universal religion, or to formulate a theosophy which would satisfy all minds; but the new race then springing up was found to be composed of such heterogeneous material that the task was too great for their accomplishment. The Western intellect has never seemed equal to the task of grasping the subtle metaphysics or the abstract reasoning of the Oriental mind, and it has been largely on this account that esoteric verities have been so grossly carnalized in accepted Christian definitions. Much of this carnalizing has proved so repulsive to spiritually-minded people that they have turned away entirely from the church and its sacraments, until they have been shown some inner meaning by some outside teacher who has possessed the necessary insight into the origin and inner meaning of the mysteries, enabling them to disentangle this from the crude materialism in which it has lain long concealed.

In the light of Gnostic interpretation, the characters in the Gospel narratives stand out clearly and instructively as permanent human types, not simply as historical personages who lived once for all at a given time in a certain place. But it is not by any means chiefly on that account that the Gnostic clue

to the New Testament is needed, but by reason of
the profound verities veiled in the doctrine of the
Trinity and other arcane mysteries that we most
need this elucidation.   In the popular notion of the
Divine Trinity, there are three Persons but only
one God.   This is said to be a mystery too deep
for the human intellect to probe; therefore, outside
the Athanasian Creed we find no ambitious attempts to define the concept.   But we cannot afford
to remain silent as to the pernicious influence exerted throughout Christendom by the prevalent idea
that the three Divine Persons are exclusively male.
Much older, purer, and far more natural ideas of
a Trinity are to be found among the records of
ancient Egypt, where Osiris, Isis, and Horus were
regarded as Father, Mother, and Offspring.   Some
aspects of Horus are male and others female; showing that the highest and purest religious concepts
of the Egyptians gave to the feminine a place of
honor equal with the masculine in all things.   People cannot entertain an exclusively masculine idea
of Deity and at the same time believe that motherhood is as divine as fatherhood.   The degradation
of woman is always supported most strongly where
the belief is pregnant that only males are fit to
officiate at sacred altars.   Mohammedanism has kept
women in much greater servitude than Christianity,
because it has never tolerated the idea of a Queen
as well as a King of Heaven, an idea which the
Church of Rome has always fostered, thereby
largely counteracting the baneful effect of suppress-
ing the vision of the Divine Mother standing between the Father and the Child.

Judaism has never tolerated pictorial representations of the Divine One, for to the pious Israelite
any attempted picturing of Deity would be regarded
as a flagrant violation of the Decalogue; but in many
Christian churches, and in illustrated Bibles, we
see attempts to portray the Holy Trinity, and always by three figures—one of an elderly man, one
of a younger man, and one of a dove.   Now the
dove hides the face of the Divine Mother, and is
her emblem.   Were the representation to be restored to its original form, it would be far better
than it is now, and when thus restored it could be
readily interpreted to mean simply three distinct
manifestations of Deity accommodated to human
necessity, while, as H. P. Blavatsky suggested after
gazing upon Gustave Doré's famous painting, the
silence of the formless mystery in the background
symbolled the Ineffable One far more than the three
limited figures in the foreground.

If we must have representations of human conceptions of Deity, we certainly have the right to
urge that they be of the most elevating character
possible, and this they never can be if they exclude
the mothers from equal rank with the fathers of
our race.   It is to Art that we must largely look to
carry the gospel of the coming age to the utmost regions of the earth, as works of art appeal to multitudes to whom didactic teaching makes no appeal
whatever.   What is now often called the state of
Super-man is called by Gnostics the state of "the
woman perfected, who comprises and surmounts
man."   This is, of course, an extreme view, but in
the interests of better race-propagation it is much

safer to exalt woman above man than to elevate
man above woman, because mothers exert a far
greater influence over the unborn, and over little
children, than do fathers. . The Gnostic doctrine of
the Forgiveness of Sins is an important one, and
quite at variance with all belief in "vicarious" atonement, for to the Gnostic it is indeed true that Christ
*within* is "the hope of glory." Jacob Boehme went
very far toward explaining the Gnostic attitude when
he said: "God in man gives that which is sinful
away. Nobody can forgive sins except Christ in
Man. Whenever Christ lives in Man, there is the
absolution." One can very readily detect in the
above utterance of a modern German mystic a form
of esoteric teaching which does away entirely with
all disputations concerning genealogies and other
purely external matters against which all Gnostic
writers in primitive Christian days continually
warned their catechumens. It was not earlier than
the fourth century that the dominant exoteric party
in the Church gained the upper hand to such an
extent that they forcibly repressed all public teaching of Gnosticism and spread the infamous report
that Gnostics were shockingly immoral persons, who
sought to pervert the Gospel to the ends of licen-
tiousness, a statement which is a flagrant contradic-
tion of well-attested fact. As no persecution or opposition of any sort to esoteric teaching has ever
arisen without some superficial show of justification, it is quite probable that some sincere persons
in bygone days did actually so far misunderstand
the real trend of Gnostic philosophy as to believe
that it advocated immorality; but no ripe scholar

could at any time have held so utterly erroneous a
view unless he had become so warped by prejudice
and fanaticism as to have rendered himself altogether incompetent to weigh evidence in that particular, or consider statements in the light of calm
judicial reasoning.   Gnosticism had long preceded
Christianity, and it was no doubt often feared by
dominating ecclesiastics that the real original of
Christian rites and ceremonies might be discovered
by the people at large, if Gnostic "heresies" were
tolerated.   The great sin of Christendom has been
its arrogant attitude toward all religious systems
older or other than orthodox Christianity, and
though it has so far endorsed ancient Judaism as to
declare that it was a Divinely instituted religion, its
attitude to modern Judaism has been one of relentless and unending opposition and persecution.   It
would be a happy day for persecuted Israel in Russia
and several other nominally Christian lands were
the light of Gnosticism to break through the dense
fog of prevailing literalism, for then the Crucifixion
of the Christ, being understood esoterically and universally, on no pretext whatever could Jews be
execrated as "Christ-killers," a title often applied
to them as an excuse for the gross injustice with
which they are treated many times by their avowedly Christian neighbors.

Emancipated womanhood in the light of Gnostic
teaching represents "Pistis Sophia" liberated from
all bondage to carnal lusts, and exalted to the throne
of dominion where she rightfully belongs.   Goethe,
in the second part of his mystic drama, "Faust,"
finds "Mater Gloriosa," the centre of 183 Spheres

of light; this is indeed "the Divine Feminine that ever leads us on." Jealousy on the part of male disciples of a Master who appointed women to instruct them in the mysteries of Anastasis (resurrection and regeneration), must have had much to do with the rigorous exclusion of women from the Christian priesthood, for nothing can well be plainer than the words attributed to the risen Master in the Fourth Gospel, where he tells Mary Magdalene to tell his disciples, and especially Peter (the nominal head of the Roman Church), that he has risen from the sepulchre. Entirely apart from an immense mass of extra-Christian testimony, the accepted Gospels and Epistles of the New Testament furnish abundant evidence that the Master gave many of his deepest instructions to women, thereby initiating them into the "mysteries of the kingdom of heaven," a phrase well understood by Gnostics, who understand it to mean a living realization of truth inwardly apprehended, not outwardly witnessed to on historic grounds, as in the case of all who depend on extraneous testimony and not on interior realization. The transmutation of all energy is the dominant aspiration of the Gnostics, and no one can be a practical, experienced Gnostic who has not learned to so subdue the flesh to the spirit that the "old serpent" becomes transformed from the death-dealer to the life-bringer. Thus will the prophecy be at length completely fulfilled, "They shall take up serpents," and thus also will many equally enigmatical scriptures be fully verified.

# CHAPTER XXIV.

## HALLEY'S COMET—ITS HISTORY AND PORTENT—VISIBLE IN 1910.

The human mind in all ages seems to have instinctively attached the idea of some mysterious agency to the appearance of comets, those erratic wanderers through fields of space whose movements now seem to be as calculable as the motions of those far less remarkable orbs and constellations which we are accustomed to call Fixed Stars, only because we have much more completely comprehended their behavior. Halley's Comet, which has reappeared this year (1910), after an absence of seventy-five years since its last appearance, has a most eventful history, one which seems in large degree to justify the superstitious awe with which it was regarded during the Middle Ages, when it struck terror into the population of many lands, and, according to Draper's narrative, contained in his well-known "History of the Conflict Between Religion and Science," was at one time solemnly anathematized by the highest ecclesiastical authorities and bidden to depart from the skies, as its presence suggested to their minds some diabolical agency. Though the masses of the people every-

where are supposed to be better educated, and therefore less superstitious, now than formerly, it is by
no means uncommon to hear fears expressed to-
day that a comet may work serious disaster.   This
alarm is very ancient, and, according to Ignatius
Donnelly, and some other well-known authors, is
traceable to a great cosmic catastrophe which occurred many ages ago, when our planet collided with
a comet, and the Age of Fire and Gravel resulted.
Whatever foundation there may be for such a tradition, there seems to be nothing in the career of
Halley's Comet thus far to justify any morbid ap-
prehensions of physical destruction; but history furnishes us with abounding evidence that truly great
events in human history have taken place when this
brilliant wanderer has illumined the midnight sky.
There seems valid ground for declaring that events
move in cycles, that human affairs, like all else in
Nature, are subject to a Law of Periodicity, and
when this law is more fully understood, we shall
be able to read the book of history far more intelligently than most of us are reading it at present.

To the untutored and unscientific mind, the unusual and the unexpected seem always to presage
evil, but to the better-informed, change by no means
necessarily spells disaster.   Granted that great up-
heavals in the affairs of nations have been persistently contemporary with the appearance of this beautiful celestial traveller, alterations in the map of
the world are often unmistakable signs of welcome
progress, and far from causing us to believe that
when mighty changes impend, disaster is upon us,
we may learn to lift up our heads with joy, feel-

ing that deliverance from many curses draweth nigh.
The perihelion of our fascinating visitor whose presence in our skies is now attracting immense attention, was calculated by the illustrious astronomer,
Edmund Halley, as having occurred August 26,
1531.   This same comet reappeared, according to the
same authority, October 27, 1607, and then September 15, 1682, at which time Halley himself observed it.   Again it made its periodic appearance
March 13, 1759, and November 16, 1835, a date
within the memory of many witnesses now living.
Probably much of the historic interest attaching to
its periodic visits is due to the fact that it was in
evidence at the time of the Norman Conquest of
Great Britain, in 1066, and it has been observed
that momentous events have always occurred during
periods when it has since been visible.   This year of
its latest return visit, 1910, has certainly done much
to sustain the comet's reputation as an accompanier
of startling occurrences, for very early in the year
disturbances of every sort became rife in many lands,
and, particularly in America, Labor difficulties have
proved extremely difficult to handle.   It is certainly
far from foolishly superstitious to investigate, as far
as we are able, striking coincidences which may
throw some light on the always interesting problem
of the sympathetic relation between our planet and
other members of the stellar universe, though it is
inexcusable on the part of any who know how injurious is morbid apprehension of coming calamities,
to play upon the fears of the weak-minded and
credulous by telling them that a comet in the sky
is an augury of coming fell disaster.

For convenience of reference, should any of our readers wish to look up the leading events of the subjoined years and months, we append a list of the dates when Halley's Comet has been observed, from 11 B. C., to 1910 of our era. We are indebted to an article in the "Popular Science Monthly" (Jan., 1910) for this precise information. There have been twenty-six observed perihelia of this famous comet, the first of which carries us back to 11 B. C. During the present era the perehelion dates have been: January 26, 66; March 29, 141; April 6, 218; April (date not supplied), 295; November 7, 530 (beg.); July 3, 451; November 7, 530 (beg.); October, 684 (date omitted); June 11. 760; March 1, 837 April, 912 (early in month); September 1, 989; April 1, 1066; April 19, 1145; August 22, 1222; October 23, 1301; November 9, 1378; June 8, 1456; August 26, 1531 (all above dates are according to Julian reckoning); October 27, 1607; September 15, 1682; March 13, 1759; November 16, 1835; May 18, 1910. Many and varied have been the conjectural theories advanced concerning comets in general and in particular, but the theory most widely accepted by astronomers to-day is that they are worlds burning out—worlds which have long since accomplished such active missions as our earth is now accomplishing; for it is surely the purpose of the all-wise Designer of the Universe to appoint to every star its place and mission, and as all outward existences have a beginning, so at some time and in some way they must have an end. Astronomy is unquestionably at once the sublimest and most awe-inspiring of all the sciences, and well may we exclaim with the Hebrew poet of old, "The heavens declare the glory of God; the firmament showeth forth the handiwork of the Eternal One."

It was by scanning the skies that ancient peoples gained all their external ideas of order in the universe; therefore we find that all venerated Scriptures are largely astronomical in their references, and it has even been stated that every Bible story can be traced to an astronomical origin. Whether this be so or not, it is beyond reasonable dispute that a study of the visible heavens was intimately bound up with the duties and occupations of all venerable priesthoods, the members of which, in all renowned ancient countries, were the scientific as well as the religious leaders of the multitude; and now with the revolution of the cycles bringing us again to a point of fresh explorations and revelations, we are reviewing the records of the remote past with ever-increasing interest and fulness, and at the same time witnessing a new cult, or several new cults, springing up among us, seeking to embody the wisdom of the past in consonance with the discoveries of the present. As the new time ripens and the modern spirit matures, we shall certainly grow to appreciate much of the religion and science of our long-departed ancestors, while the brighter light and ampler opportunities for discovery and comparison which will characterize the advancing epoch will enable us to systematize and synthesize the knowledge now available to the end of constructing a synthetic philosophy embracing all the excellences of past systems without their inevitable limitations. At any rate, let such be our fearless aim and quest, then whatever legitimate study or research aids us on our way we shall gladly welcome and embrace it.

**FINIS.**

# PSYCHOPATHIC TREATMENT

OR

SUGGESTIVE THERAPY IN PRACTICAL APPLICATION.

By W. J. Colville.

Having recently made a fourth visit to Kingston-on-Hudson (a charming resort at all seasons, within easy access of New York City, 85 miles distant, reached in two and a quarter hours), by special invitation of Dr. Charles Oliver Sahler, founder and president of the world-famous Sanitarium at that place, I am now in a position to speak from direct personal observation concerning the practicability of employing modern suggestive methods in the conduct of a large and ever-growing institution.

Practically everybody admits to-day that mental treatment is available and useful in certain classes of disorders, technically styled "Nervous ailments," but a widespread impression prevails that what are designated Functional and Organic derangements are not to be conquered by other than distinctly physical methods.

Much good work is now being accomplished all over America and in other lands by distinguished doctors of theology as well as of medicine who incline to this popular restricted view, but such opinions must inevitably hamper the proficiency of the work of all who entertain them.

Dr. C. O. Sahler, a regular physician who graduated from the Medical Department of Columbia University, New York City, in 1878, and practiced in the older ways for many years with great success, made a singularly bold venture in 1893 when he

started out as pioneer demonstrator of Suggestive
Therapeutics in connection with the work of a newly
organized Sanitarium which commenced its career
in very modest style, with little to support it beyond
the ardent enthusiasm of its founder, who was then
intuitively certain that a work of the kind he had
so bravely undertaken was not only calculated to
supply a great necessity, but also destined to grow
and thrive until it should command the respect and
interests of thoughtful people everywhere.

At Kingston-on-Hudson a pleasant, roomy house
was secured in the quietest section of the town,
within easy walking distance of the business center.
Twenty rooms were available for the accommodation of students and patients seeking instruction and
treatment, and very shortly the demand of visitors
far exceeded the supply. By 1899 many important
additions and improvements had been made and the
number of rooms was raised to 42.

Still the work kept growing and demanding larger
and larger accommodations, till in 1906 the present
large and beautiful institution was completed, still
on the old site, containing 160 rooms. One hundred
and twenty patients are often in the various buildings at the same time, and including workers in the
various departments the population of the Home
(for such it truly is) is seldom under 200. Dr.
Sahler is now ably assisted in his enormous work by
Dr. C. P. Wescott.

It requires marvelous energy and insight to direct
and oversee so great an organization, but apparently
without any strainful effort Dr. Sahler regularly
accomplishes this mighty task, and so effectively

that everything runs on so smoothly that one is led to wonder what magical force is directing the affairs from some unseen sanctuary.

The open secret of the whole business is the powerful individuality of the director, whose whole interest is in the work, which he dearly loves, and which never could be accomplished by any human being, no matter how highly trained and naturally gifted, who did not truly enjoy doing the numerous interesting and important things that must be systematically done continually.

One who has been a great factor in developing and organizing this unique system is the present Superintendent, Miss Charlotte Atkins, who has been with the Sanitarium since 1895.

There do we witness the mighty power of self-discipline in active operation. Theroists abound, but highly successful demonstrators are still but few. It is ever *the doctor himself,* rather than any particular method which can be concretely formulated, which proves the success-compelling factor, and in Dr. Sahler we witness in pre-eminent degree an embodiment of spiritual ardor exquisitely blended with intellectual vigor and sober common sense.

A distinctly distinguishing feature of the Sanitarium is that it is truly what its name declares, an abode of health. Every equipment suggests cheerfulness, the indwellers are all at home in a beautifully-situated mansion where they enjoy the largest possible amount of reasonable liberty, and where they are treated as healthy intellectual human beings, and, as such, provided with abundant means for instruction and entertainment.

Though there are always a large number of patients at Kingston, quite a considerable percentage of the residents are elderly people who are enjoying the blessings of a cheerful home and who find the genial atmosphere, both mental and physical, particularly conducive to their continued welfare and rejuvenation.

Though Dr. Sahler practices suggestion regularly and systematically in specially adapted apartments where patients, while receiving treatment, are secluded from all disturbing sights and sounds, his system is so widely comprehensive that it embraces all that enters into the entire scheme of a comprehensive Sanitarium and the routine of its management.

Love of the beautiful is everywhere in evidence. Simplicity combined with comfort and elegance confronts the visitor at every turn. All the rooms are beautifully but quietly decorated and furnished There are no glaring colors, but soft, melodious tints everywhere meet the eye, suggesting rest combined with healthy activity. Nobody is idle, and all forms of healthful exercise are carried on to meet the needs of various temperaments.

A great charm of the institution is its thoroughly liberal and up-to-date equipment in all particulars. Gymnastic exercises are encouraged, under an able and experienced director, Miss Louise Gowan, who is an expert demonstrator of the Delsarte and all other refined and delicate modes of physical culture. All exercises are wisely adapted to the exact requirements and present strength of the participants.

The Turkish and Russian baths form a very valuable and attractive feature, and for their management Dr. Sahler has secured a singularly proficient director in George Barnard.

The Craft and Arts Department occupies a large three-story building consisting of Workshops, Art Rooms, Kitchen and Tea Room, under the able directorate of Miss L. F. Wait.

An unassuming, but none the less a valuable worker, is the handy man, Sam, who has been in the Sanitarium since 1901 attending at all times to everybody's comfort by keeping the furnaces going, carrying trays and ministering in many ways to the creature comforts of all within the house.   Dr Sahler regards him as a very important factor in his staff of assistants.

Another very responsible worker is the outside overseer, Ernest Deyo.

Miss Nell Sahler very ably conducts the Department of Domestic Science and Household Economics.

Mrs. Keith-McClintock, Assistant Healer, arrived in 1906 and has proved herself particularly successful with those who require intelligent encouragement and well directed sympathy.   Her musical services are also of great value.   This highly gifted woman is largely responsible for the many good results which follow upon continued application of theory in practice, her special efforts being always directed toward helping the weak in will and those lacking in necessary self-confidence to comprehend their own interior qualities, which judicial mental treatment always arouses.

While receiving suggestion, either from Dr. Sahler or one of his assistants, the patient reclines on an easy couch in a cozy cabinet, and listens to the comforting assurances of the psychopathist who addresses the sub-consciousness, as well as the outward ear, and explains the method so that teaching is combined with treating.

Considering the highly important work of the Matron of so large an institution, where so many needs have constantly to be met, great praise is due to Miss Rosina Atkins, who is rendering faithful and efficient service in that capacity. Much praise is also due to William Atkins, who admirably fills the post of steward.

Since the opening in 1898 the influential and highly responsible position of Business Manager has been filled by Miss H. M. Terpenning, who is an excellent financier, a true economist in the best meaning of the term, and at the same time one who fully indorses Dr. Sahler's esthetic contention that grace, utility and liberality must always be made manifest in unity.

The tireless housekeeper, Mrs. Isora Lewis, has also been in her position since 1893, and to her continuous watchful care far more that makes for success is rightly attributable than generally meets the eye.

Another very useful worker, and one who contributes greatly to the comfort of all concerned, is Miss Charlotte Muir, who has had full charge of the dining room since 1903. This active, good-natured young woman accomplishes successfully the difficult task of accommodating all the patients and

visitors within necessarily prescribed time limits, in
such a manner as to cause no friction among the extremely varied inmates of the house. Punctuality in
all things is an inflexible rule, and Dr. Sahler is
much to be congratulated on the efficient aid he receives from his large corps of assistants in carrying
out this most important rule.

Having now sketched the history and the per-
sonnel, let us take a brief but comprehensive glance
at the main building and its general floors. In the
spacious, light, airy and perfectly ventilated base-
ment we find a lecture room provided with 200
chairs, a spacious platform and a fine piano. In this
apartment lectures and excellent entertainments are
constantly being given, which are largely attended
by townspeople and visitors as well as by those who
are dwelling under the Sanitarium roof or domi-
ciled in one of its many auxiliary cottages. On this
floor also we find the Turkish Baths, Gymnasium,
Billiard Rooms, etc.

The kitchens, in a wing by themselves, are splen-
didly equipped with every modern appliance for
health and utility. These important offices are
flooded with sunlight, kept scrupulously clean and
presided over by a thoroughly efficient and competent
staff of assistants.

On the main entrance floor we find business offices
fitted with every appliance for doing a maximum of
work with a minimum of effort. Spacious reception
rooms, beautifully furnished, containing everything
requisite to make guests and patients feel as though
they were residing at an excellent family hotel, occupy a large portion of this floor, which in its newest

portion contains the private apartments of Dr. Sahler and his family.

Mrs. Sahler, though given to artistic pursuits rather than to domestic oversight, is a charming hostess, at whose private board it is a great privilege to sit.

The public dining room equals in size and general appointments a similar refectory in a thoroughly first-class hotel. The cuisine is excellent and liberal, and though some food specialists might pronounce the dietary all too varied, there is much to commend it from the suggestive standpoint, as it suggests nothing of the conventional sanitarium, and everything of a feeding place for healthy people, with normal appetites and good powers of digestion.

Special food is always supplied under Dr. Sahler's supervision to those whose immediate condition renders specific diet necessary.

The second and third floors are devoted to sleeping apartments, bathrooms and sun parlors. As the view over the adjacent hills is wide and exhilarating the sun parlors are a particularly delightful and health-inspiring feature.

The fourth floor is given over to dormitories entirely, and though accommodation is less expensive in the skylight regions than lower down, it is excellent in all respects, and affords the highest view of the surrounding country, which is extremely picturesque.

In addition to all public and semi-public portions of the establishment, there is an inner sanctum—Dr. Sahler's private library and treating rooms. This sheltered nook, to which only the specially invited are admitted, reveals the temperament and character of its presiding genius in singularly marked degree; here are art treasures from nearly all over the earth, many of them gems which might adorn cathedrals. These extremely beautiful objects are for the most part offerings sent by grateful patients who owe their restoration to health and their introduction to new-born liberty to the noble work carried on within the sanctuary which their gratitude impels them to adorn.

Graduates from Kingston are doing good work in many places. Among these should be mentioned Mrs. Mary Seaton, now practising very successfully as a mental therapeutist in Washington.

This lady was completely healed of chronic difficulties by Dr. Sahler's treatment many years ago, and has enjoyed robust health ever since.

We will conclude this sketch of a singularly useful work with a quotation from one of Dr. Sahler's lectures, which gives a good outline of what is exactly his position.

"The words, 'Suggestive Therapeutics,' are so carelessly or loosely used, so misunderstood, that a careful consideration of them is necessary as befitting so important a subject. The combination of these two words does not give a clear meaning or throw a true light on the subject unless they are at first disconnected and analyzed.

First, THERAPEUTICS means that department of medical science that relates to the treatment of disease and action of remedial agents on the human organization. SUGGESTION when spoken of as a remedial agent stands for a truth, although it is not a drug. When one understands or is versed in the use of drugs and their effect upon the human organism, he is known as a THERAPEUTIST or a practitioner of medicine, hence he is called a physician. In truth, a physician is one legally authorized to treat diseases. A true physician is one who is broad-minded, who will treat diseases by any rational method; so the true physician would use SUGGESTION as a curative agent. Here we must study this curative agent. SUGGESTION is not a drug, and to understand first its curative power we ask, What is SUGGESTION?

SUGGESTION is an idea received by an individual consciousness. It may come from any source, by any process, or through any channel. We thus see it is not a material remedy, so we are understandingly directed into the channel of metaphysics. For to use SUGGESTION as a remedial agent we must have an understanding of metaphysics, as he who applies the metaphysical idea of treating is known as a metaphysician, which, in truth, means one versed in the philosophy of the ultimate nature, cause and reason of things. So the ideal physician must of necessity be a metaphysician as well, before he is able to cope with all the ailments or diseases of mankind successfully. Thus we see SUGGESTION and THERAPEUTICS combined really imply a therapeutical practice by a metaphysician or physician who understands the nature, cause and reason of things, and the remedy needed.

Man is a suggestible creature. In fact all animals, as well as man, live, move and have their being by the law of suggestion. The advancement of civili-

zation is due to the larger and better understanding
of this law.  So it follows, logically, that SUGGES-
TIVE THERAPEUTICS holds a prominent place.

Practically it is little understood in its real essence as a curative agent by the medical profession,
for ,as members of the profession we have been educated along material lines, treating the body with its
intellect as the man, wholly affected by external
causes and through external agents, such as drugs,
appliances, etc.

We lose sight of the fact that within man, besides
his body and intellect, there is a consciousness, and
through the latter, according to involuntary law, the
body is builded and sustained.  It is because of this
lack of understanding or knowledge of psychic
forces in man, which seems to so shroud this subject with mysticism, that it cannot be explained by
the general practitioner.

SUGGESTION as commonly understood is simply persuasion, which may or may not carry much
force with it; but from a psychic point of view SUG-
GESTION becomes a mighty power and so dis-
similar to the commonly used word SUGGESTION
that when the subject is once understood the former
seems to bear no relation to the latter.  Unfortu-
nately, it is difficult to explain or express the very
truth or life of this subject by an article or a book.
One can scarcely form a true idea of its meaning or
worth through reading.  In fact, the most intelligent
or educated patient cannot explain or so understand
it as to tell another even after being treated.  Still,
he has a thorough realization and knowledge in his
own consciousness of its influence o rpower.  This is

an experience expressed by hundreds of our patients. At no time is the patient unconscious in intellect or feeling while taking treatment, still he has the realization that something is far different from the normal state.   He also understands that its force depends upon his own attitude in his consciousness and his relationship to the physician or operator."

Speaking for myself, I have only to add that my several lecture courses at Kingston have proved phenomenally successful.   I trust I may again be privileged to visit that delightful spot, which is a center from which healing radiations are extending immeasurably further than our knowledge can estimate.

W. J. COLVILLE.

June, 1910.

www.ingramcontent.com/pod-product-compliance
Lightning Source LLC
Chambersburg PA
CBHW020420030726
47495CB00006B/1591